Lecture Notes in Computer Science 12401

More information about this series at http://www.springer.com/series/7409

Ruifeng Xu · Wang De ·
Wei Zhong · Ling Tian ·
Yongsheng Bai · Liang-Jie Zhang (Eds.)

Artificial Intelligence and Mobile Services – AIMS 2020

9th International Conference
Held as Part of the Services Conference Federation, SCF 2020
Honolulu, HI, USA, September 18–20, 2020
Proceedings

Springer

Editors
Ruifeng Xu ⓘ
Harbin Institute of Technology
Shenzhen, China

Wang De
Sunmi US Inc.
Pleasanton, CA, USA

Wei Zhong
University of South Carolina Upstate
Spartanburg, SC, USA

Ling Tian
University of Electronic Science
and Technology of China
Chengdu, China

Yongsheng Bai
Eastern Michigan University
Ypsilanti, MI, USA

Liang-Jie Zhang ⓘ
Kingdee International Software
Group Co., Ltd.
Shenzhen, China

ISSN 0302-9743   ISSN 1611-3349 (electronic)
Lecture Notes in Computer Science
ISBN 978-3-030-59604-0   ISBN 978-3-030-59605-7 (eBook)
https://doi.org/10.1007/978-3-030-59605-7

LNCS Sublibrary: SL3 – Information Systems and Applications, incl. Internet/Web, and HCI

This Springer imprint is published by the registered company Springer Nature Switzerland AG
The registered company address is: Gewerbestrasse 11, 6330 Cham, Switzerland

Preface

The International Conference on AI & Mobile Services (AIMS 2020) aims at providing an international forum that is dedicated to exploring different aspects of AI (from technologies to approaches and algorithms) and mobile services (from business management to computing systems, algorithms, and applications) to promoting technological innovations in research and development of mobile services, including, but not limited to, wireless and sensor networks, mobile and wearable computing, mobile enterprise and ecommerce, ubiquitous collaborative and social services, machine-to-machine and Internet-of-Things clouds, cyber-physical integration, and big data analytics for mobility-enabled services.

AIMS 2020 is a member of the Services Conference Federation (SCF). SCF 2020 had the following 10 collocated service-oriented sister conferences: the International Conference on Web Services (ICWS 2020), the International Conference on Cloud Computing (CLOUD 2020), the International Conference on Services Computing (SCC 2020), the International Conference on Big Data (BigData 2020), the International Conference on AI & Mobile Services (AIMS 2020), the World Congress on Services (SERVICES 2020), the International Conference on Internet of Things (ICIOT 2020), the International Conference on Cognitive Computing (ICCC 2020), the International Conference on Edge Computing (EDGE 2020), and the International Conference on Blockchain (ICBC 2020). As the founding member of SCF, the First International Conference on Web Services (ICWS 2003) was held in June 2003 in Las Vegas, USA. Meanwhile, the First International Conference on Web Services - Europe 2003 (ICWS-Europe 2003) was held in Germany in October 2003. ICWS-Europe 2003 was an extended event of ICWS 2003, and held in Europe. In 2004, ICWS-Europe was changed to the European Conference on Web Services (ECOWS), which was held in Erfurt, Germany. To celebrate its 18th birthday, SCF 2020 was successfully held in Hawaii, USA.

This volume presents the accepted papers for the AIMS 2020, held as a fully virtual conference during September 18–20, 2020. The major topics of AIMS 2020 included but were not limited to: AI Modeling, AI Analysis, AI and Mobile Applications, AI Architecture, AI Management, AI Engineering, Mobile Backend as a Service (MBaaS), User Experience of AI and Mobile Services.

We accepted 13 papers, including 11 full papers and 2 short papers. Each was reviewed and selected by three independent members of the AIMS 2020 International Program Committee. We are pleased to thank the authors whose submissions and participation made this conference possible. We also want to express our thanks to the Program Committee members for their dedication in helping to organize the conference and reviewing the submissions. We thank all volunteers, authors, and conference participants for their great contributions to the fast-growing worldwide services innovations community.

July 2020

Ruifeng Xu
De Wang
Wei Zhong
Ling Tian
Yongsheng Bai
Liang-Jie Zhang

Organization

General Chairs

Teruo Higashino	Osaka University, Japan
Rafal Angryk	Georgia State University, USA
Youping Deng	University of Hawaii, USA

Program Chairs

Ruifeng Xu	Harbin Institute of Technology, China
De Wang	Sunmi US Inc., USA
Wei Zhong	University of South Carolina Upstate, USA
Ling Tian	UESTC, China
Yougsheng Bai	University of Michigan, USA

Services Conference Federation (SCF 2020)

General Chairs

Yi Pan	Georgia State University, USA
Samee U. Khan	North Dakota State University, USA
Wu Chou	Vice President of Artificial Intelligence & Software at Essenlix Corporation, USA
Ali Arsanjani	Amazon Web Services (AWS), USA

Program Chair

Liang-Jie Zhang	Kingdee International Software Group Co., Ltd, China

Industry Track Chair

Siva Kantamneni	Principal/Partner at Deloitte Consulting, USA

CFO

Min Luo	Huawei, USA

Industry Exhibit and International Affairs Chair

Zhixiong Chen	Mercy College, USA

Operations Committee

Jing Zeng	Yundee Intelligence Co., Ltd, China
Yishuang Ning	Tsinghua University, China
Sheng He	Tsinghua University, China
Yang Liu	Tsinghua University, China

Steering Committee

Calton Pu (Co-chair)	Georgia Tech, USA
Liang-Jie Zhang (Co-chair)	Kingdee International Software Group Co., Ltd, China

AIMS 2020 Program Committee

Cheng Cai	Northwest A&F University, China
Yongtian He	University of Houston, USA
Fabrizio Lamberti	Politecnico di Torino, Italy
Zakaria Maamar	Zayed University, UAE
Rong Shi	The Ohio State University, USA
Zhen Xu	Google, USA
Yuchao Zhang	Beijing University of Posts and Telecommunications, China
Hongbo Zou	Petuum Inc., USA

Conference Sponsor – Services Society

Services Society (S2) is a nonprofit professional organization that has been created to promote worldwide research and technical collaboration in services innovation among academia and industrial professionals. Its members are volunteers from industry and academia with common interests. S2 is registered in the USA as a "501(c) organization," which means that it is an American tax-exempt nonprofit organization. S2 collaborates with other professional organizations to sponsor or co-sponsor conferences and to promote an effective services curriculum in colleges and universities. The S2 initiates and promotes a "Services University" program worldwide to bridge the gap between industrial needs and university instruction.

The services sector accounted for 79.5% of the USA's GDP in 2016. The world's most service-oriented economy, with service sectors accounting for more than 90% of GDP. S2 has formed 10 Special Interest Groups (SIGs) to support technology and domain specific professional activities:

- Special Interest Group on Web Services (SIG-WS)
- Special Interest Group on Services Computing (SIG-SC)
- Special Interest Group on Services Industry (SIG-SI)
- Special Interest Group on Big Data (SIG-BD)
- Special Interest Group on Cloud Computing (SIG-CLOUD)
- Special Interest Group on Artificial Intelligence (SIG-AI)
- Special Interest Group on Edge Computing (SIG-EC)
- Special Interest Group on Cognitive Computing (SIG-CC)
- Special Interest Group on Blockchain (SIG-BC)
- Special Interest Group on Internet of Things (SIG-IOT)

About the Services Conference Federation (SCF)

As the founding member of the Services Conference Federation (SCF), the First International Conference on Web Services (ICWS 2003) was held in June 2003 in Las Vegas, USA. Meanwhile, the First International Conference on Web Services - Europe 2003 (ICWS-Europe 2003) was held in Germany in October 2003. ICWS-Europe 2003 was an extended event of ICWS 2003, and held in Europe. In 2004, ICWS-Europe was changed to the European Conference on Web Services (ECOWS), which was held in Erfurt, Germany. SCF 2019 was held successfully in San Diego, USA. To celebrate its 18th birthday, SCF 2020 was held virtually during September 18–20, 2020.

In the past 17 years, the ICWS community has been expanded from Web engineering innovations to scientific research for the whole services industry. The service delivery platforms have been expanded to mobile platforms, Internet of Things (IoT), cloud computing, and edge computing. The services ecosystem is gradually enabled, value added, and intelligence embedded through enabling technologies such as big data, artificial intelligence (AI), and cognitive computing. In the coming years, all the transactions with multiple parties involved will be transformed to blockchain.

Based on the technology trends and best practices in the field, SCF will continue serving as the conference umbrella's code name for all service-related conferences. SCF 2020 defines the future of New ABCDE (AI, Blockchain, Cloud, big Data, Everything is connected), which enable IoT and enter the 5G for the Services Era. SCF 2020's 10 collocated theme topic conferences all center around "services," while each focusing on exploring different themes (web-based services, cloud-based services, big data-based services, services innovation lifecycle, AI-driven ubiquitous services, blockchain driven trust service-ecosystems, industry-specific services and applications, and emerging service-oriented technologies). SCF includes 10 service-oriented conferences: ICWS, CLOUD, SCC, BigData Congress, AIMS, SERVICES, ICIOT, EDGE, ICCC, and ICBC. The SCF 2020 members are listed as follows:

[1] The International Conference on Web Services (ICWS 2020, http://icws.org/) is the flagship theme-topic conference for Web-based services, featuring Web services modeling, development, publishing, discovery, composition, testing, adaptation, delivery, as well as the latest API standards.

[2] The International Conference on Cloud Computing (CLOUD 2020, http://thecloudcomputing.org/) is the flagship theme-topic conference for modeling, developing, publishing, monitoring, managing, delivering XaaS (Everything as a Service) in the context of various types of cloud environments.

[3] The International Conference on Big Data (BigData 2020, http://bigdatacongress.org/) is the emerging theme-topic conference for the scientific and engineering innovations of big data.

[4] The International Conference on Services Computing (SCC 2020, http://thescc.org/) is the flagship theme-topic conference for services innovation lifecycle that includes enterprise modeling, business consulting, solution creation, services

orchestration, services optimization, services management, services marketing, and business process integration and management.

[5] The International Conference on AI & Mobile Services (AIMS 2020, http://ai1000.org/) is the emerging theme-topic conference for the science and technology of AI, and the development, publication, discovery, orchestration, invocation, testing, delivery, and certification of AI-enabled services and mobile applications.

[6] The World Congress on Services (SERVICES 2020, http://servicescongress.org/) focuses on emerging service-oriented technologies and the industry-specific services and solutions.

[7] The International Conference on Cognitive Computing (ICCC 2020, http://thecognitivecomputing.org/) focuses on the Sensing Intelligence (SI) as a Service (SIaaS) which makes systems listen, speak, see, smell, taste, understand, interact, and walk in the context of scientific research and engineering solutions.

[8] The International Conference on Internet of Things (ICIOT 2020, http://iciot.org/) focuses on the creation of IoT technologies and development of IoT services.

[9] The International Conference on Edge Computing (EDGE 2020, http://theedgecomputing.org/) focuses on the state of the art and practice of edge computing including but not limited to localized resource sharing, connections with the cloud, and 5G devices and applications.

[10] The International Conference on Blockchain (ICBC 2020, http://blockchain1000.org/) concentrates on blockchain-based services and enabling technologies.

Some highlights of SCF 2020 are shown below:

- **Bigger Platform:** The 10 collocated conferences (SCF 2020) are sponsored by the Services Society (S2) which is the world-leading nonprofit organization (501 c(3)) dedicated to serving more than 30,000 worldwide services computing researchers and practitioners. Bigger platform means bigger opportunities to all volunteers, authors, and participants. Meanwhile, Springer sponsors the Best Paper Awards and other professional activities. All 10 conference proceedings of SCF 2020 have been published by Springer and indexed in ISI Conference Proceedings Citation Index (included in Web of Science), Engineering Index EI (Compendex and Inspec databases), DBLP, Google Scholar, IO-Port, MathSciNet, Scopus, and ZBlMath.
- **Brighter Future:** While celebrating the 2020 version of ICWS, SCF 2020 highlights the Third International Conference on Blockchain (ICBC 2020) to build the fundamental infrastructure for enabling secure and trusted service ecosystems. It will also lead our community members to create their own brighter future.
- **Better Model:** SCF 2020 continues to leverage the invented Conference Blockchain Model (CBM) to innovate the organizing practices for all the 10 theme conferences.

Contents

Short Paper Track

Research Track

Infant Sound Classification on Multi-stage CNNs with Hybrid Features and Prior Knowledge

Chunyan Ji⬤, Sunitha Basodi⬤, Xueli Xiao⬤, and Yi Pan⁽✉⁾⬤

Georgia State University, Atlanta, GA 30303, USA
{cji2,sbasodi1,xxiao2}@student.gsu.edu, yipan@gsu.edu

Abstract. We propose an approach of generating a hybrid feature set and using prior knowledge in a multi-stage CNNs for robust infant sound classification. The dominant and auxiliary features within the set are beneficial to enlarge the coverage as well as keeping a good resolution for modeling the diversity of variations within infant sound. The novel multi-stage CNNs method work together with prior knowledge constraints in decision making to overcome the limited data problem in infant sound classification. Prior knowledge either from rules or from statistical results provides a good guidance for searching and classification. The effectiveness of proposed method is evaluated on commonly used Dustan Baby Language Database and Baby Chillanto Database. It gives an encouraging reduction of 4.14% absolute classification error rate compared with the results from the best model using one-stage CNN. In addition, on Baby Chillanto Database, a significant absolute error reduction of 5.33% is achieved compared to one-stage CNN and it outperforms all other existing related studies.

Keywords: Hybrid features · Multi-stage CNNs · Prior knowledge

1 Introduction

Crying is the only way that infants communicate with the world. There are many reasons behind the baby crying such as pain, discomfort, and hunger, etc. Previous work shows that baby crying is a short-term stationary signal and only contains non-speech information [1]. In recent years, Priscilla Dustan shows that baby crying is a complicated procedure consisting of baby language and baby crying parts [2]. The Infant sound concept is proposed to cover both baby language and crying. In addition, Dustan's theory points out that baby language consists of five words associated with infants' five basic needs. Many researchers focus on using Dustan theory for baby sound analysis and processing, especially in the area of testing the universal baby language hypothesis using speech recognition methods such as GMM, HMM, and CNN for classification [2].

© Springer Nature Switzerland AG 2020
R. Xu et al. (Eds.): AIMS 2020, LNCS 12401, pp. 3–16, 2020.
https://doi.org/10.1007/978-3-030-59605-7_1

4   C. Ji et al.

Priscilla Dunstan discovered that babies use a proto-language with five "words" to express their needs [2]. It is shown that the proto-language is universal. Dustan translated the words as "Neh" = hungry; "Eh" = need to burp; "Oah" = tired; "Eairh" = low belly pain; and "Heh" = physical discomfort. Infants first express a certain need with one of these phonemes. If the need is not taken care of, they will soon start to cry. Mel Frequency Cepstral Coefficients (MFCC) together with K-Nearest Neighbor (KNN) was used to achieve 79% for Dunstan five-word classification. Linear Frequency Cepstral Coefficient (LFCC) was proven to be effective and the classification accuracy reached around 90% on limited testing data [2]. Other researchers collected the raw data using Dustan definition and used MFCC with KNN classifier to obtain around 70% accuracy [3]. An automatic method for infant cry classification was proposed in [1]. The author used GMM-UBM as well as i-vectors modeling methods to achieve average accuracy around 70%. A method of converting infant crying audio samples to spectrogram images as the input for neural networks achieved 89% accuracy [2]. In this method, a Convolutional Neural Network (CNN) was used to classify the five "words" with a fixed specific testing data. More recently, machine learning methods together with prosodic features for infant cry processing have been proposed. It is shown that fundamental frequency F0 is an essential feature for baby crying classification [4,5]. Recently, frame level features including MFCCs, pitch, and short-time energy were used for infant cry analysis and detection [6].

Using different features or spectrogram images together with machine learning approaches addresses the fundamental work of infant crying classification. Challenges remain in these approaches, especially for infant speech classification tasks. Infant speech is different from infant crying. Baby crying is considered more stationary than speech since infants cannot fully control the vocal tract [1]. Applying speech recognition approaches leads to inferior performance due to the difference between speech and non-speech signals. Infant sound is a time sequence with four steps, including infant speech and crying [1]. The use of either speech coefficients such as MFCC/LPC/LFCC or converted spectrogram images solely as input for the machine learning models is not able to capture the diversity of variations within the sound produced by different age infants. In addition, the size of the Dustan infant speech database is small. The total amount of transcribed samples is very limited for robust neural network classification structure. Automatic infant speech classifier with CNN approach improved the performance for infant speech classification on the Dustan database [2]. Whereas, the testing environment is set to be very specific and both test set and configurations are fixed strictly. It is essential to have an efficient approach for processing both infant speech and infant crying under limited data samples.

In this paper, we propose generating a hybrid feature set and using prior knowledge to guide the training of a multi-stage CNNs model for robust infant sound classification. We investigate the detailed difference between infant speech and crying both in time domain and frequency domain. We compare infant speech and crying to traditional normal speech to discover the hidden characteristics in the sound. We establish dominant and auxiliary features to form a hybrid feature set to take advantage of different discrimination ability of each CNN. Compared to using traditional features solely, the hybrid feature set uses the auxiliary features as supplement to capture the diversity of variations within infant speech and crying. Furthermore, the prior knowledge either from rules or from statistical results is used to guide the multi-stage CNNs classification. With the use of prior knowledge and hybrid feature set, the searching space of CNN classification is constrained so the system is robust under limited data samples. The effectiveness of the proposed method is evaluated on commonly used Dustan Baby Language Database and Baby Chillanto Database. In this paper, our major contributions include the following:

- We propose a novel approach of generating hybrid features including prosodic feature images;
- We introduce a method to use different feature images to feed into multiple CNN models for robust classification;
- We propose a multi-stage CNNs model that can take advantage of the discriminative ability of each individual model;
- We use prior knowledge in decision making to guide the training process in the multi-stage model.

The remainder of the paper is organized as follows. In Sect. 2, infant sound analysis and mixed feature set generation are described. Section 3 outlines our method of establishing multi-stage CNNs as well as prior knowledge generation. In Sect. 4, experimental results on Dustan Baby Language Database and Baby Chillanto database are presented. We conclude in Sect. 5.

2   Infant Sound Analysis and Hybrid Features

2.1   Infant Sound Analysis

Infant sound is associated with infant speech and infant crying. Pediatricians and professionals can distinguish different types of infant sounds. It is shown that an infant sound is made of four types of sounds: each of them coming from the expiration phase, a brief pause, and a sound coming from the inspiration phase followed by another pause. An infant sound signal is assumed more stationary than a speech signal because of infants' lack of full control of the vocal tract. Figure 1 gives a comparison of spectrograms from infant sound and adult speech. We can see that the variations within waveform and spectrum are quite different, especially in the areas of energy, intensity, and formants.

Variations in intensity, fundamental frequency (F0), formants, and duration are typical acoustic cues for infant sound and speech [7]. Adult speech's F0 ranges 85 Hz 200 Hz while infant crying signal is characterized by its high F0 within 250–700 Hz. F0 is commonly computed using an auto correlation-based method provided by Praat [8]. In Fig. 1b, we can see that the corresponding clear harmonics in the lower frequency region are below 2 KHz in adult speech, whereas the harmonic structure becomes drastically weaker as the frequency increases. In other words, the lower frequency region covers more energy and the transitional pattern of speech manifold in that region. This is the reason why mel-scale frequency warping is promising for speech recognition. Figure 1a shows that the envelop of the intensity of normal baby cry signal is rhythmic and has cyclic changes due to the natural breath. It has a high pitch of 500 Hz. Further, the infant sound is characterized by its periodic nature, alternating crying and respiration.

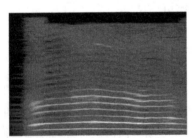

(a) Waveform and spectrogram of infant sound.

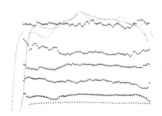

(b) Waveform and spectrogram of an adult speech.

Fig. 1. Adult speech vs. infant sound in time and frequency domain.

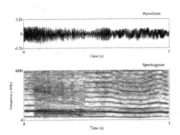

(a) The spectrogram image for infant word of "Neh"

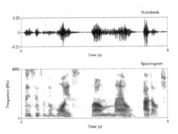

(b) The prosodic lines image for infant word of "Neh"

Fig. 2. The spectrogram and prosodic lines for infant word of "Neh".

As discussed before, Priscilla Dunstan states that babies use a proto-language with five "words" to express their needs [2]. The proto-language is universal and is regarded as the infant speech. Dustan translates the words as "Neh" = hungry; "Eh" = need to burp; "Oah" = tired; "Eairh" = low belly pain; and "Heh" = physical discomfort. In order to see the differences of five words of infant speech, we plot both spectrograms and prosodic feature lines including F0, intensity and F12345.

We investigate the above figures and find out the following:

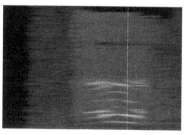
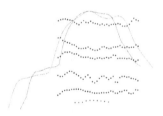

(a) The spectrogram image for infant word of "Eh"

(b) The prosodic lines image for infant word of "Eh"

Fig. 3. The spectrogram and prosodic lines for infant word of "Eh".

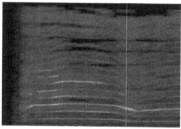
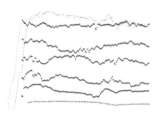

(a) The spectrogram image for infant word of "Oah"

(b) The prosodic lines image for infant word of "Oah"

Fig. 4. The spectrogram and prosodic lines for infant word of "Oah".

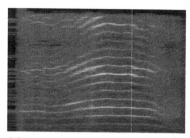
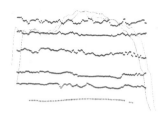

(a) The spectrogram image for infant word of "Eairh"

(b) The prosodic lines image for infant word of "Eairh"

Fig. 5. The spectrogram and prosodic lines for infant word of "Eairh".

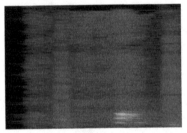

(a) The spectrogram image for infant word of "Heh"

(b) The prosodic lines image for infant word of "Heh"

Fig. 6. The spectrogram and prosodic lines for infant word of "Heh".

1. The energy shown in the spectrograms at different frequency of five infant words is quite different. For example, the word "Heh" has the lowest energy in all frequency band while "Eairh" has the highest, which is in accordance with the infant status of physical discomfort and stomach cramp. In addition, the figures also present that infants can pronounce vowels.
2. Prosodic features have good resolution to characterize the difference within infant sound. For instance, the envelop of the intensity of "Eh" is approximate rhythmic and has cyclic changes due to the reason of the need of burp. The tendency of "Oah" is gradient descent caused by tiredness of the infant. The F0 as well as the envelop of formants have good discriminative ability to classify five infant words.
3. The spectrogram is a good feature to describe the characteristics of infant sound signals. It is assumed that both acoustic and prosodic information are included in spectrograms. The combined prosodic features are good auxiliary features with fine resolution to describe the variations hidden in the infant sound.

2.2 Hybrid Features of Infant Sound

An automatic method of infant sound classification uses speech features as the input. Infant crying is a combination of vocalization, silence, coughing, choking, and interruptions, which includes a diversity of acoustic and prosodic information at different levels. We establish dominant and auxiliary features to form a hybrid feature set to take advantage of their different discrimination abilities. The spectrogram is set to be the dominant feature because it has a strong ability to present the signal including both acoustic and prosodic information. The spectrogram can be extracted through framing, Fast Fourier Transform, and calculating the log of the filtered spectrum steps illustrated in Fig. 7.

The infant sounds from the Dunstan Baby Language Database have different durations. In order to keep the same size for all the spectrogram images, the images generated are normalized instead of zero padded. Besides the dominant feature of spectrogram, we also generate auxiliary features including waveform

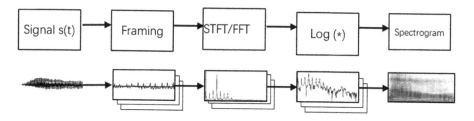

Fig. 7. The flowchart of spectrogram generation

images and prosodic feature images. The spectrogram regarding as the dominant feature gives a comprehensive description of infant sound while other features have discrimination abilities for different infant sound. The waveform of the acoustic signal and the high-level prosodic information have different discriminative ability of modeling the diversity of variations in infant sound samples. The waveform image and the prosodic feature image are both extracted from the Praat tool [8]. The waveform images sometimes are used by researchers for audio classification while the prosodic feature images are novel images that we introduce. The prosodic feature line image, as shown in Figs. 2, 3, 4, 5 and 6, contains C0, intensity, F0, and F12345. C0 is based on MFCC coefficients representing the energy information, defined by:

$$C(n) = \sum_{m=0}^{N-1} s(m) \times cos(\pi \times n(m - 0.5)/M) \quad n = 1, 2, ..., L \qquad (1)$$

where L is the order of MFCC. When $n=0$, the whole part of $cos(0)$ equals to 1, the equation is the sum of $s(\mathrm{m})$. These auxiliary features complement well to describe the difference within infant sound for multi-stage classification as shown in the next section.

3   Multi-stage CNNs Model and Prior Knowledge Generation

Data limitation is always a challenge for neural network classification tasks. The search space constraint approaches are effective for better performance. Our multi-stage CNNs model uses the hybrid features set and applies the rule-based or statistic-based prior knowledge during the decision-making process. The searching space of CNN classification is narrowed, and hence the performance of classification is improved.

3.1   Hybrid Feature Multi-stage CNNs Model

For speech recognition tasks, phoneme units are commonly used. Acoustic coefficients are concatenated and trained at frame level by CNN based classification structure [9]. On the other hand, infant speech and crying are different regarding as non-speech signals. It is not confirmed that phoneme-based structure is suitable for classifying such non-speech signals. Inadequate hand labeled transcriptions cannot support robust model training under CNN framework. Usually, different feature sets have different discrimination ability for different audio signals. So, we analyze the confidence measure of each feature set with all test samples along with the corresponding model. We calculate the confidence measure of each feature i to identify that feature i has higher accuracy on target k, but not strong in other targets. Here i = 1, 2, ···, N, where N is the number of feature sets. k=1, 2, ···, M, where M is the total number of the categories. Based on the order of the classification accuracy on each target k using each feature set i, we can consider using a N-stage classifier to combine the ability of all N feature sets. In the N-stage classifier, each feature set is only used in its corresponding model to classify the categories that has higher confidence. The confidence measure can be the classification accuracy of each category. We use a multi-stage classifier to find such comparative advantages among different feature sets.

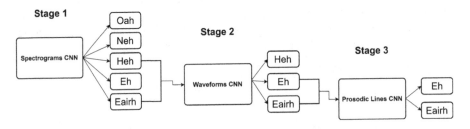

Fig. 8. Hybrid-feature Multi-stage method

Figure 8 shows the hybrid feature multi-stage method used in Dustan baby language classification. We use spectrogram CNN model to perform the 5-category classification. The accuracy for each category is calculated as the confidence measure. The best two categories will not involve in the second stage. In the case of Fig. 8, the Oah and Neh can be classified well in the first stage. Then, Heh, Eh, and Eairh's waveform images will be fed into the second stage CNN for the 3-category classification. In the third stage, only the Eh and Eairh's prosodic line images will be used in the third CNN for binary classification since the Heh sound has been classified relatively well in the second stage.

3.2   Prior Knowledge Generation

Prior knowledge can be defined either from statistic method or from rules. Statistic-based knowledge is used to decide which model should be used to classify the relevant categories. Other rule-based knowledge, such as, a vowel sound should be easier to differentiate from a consonant sound, is also used in the decision-making process. Due to limited data in our task, an efficient multi-stage classifier is performed to see if we can find such comparative advantage among different feature sets.

Different feature sets have different discrimination ability for different targets. Hence, we train and validate the individual spectrogram CNN, waveform CNN as well as prosodic lines CNN separately to obtain different classification accuracies. The prior knowledge gained indicates that the spectrograms can predict certain signals more accurately while waveforms can predict another type of signal better. Similarly, this applies to other input images as well. The accuracy can be regarded as confidence measure for prior knowledge. We use the calculated statistic-based prior knowledge to decide which model should be used to classify which categories. In addition, rule-based knowledge from linguistic information is added as another prior knowledge. For example, high energy sound should be easier to differentiate from low energy sound, a vowel sound should be easier to differentiate from a consonant sound. These rules are used to decide which category should be classified together with relevant categories. The prior knowledge is integrated into multi-stage CNN classification task as follows:

1. First stage: use the best network, the spectrogram model, to perform five-category classification. The classification accuracy of each category is calculated. The weakest three categories will be classified in the following stages.
2. Second stage: use waveform model to perform three-categories based on the confidence measure calculated in the first stage. In the case of Fig. 8, the waveform model is selected because it can recognize "Eairh" sound better than other two models. In the case of Baby Chillanto database, which is described in Sect. 4, the binary classification is decided based on the prior knowledge by analyzing the differences among images. The high energy sounds pain and hunger should not be classified together but they can be classified very well separately with another low energy sound such as asphyxia.
3. Third stage: use the last model to classify the last two types of sound.

With the mixed feature set and the use of prior knowledge during decision-making process, the searching space of CNN classification is constrained, and hence the system is more robust under limited data samples. Meanwhile, with the guidance of prior knowledge, the remaining steps of classification can be divided with different discrimination.

4   Experiments and Results

4.1   Datasets

The effectiveness of the proposed method is evaluated on both Dunstan baby language Database and Baby Chillanto Database for infant speech and infant crying classification. As shown in Table 1, Dunstan database consists of 315 wave files, sampled at 16 KHz, with a variable length between 0.3 to 1.6 s. Each utterance is a word of infant speech corresponding to one of the five "Dunstan words" transcribed by Dunstan herself or other Dunstan certified experts [2]. Baby Chillanto Database was collected by National Institute of Astrophysics and Optical Electronics, CONACYT Mexico [10]. This database consists of 2268 baby cry samples in five categories as shown in Table 2. The duration of each sample is one second.

For both datasets, we perform five-fold cross validation classificatiison due to the limitation of available samples. We use 80% samples for training and 20% samples for testing in all experiments. Spectrograms are generated by Sound eXchange (Sox) software, which is a cross-platform audio editing software created by Lance Norskog [14]. The waveforms and prosodic features images are extracted using the Praat tool. The default parameters are used when extracting waveforms and prosodic feature lines including C0, pitch, intensity, and formants. All images extracted are then resized into 60 pixels in height and 90 pixels in width.

Table 1. Dunstan Baby Language data samples.

Category	Hunry	Sleepy	Need burping	Belly pain	Discomfort
No. of samples	56	106	55	37	61
Total	315				

Table 2. Baby Chillanto database data samples.

Category	Asphyxia	Deaf	Hunger	Normal	Pain
No. of samples	340	879	350	507	192
Total	2268				

4.2   Experimental Results

CNNs are implemented using Keras framework with Tensorflow backend [15]. The architecture of spectrogram CNN is shown in Fig. 9. The convolution layer uses twenty 5 * 5 filters, 2 * 2 pooling size and 2 * 2 stride are used in the max pooling layer. In the waveform model, we use five 5 * 5 filters instead to reach relatively higher accuracy. Five 3 * 3 filters are used instead in the prosodic line model for higher accuracy. Other configurations remain the same in waveform model and prosodic line model. 100 epochs were performed during the training process.

The results of using dominant feature and auxiliary feature set separately, as well as merging the three models as a CNN late fusion model are shown in Table 3. This analysis shows that the use of spectrogram as a sole feature for five infant words classification achieves the best performance of 84.08% compared with solely using waveform and prosodic feature set of 53.84% and 69.33%,

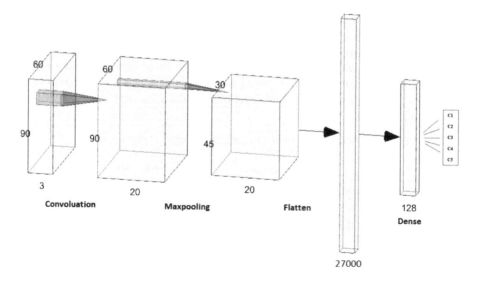

Fig. 9. CNN architecture of the baseline spectrogram model

respectively. It proves that spectrogram includes both acoustic and prosodic information and is suitable to be the dominant feature for infant speech classification under small data size. In addition, it is seen that merging spectrogram, waveform, and prosodic feature models cannot improve the performance.

Table 3. Results of using different feature combinations.

Input features and model	Accuracy	Relative changes to spectrogram
Spectrograms to CNN	84.08%	0%
Waveform to CNN	53.84%	−30.24%
Prosodic features to CNN	69.33%	−14.75%
Three CNNs late fusion model	83.48%	−0.6%
Hybrid-feature multi-stage model	88.22%	4.14%

The waveform and prosodic lines have distinguished ability to model certain infant speech as illustrated in Table 4. We observe that certain types of images are good at classifying certain types of sounds. For example, "Eairh" sound is the worst to identify in the spectrograms model, but the waveform feature can do it better; the spectrogram and waveform models both cannot recognize "Heh" sound well, but it has the 2nd best classification accuracy in the prosodic lines model. Therefore, we can use the knowledge obtained above to generate hybrid-feature set and use the multi-stage approach to achieve a better performance. The five-fold cross validation classification accuracy is 88.22%, which has a 4.14% improvement compared to the spectrogram model. Compared to the traditional CNN classification method, our multi-stage approach makes a pre-separation of searching space with prior knowledge at each step, resulting in better performance with limited data trained model. In addition, hybrid feature set consisting of dominant feature as well as auxiliary features with different discriminative ability provides different level of resolution for better classification.

Table 4. Accuracy of each category in Dunstan Baby database.

Input	Best accuracy	2nd	3rd	4th	5th
Spectrograms	Oah	Neh	Eh	Heh	Eairh
Waveforms	Oah	Neh	Eairh	Heh	Eh
Prosodic lines	Oah	Heh	Neh	Eh	Eairh

Table 5. Accuracy of each category in Baby Chillanto database.

Input	Best accuracy	2nd	3rd	4th	5th
Spectrograms	Deaf	Asphyxia	Normal	Hunger	Pain
Waveforms	Deaf	Hunger	Normal	Pain	Asphyxia
Prosodic lines	Deaf	Asphyxia	Hunger	Normal	Pain

We further evaluated our proposed approach on Baby Chillanto database. The size of this database is six times larger than the Dunstan database, but it is more unbalanced. Table 6 illustrates the results of using multi-stage classification on Baby Chillanto database. As shown in Table 5, we observe that the three networks are good at recognizing different types of crying signals. For example, the spectrograms are good at differentiating the normal crying, the waveform does a better job recognizing the hungry crying, and the prosodic feature images can classify asphyxia crying well compared to waveforms. To take advantages of all these models, we apply our hybrid multi-stage approach to classify baby crying signals. The five-category spectrogram model is used to classify deaf and normal sounds. The binary waveform model is used to classify hungry and asphyxia, and the prosodic lines are used to classify pain and asphyxia sound in the binary classification model. As shown in Table 6, Le and Kabir ensembled transfer learning CNN with SVM and reached 90.80% accuracy [11]. In [12], Wahid used MLP and Radial Basis Function Network to reach the highest accuracy, which is 93.43%. Our proposed hybrid feature with multi-stage CNNs model achieves 95.10% accuracy, which outperforms all other related studies on the Baby Chillanto database. Our results suggest that reserving the specific ability to identify from different features to form hybrid feature set is also efficient in infant crying classification tasks. Furthermore, hybrid feature set can be used to get prior knowledge information as confidence measure, which is beneficial for providing constraints in searching and classification. Our method is effective in both small database and unbalanced database and can be extend to other acoustic event databases.

Table 6. Accuracy comparison with other models on Baby Chillanto database.

Input features	Method	Accuracy
Spectrograms	CNN	89.77%
Spectrograms	Transfer Learning CNN and SVM	90.80%
MFCC and LPCC	MLP and Radial Basis Function	93.43%
Spectrograms, Waveforms, Prosodic	Hybrid-feature Multi-stage	95.10%

5   Conclusions

We have described an approach of using hybrid feature set with multi-stage CNNs for robust infant sound classification. We have shown that an infant sound is a complicated signal including infant speech and crying which have different acoustic and prosodic characteristics. Different features have different discrimination ability to model the diversity of variations within infant sound. The use of dominant and auxiliary features is beneficial to enlarge the coverage as well as keeping a good resolution. We used multi-stage CNNs method together with prior knowledge constraints in decision making to deal with limited data problem in infant sound classification. Prior knowledge information either from rules or from statistical results provide a good guidance for searching and decision making. The effectiveness of our method was evaluated on commonly used Dustan Baby Language database and Baby Chillanto database for infant speech and crying classification tasks. It gives an encouraging reduction of 4.14% absolute classification error rate compared to the results from using one-stage CNNs with spectrogram feature. On infant crying Baby Chillanto Database, our approach outperforms all other studies on this classification task. A significant absolute reduction of 5.23%, 4.30%, and 1.67% is achieved compared to the one-stage CNN, the transfer learning CNN and SVM ensemble model, and the MLP with Radial Basis Function Network, respectively. Our method generates a mechanism of hybrid features and multi-stage CNNs and can be extended to other acoustic event classification tasks. We will try other methods such as fuzzy logic to improve the performance of the infant sound detection and classification tasks. Fuzzy logic systems have been used in many applications such as wireless network routing [13]. We will introduce fuzzy logic into our learning and prediction models in the future.

Acknowledgement. We'd like to thank Dr. Eduard Franti for sharing the Dunstan Baby database and thank Dr. Orion Reyes and Dr. Carlos A. Reyes for providing the access to the Baby Chillanto database. We want to express our deepest gratitude to

Dr. Carlos A. Reyes-Garcia, Dr. Emilio Arch-Tirado and his INR-Mexico group, and Dr. Edgar M. Garcia-Tamayo for their dedication in the collection of the Infant Cry database. We also want to gratefully acknowledge the support of NVIDIA Corporation with the donation of the Tesla K40 GPU used for this research.

References

1. Banica, I.-A., Cucu, H. et al.: Automatic method for infant cry classification. In: International Conference on Communications, Kuala Lumpur, pp. 51–54. IEEE (2016)
2. Franti, E., Ispas, I., Dascalu, M.: Testing the universal baby language hypothesis automatic infant speech recognition with CNNs. In: 41st International Conference on Telecommunications and Signal Processing, Athens, pp. 424–427. IEEE (2018)
3. Bano, S., Ravikumar, K.M.: Decoding baby talk: basic approach for normal classification of infant cry signal. Int. J. Comput. Appl. **0975**, 8887 (2015)
4. Hamidi, M., Chibani, A., Osmani, A.: Machine learning approach for infant cry interpretation. In: International Conference on Tools with Artificial Intelligence, pp. 182–186. DBLP, Volos (2017)
5. Lei, Y.S., Wang, Z.Y.: The characteristic of infant cries. In: National Conference on Man-Machine Speech Communication, Xi'an (2011)
6. Varma, N., Mittal, V.K., Asthana, S.: An investigation into classification of infant cries using modified signal processing methods. In: 2nd International Conference on Signal Processing and Integrated Networks, Noida-Delhi NCR, pp. 679–684 (2015)
7. Li, Y., Kuo, K., Liu, L.: Infant cry signal detection, pattern, extraction and recognition. In: International Conference on Information and Computer Technologies, Paris, pp. 159–163 (2018)
8. Praat homepage. http://www.fon.hum.uva.nl/praat/
9. Takahashi, N., Gygli, M., Pfister, B., VanGool, L.: Deep convolutional neural networks and data augmentation for acoustic even detection. In: Interspeech, San Francisco (2016)
10. Sachin, M.U., Nagaraj, R., Samiksha, M., Rao, S., Moharir, M.: Identification of asphyxia in newborns using GPU for deep learning. In: 2nd International Conference for Convergence in Technology, India, pp. 236–239. IEEE (2017)
11. Le, L., Kabir, A.N., Ji, C., Basodi, S., Pan, Y.: Using transfer learning, SVM, and ensemble classification to classify baby cries based on their spectrogram images. In: The Sixth National Workshop for REU Research in Networking and Systems, Monterey (2019)
12. Wahid, N.S.A., Saad, P., Hariharan, M.: Automatic infant cry pattern classification for a multiclass problem. J. Telecommun. Electron. Comput. Eng. **8**(9), 45–52 (2016)
13. Liu, H., Li, J., Zhang, Y.-Q., Pan, Y.: An adaptive genetic fuzzy multi-path routing protocol for wireless ad hoc networks. In: 1st ACIS International Workshop on Self-Assembling Wireless Networks (SAWN: May 23–25, 2005, Towson, Maryland, USA, pp. 468–475 (2005)
14. Sox homepage. https://en.wikipedia.org/wiki/SoX
15. Tensorflow homepage. https://www.tensorflow.org/

Building Vector Representations for Candidates and Projects in a CV Recommender System

Adrian Satja Kurdija[(✉)], Petar Afric, Lucija Sikic, Boris Plejic, Marin Silic, Goran Delac, Klemo Vladimir, and Sinisa Srbljic

Faculty of Electrical Engineering and Computing, University of Zagreb,
Unska 3, Zagreb, Croatia
{adrian.kurdija,petar.afric,lucija.sikic,marin.silic,
goran.delac,klemo.vladimir,sinisa.srbljic}@fer.hr,
boris.plejic@ericsson.com

Abstract. We describe a CV recommender system built for the purpose of connecting candidates with projects that are relevant to their skills. Each candidate and each project is described by a textual document (CV or a project description) from which we extract a set of skills and convert this set to a numeric representation using two known models: Latent Semantic Indexing (LSI) and Global Vectors for Word Representation (GloVe) model. Indexes built from these representations enable fast search of similar entities for a given candidate/project and the empirical results demonstrate that the obtained $l2$ distances correlate with the number of common skills and Jaccard similarity.

Keywords: LSI · GloVe · Recommender systems · Nearest neighbors

1 Introduction

1.1 Recommender Systems

Recommender system is an umbrella term for various information filtering systems that tipically contain (at least) two types of entities, often *users* and *items*, and seek to infer implicit relations between them, such as user-item preference predictions, top item recommendations, and similarities between users and between items. For these purposes, two basic strategies have been developed in various ways in the past decades.

The first strategy is *content-based filtering* [1] which creates profiles for users and descriptions for items, using the obtained feature information to make connections. The downside of this strategy is the need for external information, the relevance of which is not always clear. More often, therefore, *collaborative filtering* strategies [2] are used. They are based only on the known user interactions (views, clicks, ratings, etc.) which imply their preferences and can be used to find similar users, similar items, etc. For example, users are similar if they viewed the

R. Xu et al. (Eds.): AIMS 2020, LNCS 12401, pp. 17–29, 2020.
https://doi.org/10.1007/978-3-030-59605-7_2

same items, or gave similar ratings to them; items are similar if they have been seen or rated similarly by the same set of users. The upside of this approach is domain independence: a model does not care about the meaning of "users" and "items": whether they are songs, videos, books, e-commerce products, or web services.

Recommender systems are often used in multi-user applications: in various web shops (e.g. Amazon, eBay) to recommend items for users to buy, in multimedia platforms (e.g. YouTube, Netflix, Spotify) to recommend the next song/video to stream, in social networks (e.g. Facebook, Instagram, Twitter) to recommend content in a user feed, and in dating applications (e.g. Tinder) for profile recommendation.

Apart from these popular applications, recommender systems can be employed for various technical purposes, such as financial services recommendation [3], collaboration discovery [4], and expert recommendation for digital libraries [5]. One such purpose is connecting job seekers with jobs or assignments. This paper describes a commercial recommender system built for this purpose.

1.2 CV Recommender

In our system, candidates seeking freelance or fulltime jobs upload their CVs, while employers upload job/project descriptions. In absence of other interactions between candidates and employers in the system, all relevant information is contained in a textual descriptions of a candidate (its CV document) and a textual description of a project. Therefore, a content-based recommendation must be performed based on the document contents. This paper describes the methods we used for the following recommendation tasks:

- *Finding similar candidates (CV) to a given candidate (CV).* This is useful to find candidates with similar skills to work on a same project, or to recommend missing skills to a candidate profile.
- *Finding relevant candidates (CVs) to a given project description.* In this way, candidates with skills required in the project description are recommended for possible employment.
- *Finding similar projects to a given project.* Here, past projects with similar required skills can be explored to find relevant candidates who worked on them, or to recommend missing skills to a project profile.

Our methods utilize known models of vector representations for words/documents, with the idea that candidates/projects with similar skills will map to vectors that are close to each other. The numeric representation were created from textual documents (CVs and project descriptions) using two known models: Latent Semantic Indexing (LSI) [6] and Global Vectors for Word Representation (GloVe) model [7]. Indexes built from these representations enable fast search of nearest neighbors for a given candidate/project.

The original contribution of our work is a description of methods used by our existing CV recommender system in which the numeric representation models have been successfully applied to similar entities recommendation. The experimental results will demonstrate that the obtained distances between vector representations of similar entities correlate with the number of common skills and Jaccard similarity.

The paper is organized as follows. Section 2 describes the related work. Section 3 describes our CV recommender system. Section 4 describes the conducted experiments. Conclusions are given in Sect. 5.

2   Related Work

2.1   Job Recommendation

Various job recommendation systems have been described in the literature, with various goals and different assumptions on system properties and the available data. For example, [8] presented taxonomy-based systems recommending jobs to Facebook and LinkedIn users. A job recommender based on user clustering was proposed in [9], while [10] applied other data mining techniques (such as decision trees) to a job recommender system which considers candidate job preferences. A profile-based job recommender system was proposed by [11], where user profiles were updated dynamically on the basis of previously applied jobs and their statistical features. Research work by [12] proposed enhancing a job recommender with implicit user feedback. Recently, *RecSys Challenge 2016* seeked to predict job postings that a user will interact with based on the past interactions [13].

For more comprehensive surveys on job recommender systems, please see [14] and [15]. Our recommender system assumes as little as possible, not relying on any historic/temporal data or interactions of any kind, using only textual descriptions of entities to find connections and recommendations.

The following subsection briefly describe the numerical text representation models we used in our system, and the strategy to quickly find nearest neighbors, i.e. nearest vectors to a given vector (representation).

2.2   Latent Semantic Indexing

Both LSI and GloVe models depend on the *distributional hypothesis* [16]: words which are close in meaning tend to occur in the same contexts. Therefore, to learn the relations between different words, a large set of texts (usually called *corpus*) must be processed in order to find the appropriate numerical representations which will reflect the context-based word similarities.

Latent Semantic Indexing (LSI) [6] utilizes this idea in the following way. First, it creates a word-document occurrence count matrix from a corpus of textual documents. Then a mathematical tool called Singular Value Decomposition (SVD) is employed to transform this matrix in order to reduce the number of rows while preserving the similarity structure among columns. This enables us to compare two documents using the numerical representations in their respective columns of the obtained matrix. When a new document (set of words) arrives, we can find its numerical representation by using the same rank-lowering transformation that was used on the corpus documents.

The mathematical details can be found in e.g. [17]. For this paper, we will use an abstract notation $LSI(D)$ to denote a vector which is a representation of a document (set of words) D.

2.3   GloVe Representations

Global Vectors for Word Representation (GloVe) [7] is an unsupervised machine learning algorithm whose purpose is to obtain a representation for each *word* as a numerical sequence, i.e. n-dimensional vector. Various dimensions represent various underlying concepts that give meanings to each word. Under such representations, numerical connections exist between words with connected meaning. For example, we can imagine that the words "CEO" and "spouse" might have a similar coordinate on a dimension representing the concept of *person* (as opposed to a word such as "company"), but different coordinates on a dimension representing the concept of *work* (where "CEO" will be closer to "company"). In particular, words with similar meaning have similar (close) representations.

The GloVe model is trained from a large corpus (set of texts) where first an aggregated word-word co-occurence matrix is generated, and then word vectors are learned so that their dot product corresponds to the logarithm of the words' probability of co-occurrence. The obtained representations resemble linear substructures of the word vector space.

2.4   Recent NLP Models

As part of the recent natural language processing (NLP) efforts, neural-network based models such as ELMo [18] and *Google*'s BERT [19] have been developed. They have gained a lot of popularity in the past year due to their performance on natural language processing tasks. ELMo introduces deep contextualized word representations which can model complex characteristics of word use (syntax and semantics) and the variations of its use in different contexts. Their word vectors are learned functions of internal states of a deep bidirectional language model (biLM), pretrained on a large text corpus. Unlike ELMo, BERT is designed to pretrain deep bidirectional representations from unlabeled text by jointly conditioning on both left and right context in all layers, enabling it to be finetuned with just one additional output layer in order to create state-of-the-art models for various tasks such as language inference and question answering.

However, our decision to use GloVe and LSI is based on their suitability to the specific nature of our dataset. Namely, our recommender system requires a specific dataset which does not consist of standard natural language texts, but documents of technical skills (extracted from CVs and project descriptions) which represent specific terms in the chosen models. In comparison, ELMo and BERT are generic models that do not work so well for technical skills, while the vast majority of such terms have embeddings in GloVe, and LSI learns from co-occurrence and thus does not depend of the term meaning. Therefore, since the recent and popular NLP models are too general and lack embeddings for terms that dominate our datasheet, their performance would be inferior.

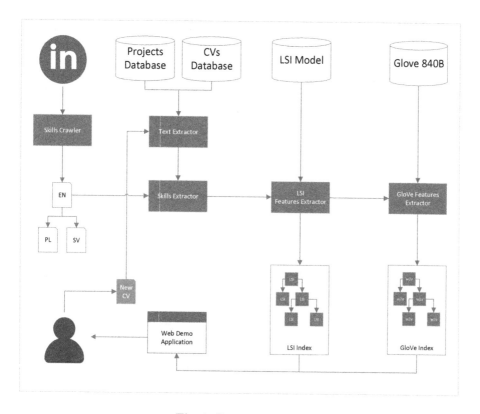

Fig. 1. System overview

2.5   Representations Index

When searching for representations (of CVs or projects) similar to a given representation v, we need to quickly find the top k nearest neighbors of v (e.g. 5, 10 or 100) from a set of representations S, according to vector distance (as an Euclidean distance or $l2$-norm). For this purpose, [20] developed an efficient and robust heuristic algorithm for approximate nearest neighbor search. Their approach (Hierarchical NSW) is graph-based and supports insertion, deletion and K-nearest-neighbors queries. An open-source implementation of this data structure (usually called an *index*) was done by [21] as a Non-Metric Space Library (NMSLIB) library which we relied on.

3   Methods

Figure 1 depicts a high-level overview of the implemented system. Its main parts will be described in the rest of this section. Briefly, each uploaded document first undergoes skill extraction, then the extracted skills are converted into numerical vector representations, which are then used to query an index of representations of existing documents to find similar entities.

By courtesy of the Ework Group AB (a consultant supplier company based in Sweden, https://www.eworkgroup.com/en/contact), we have been provided a large dataset of CV documents and project descriptions. Namely, we have collected:

– 70 321 English CVs,
– 77 736 Swedish CVs,
– 709 Polish CVs,
– 32 488 English project descriptions,
– 33 484 Swedish project descriptions,
– 342 Polish project descriptions.

The following subsections describe the main parts of our CV recommender system.

3.1   Skill Extraction

The basic idea of our CV recommender system was to compare the entities based on their *hard skills* (competences) which can be extracted from the textual document. The examples of hard skills include "C++", "3G", "Web Design", "Project Management", "Colorimetry", "Welding", etc.

For this purpose, we have implemented a crawler over the Linkedin database of topics and skills[1] and thus obtained a list of 20 000+ skills which we then manually filtered to exclude erroneous or irrelevant entries.

Using Google Translate API, we have translated all skills into the relevant foreign languages (Swedish and Polish). We have thus obtained separate lists of hard skills for English, Swedish and Polish languages. When a skill did not have a corresponding translation, an original (English) version of the skill was used for Swedish/Polish list. A list of skills for each language was stored as a standard *set* data structure (which is internally implemented by a variant of balanced binary search tree) so that a query of the form "does string x belong to the set?" can be performed fast, in the time complexity equal to the logarithm of the number of skills.

For each uploaded CV or project description, we first check the language it was written in. For this purpose we utilized the Polyglot library [22]. Then we perform a single pass over the document words and extract all hards skills that are present. Whether a word (or two/three consecutive words) is a hard skill can be efficiently checked by querying a set of all hard skills as mentioned in

---

[1] https://www.linkedin.com/directory/topics/[letter].

the previous paragraph. When a list of hard skills for a document is ready, it is forwarded to the LSI or GloVe model which converts it into a numeric vector, which is described in the following subsections.

3.2 Extracting LSI Features

The LSI model assumes a collection of documents containing words. Instead of considering each word, in our model, each CV and project description is seen as a set of extracted skills (see the previous subsection). Such a choice was made for two reasons. An obvious reason is a significant reduction in time and space complexity of the LSI model. Also, considering each word would make our model dependent on many irrelevant aspects of a document (such as vocabulary). By focusing on what is truly relevant (objective competences of a candidate and required competences in a project) we are able to filter out much noise and make our model more robust.

The core of LSI model is a transformation matrix which converts a document (encoded as a vector of skill occurrences) into a vector with a given number of dimensions. Notice that the skill occurence vector encoding does not depend on a language. To see this in an example, assume that a CV was translated from Swedish to English. Assume that the Swedish version contains skill #5 ("Svetsning"). Then the translated version will also contain skill #5 ("Welding"). Therefore, both skill occurence vectors will have 1 in the fifth position, i.e., they will be equal.

For these reasons, we used a single LSI model for all languages. The model was precomputed from the available documents and the number of dimensions was set to 25. To calculate LSI we used the Gensim library [23]. The LSI representations are added to a set (an index) which can be efficiently queried to find nearest neighbors to a given representation. We used the NMSLIB index [21].

When the model is up and running, for each query (new uploaded CV or a project description) we first calculate the skill occurence vector x and then calculate $LSI(x)$, obtaining a 25-dimensional numerical representation of a document. Using this representation, a nearest neighbors query can be performed on an index of existing LSI representations, in order to find e.g. 10 most similar candidates (in terms of competence) to a given CV/project. Also, an LSI representation of a newly uploaded document is added to the LSI index.

3.3 Extracting GloVe Features

For a vocabulary of about 2.2 milion words we have downloaded pre-trained word vectors[2]. These vectors have 300 dimensions. Using these vectors, a GloVe representation vector of a document was created by averaging the GloVe word vectors for all skills which were extracted from a document. The final vector was normalized to have an $l2$ norm equal to 1. The GloVe representations are added

---

[2] http://nlp.stanford.edu/data/glove.840B.300d.zip.

to a set (an index) which can be efficiently queried to find nearest neighbors to a given representation. We used the NMSLIB index [21].

For each query x (new uploaded CV or a project description), its extracted skills (in English) are converted to its pre-trained 300-dimensional GloVe representation, only for those skills which appear in the pre-trained vocabulary of 2.2 million words. These skill representations are averaged using weighted average, such that frequent skills have less weight in the average. More precisely, weight of each skill s is inversely proportional to its total number of occurences in the available documents. The final vector was normalized to have an $l2$ norm equal to 1. To summarize:

$$GloVe(x) = \frac{\sum_{s\in x} GloVe(s)/\text{totalCount}(s)}{||\sum_{s\in x} GloVe(s)/\text{totalCount}(s)||} \tag{1}$$

A GloVe representation of each newly uploaded document is added to the GloVe index.

4   Evaluation

In order to evaluate the quality of our similar entities recommendation, we decided to compare the Euclidean ($l2$) distances of the vector representations with the more explicit and straighforward similarity measures. Namely, the chosen similarity measures/distance were:

1. *Jaccard distance.* For two documents viewed as two sets of skills S_1 and S_2, their Jaccard distance is calculated as

$$Jaccard(S_1, S_2) = 1 - \frac{|S_1 \cap S_2|}{|S_1 \cup S_2|}. \tag{2}$$

2. *Intersection.* For two documents viewed as two sets of skills S_1 and S_2, their *intersection* is the number of skills they have in common. By its nature, this is a measure of similarity, so we need to invert it (e.g. by using a minus sign) to convert it into a distance measure:

$$Intersection(S_1, S_2) = -|S_1 \cap S_2|. \tag{3}$$

3. *Weighted intersection.* This is similar to the previous measure, but it weights each skill in the intersection so that less frequent skills contribute more to the similarity. (For example, a specific skill such as "NumPy" carries more information than a generic skill such as "Python", and both are more relevant than e.g. "Programming".) Namely,

$$WeightedIntersection(S_1, S_2) = - \sum_{s\in S_1 \cap S_2} 1 - \frac{\text{totalCount}(s)}{C}, \tag{4}$$

where C is the maximal *totalCount* for all skills in a dataset.

For each model (GloVe and LSI) we have performed all queries for all documents, namely:

- Finding top 100 similar CVs to a given CV.
- Finding top 100 similar CVs to a given project.
- Finding top 100 similar projects to a given project.

For each query document, $l2$ distances from this document to the retrieved similar documents' representations were calculated, and correlated with other described distances (Jaccard, Intersection, Weighted Intersection). Namely, standard Pearson correlation coefficient (between -1 and 1) was calculated, and its median value (over all queries of the same type for a given language) was taken as a representative correlation value.

To expand our experiments to the entities which are not very similar to each other, we also decided to examine the representation distances to *random* 100 (instead of nearest 100) entities to a given query, in order to further verify our hypothesis that the representation distances correlate with other distances, regardless of the amount of their similarity.

Figure 2 depicts the results for GloVe model. Significant positive correlations are found in all cases, with median p-value < 0.001, except for "nearest CVs for project" experiment where the correlations are less significant (≈ 0.2 correlations with median p-values ≈ 0.1). The strongest correlations are found in the "nearest CVs for CV" experiment (above 0.8). There are no significant differences with respect to three alternative measures, which is explained by the fact that they are all based on common skills. Also, there no significant differences with respect to languages.

Figure 3 depicts the results for LSI model. Here the correlations are lower than for the GloVe model, but still significant (≈ 0.4 or higher) in four out of six experiments. Median p-value is < 0.001 for all experiments except for "nearest CVs for project" and "nearest projects for project" experiments, where no correlations were found. Since the "random" experiments for the same entities give strong correlations, a lack of distance correlations in the "nearest" case could be explained by the inability of the model to differentiate between very similar entities. In other words, LSI gives much stronger correlations when the entities are more apart from each other, and behaves less fine-grained than GloVe. Again, as in the GloVe experiments, there are no significant differences with respect to three alternative measures and no significant differences with respect to languages.

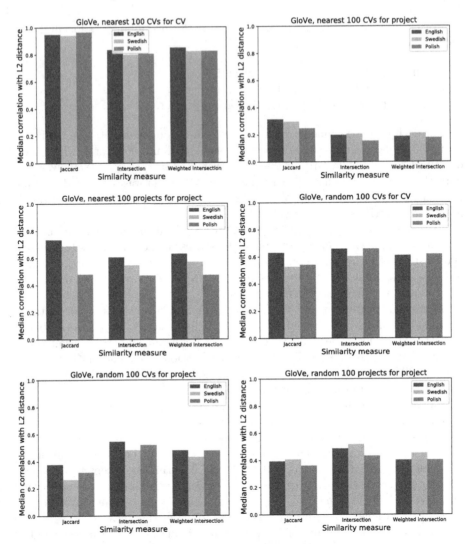

Fig. 2. Results for GloVe model

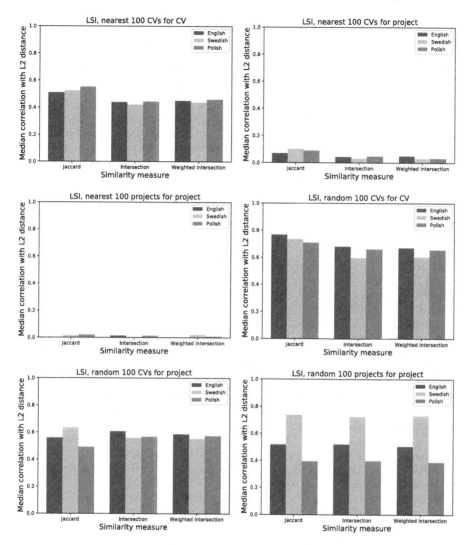

Fig. 3. Results for LSI model

5   Conclusion

We have presented a CV recommender system capable of efficient retrieval of similar entities based on their numeric representations. A list of hard skills (competences) is extracted from each candidate CV or a project description, and then converted into a numerical vector using GloVe or LSI model. The numeric representations are stored in an index which enables fast retrieval of closest neighbors – GloVe or LSI vectors with the smallest $l2$ distance from the given query CV or a project description. The experiments have shown that the obtained distances strongly correlate with standard explicit similarity measures (such as Jaccard distance) which are based on the list of hard skills (competences) retrieved from the document. This proves the effectiveness of the presented methods in recommending similar entities and shows their benefits in recommender systems based on textual documents.

Acknowledgment. The dataset for this research has been collected by EWORK (https://www.eworkgroup.com/en/contact). The authors acknowledge the support of the **Croatian Science Foundation** through the *Reliable Composite Applications Based on Web Services* (**IP-01-2018-6423**) research project. The Titan X Pascal used for this research was donated by the NVIDIA Corporation.

References

1. Pazzani, M.J., Billsus, D.: Content-based recommendation systems. In: Brusilovsky, P., Kobsa, A., Nejdl, W. (eds.) The Adaptive Web. LNCS, vol. 4321, pp. 325–341. Springer, Heidelberg (2007). https://doi.org/10.1007/978-3-540-72079-9_10

2. Su, X., Khoshgoftaar, T.M.: A survey of collaborative filtering techniques. Adv. Artif. Intell. **2009**, 4:2 (2009)

3. Felfernig, A., Isak, K., Szabo, K., Zachar, P.: The vita financial services sales support environment. In: Proceedings of the 19th National Conference on Innovative Applications of Artificial Intelligence, IAAI 2007, vol. 2, pp. 1692–1699. AAAI Press (2007)

4. Chen, H.H., Gou, L., Zhang, X., Giles, C.L.: CollabSeer: a search engine for collaboration discovery. In: Proceedings of the 11th Annual International ACM/IEEE Joint Conference on Digital Libraries, JCDL 2011, pp. 231–240. Association for Computing Machinery, New York (2011)

5. Chen, H., Ororbia II, A.G., Giles, C.L.: ExpertSeer: a keyphrase based expert recommender for digital libraries. CoRR abs/1511.02058 (2015)

6. Deerwester, S., Dumais, S., Furnas, G., Landauer, T., Harshman, R.: Indexing by latent semantic analysis. J. Am. Soc. Inf. Sci. **41**, 391–407 (1990)

7. Pennington, J., Socher, R., Manning, C.D.: Glove: global vectors for word representation. In: Empirical Methods in Natural Language Processing (EMNLP), pp. 1532–1543 (2014)

8. Diaby, M., Viennet, E.: Taxonomy-based job recommender systems on Facebook and Linkedin profiles. In: 2014 IEEE Eighth International Conference on Research Challenges in Information Science (RCIS), pp. 1–6. IEEE (2014)

9. Hong, W., Zheng, S., Wang, H., Shi, J.: A job recommender system based on user clustering. JCP **8**(8), 1960–1967 (2013)

10. Gupta, A., Garg, D.: Applying data mining techniques in job recommender system for considering candidate job preferences. In: 2014 International Conference on Advances in Computing, Communications and Informatics (ICACCI), pp. 1458–1465. IEEE (2014)

11. Hong, W., Zheng, S., Wang, H.: Dynamic user profile-based job recommender system. In: 2013 8th International Conference on Computer Science & Education, pp. 1499–1503. IEEE (2013)

12. Hutterer, M.: Enhancing a Job Recommender with Implicit User Feedback. Citeseer (2011)

13. Abel, F., Benczúr, A., Kohlsdorf, D., Larson, M., Pálovics, R.: RecSys challenge 2016: job recommendations. In: Proceedings of the 10th ACM Conference on Recommender Systems, pp. 425–426. ACM (2016)
14. Siting, Z., Wenxing, H., Ning, Z., Fan, Y.: Job recommender systems: a survey. In: 2012 7th International Conference on Computer Science & Education (ICCSE), pp. 920–924. IEEE (2012)
15. Al-Otaibi, S.T., Ykhlef, M.: A survey of job recommender systems. Int. J. Phys. Sci. **7**(29), 5127–5142 (2012)
16. Harris, Z.S.: Distributional structure. Word **10**(2–3), 146–162 (1954)
17. Dumais, S.: Latent semantic analysis. ANnual Rev. Inf. Sci. Technol. **38**, 188–230 (2004)
18. Peters, M.E., et al.: Deep contextualized word representations. CoRR abs/1802. 05365 (2018)
19. Devlin, J., Chang, M., Lee, K., Toutanova, K.: BERT: pre-training of deep bidirectional transformers for language understanding. CoRR abs/1810.04805 (2018)
20. Malkov, Y.A., Yashunin, D.A.: Efficient and robust approximate nearest neighbor search using hierarchical navigable small world graphs. CoRR abs/1603.09320 (2016)
21. Boytsov, L., Naidan, B.: Engineering efficient and effective non-metric space library. In: Brisaboa, N., Pedreira, O., Zezula, P. (eds.) SISAP 2013. LNCS, vol. 8199, pp. 280–293. Springer, Heidelberg (2013). https://doi.org/10.1007/978-3-642-41062-8_28
22. Al-Rfou', R., Perozzi, B., Skiena, S.: Polyglot: distributed word representations for multilingual NLP. In: Proceedings of the Seventeenth Conference on Computational Natural Language Learning, Sofia, Bulgaria, Association for Computational Linguistics, pp. 183–192, August 2013
23. Řehůřek, R., Sojka, P.: Software framework for topic modelling with large corpora. In: Proceedings of the LREC 2010 Workshop on New Challenges for NLP Frameworks, Valletta, Malta, ELRA, May 2010, pp. 45–50. http://is.muni.cz/publication/884893/en

Candidate Classification and Skill Recommendation in a CV Recommender System

Adrian Satja Kurdija$^{(\boxtimes)}$, Petar Afric, Lucija Sikic, Boris Plejic, Marin Silic, Goran Delac, Klemo Vladimir, and Sinisa Srbljic

Faculty of Electrical Engineering and Computing, University of Zagreb, Unska 3, Zagreb, Croatia
{adrian.kurdija,petar.afric,lucija.sikic,marin.silic,goran.delac, klemo.vladimir,sinisa.srbljic}@fer.hr, boris.plejic@ericsson.com

Abstract. In this paper, we describe a CV recommender system with a focus on two properties. The first property is the ability to classify candidates into roles based on automatic processing of their CV documents. The second property is the ability to recommend skills to a candidate which are not listed in their CV, but the candidate is likely to have them. Both features are based on skills extraction from a textual CV document. A spectral skill clustering is precomputed for the purpose of candidate classification, while skill recommendation is based on various similarity-based strategies. Experimental results include both automatic experiments and an empirical study, both of which demonstrate the effectiveness of the presented methods.

Keywords: Recommender systems · Skill recommendation · Spectral clustering · Classification

1 Introduction

1.1 Recommender Systems

Recommender system is an umbrella term for various information filtering systems that tipically contain two types of entities (*users* and *items*), seeking to infer implicit relations between them, such as user-user and item-item similarities, user-item preference predictions, and top item recommendations for a particular user.

For these purposes, two basic strategies have been developed in various ways in the past decades. The first strategy is *content-based filtering* [1] which creates profiles for users and descriptions for items, using the obtained feature information to infer relations. The downside of this strategy is the need for external information, the relevance of which is not always clear. Therefore, more often, *collaborative filtering* strategies [2] are used. They view users and items as "black boxes" without the need for their internal descriptions, relying on the interactions between them

© Springer Nature Switzerland AG 2020
R. Xu et al. (Eds.): AIMS 2020, LNCS 12401, pp. 30–44, 2020.
https://doi.org/10.1007/978-3-030-59605-7_3

(such as views, clicks, ratings) to infer preferences and find user-user and item-item similarities. From this perspective, users are similar if they clicked on the same items or gave similar ratings; items are similar if they have been clicked (or rated similarly) by the same users. The upside of this approach is domain independence: a model does not rely on the meaning of "users" and "items", which can be films, books, web shop products, job candidates, or their skills.

Recommender systems are commonly used in multi-user applications: in e-commerce (e.g. eBay, Amazon) for product recommendations, in multimedia sites (e.g. Netflix, YouTube, Spotify) to recommend the next streaming song/video, in social media (e.g. Instagram, Twitter, Facebook) for content recommendation, and in dating applications (e.g. Tinder) for matching profile recommendations. Recommender systems can also be employed for various less widespread purposes, such as recommendation of financial services [3], collaboration discovery [4], and expert recommendation for digital libraries [5]. An area which gains more and more attention is job recommendation, which is a primary purpose of the commercial system built by the authors and described in this paper.

1.2   CV Recommender

In our system, user candidates seeking fulltime or freelance jobs upload their CV documents in a freely chosen format, while employers upload textual descriptions of projects/jobs. In absence of other interactions between candidates and employers in the system, the information relevant for recommendations is contained in the uploaded documents. For this reason, a content-based recommendation is performed, relying on the document contents to infer relations and predictions. This paper describes the methods we used for the following recommendation tasks:

- *Candidate classification.* Using the candidate CV document, recommend the most likely roles (positions) for which the candidate is competent based on the skills they have listed in the CV text. The recommended role can be used as a handy reference point by both the candidate and an employer.
- *Skill recommendation.* Recommend missing skills to a candidate profile. In other words, find skills that are likely to appear together with the skills listed in the candidate's CV document, in order to make the candidate's profile more accurate and complete, which increases its probability of being selected for the appropriate position.

For candidate classification, we devised an appropriate notion of skill similarity and utilized spectral clustering with various enhancements. Skill recommendation was based on several strategies, where some were based on the ideas that similar candidates share common skills and that similar skills/candidates can be found by using their appropriate vector representations. In other words, numeric representations of skills or candidate CV documents will be close to each other when the original skills/candidates are similar.

The original contribution of this work is a description of methods used by our implemented CV recommender system in which the existing algorithm were successfully applied to candidate classification and skill recommendation problems. Our methods have been verified in both manual and automatic testing scenarios.

The paper is organized as follows. Section 2 describes the related work. Section 3 describes the methods used for the recommendation tasks. In Sect. 4 we describe the conducted experiments to verify the effectiveness of our methods. Section 5 presents our conclusions.

2   Related Work

2.1   Job Recommendation

Various job recommendation systems have been described in the literature. They have different goals and various assumptions on system properties and the available data. Let us name a few approaches. Work by [6] presented taxonomy-based systems which recommend jobs to users of social networks (LinkedIn and Facebook). A job recommender based on user clustering was proposed in [7], while [8] applied other data mining techniques (such as decision trees) to a job recommender system which considers candidate job preferences. Work by [9] proposed a profile-based job recommender system, where user profiles were dynamically updated based on the previously applied jobs and their statistical features. In [10], the authors proposed enhancing a job recommender with implicit user feedback. Recently, *RecSys Challenge 2016* was to predict job postings that a user will interact with based on their past interactions [11].

For comprehensive surveys on job recommender systems, please see [12] and [13]. Our recommender system assumes as little as possible: it does not rely on any temporal/historic data or interactions of any kind. It uses only textual descriptions of entities (CV documents) to infer connections and recommendations. As a side difference, unlike the work by [7] which uses user clustering, we performed clustering of their *skills* as more exact objects.

2.2   Numeric Representations

Some of our methods utilize known models of vector representations for words/documents, with the idea that related skills will map to vectors that are close to each other, and that candidates with similar skills will, therefore, also map to vectors that are close to each other. Numeric representation were created from textual documents (CVs and project descriptions) using two known models: Latent Semantic Indexing (LSI) [14] and Global Vectors for Word Representation (GloVe) model [15]. The obtained vector representations were saved into data structures called *index*. An index enables fast search of nearest neighbors for a given vector [16]. An open-source implementation of such an index is present in the Non-Metric Space Library (NMSLIB) [17] which we used in our system. The details on creating LSI and GloVe representations of entities in our CV recommender system are beyond the scope of this paper and will be presented in another paper [29].

2.3   Clustering Algorithms

Clustering is an unsupervised learning method. Its purpose is to join (unlabeled) data items into groups (called clusters) such that items in the same group are similar to each other and items from different groups are dissimilar. The notion of similarity is often unclear and depends on the chosen definition. The notion of good clustering is also vague and different clustering algorithms have been developed in order to optimize different clustering quality measures. We can name K-Means [18] and hierarchical clustering [19] as the most common clustering approaches. In K-Means, the number of clusters must be given in advance. Hierarchical clustering is usually more time consuming, but creates a whole cluster hierarchy where a "cut" can be made at any point to produce any number of clusters. Over the years, many other clustering algorithms have been proposed and used for different purposes. As examples, we can mention the Mean Shift approach [20] which is centroid-based (like K-Means), but automatically sets the number of clusters; the DBSCAN algorithm [21] and its generalization OPTICS algorithm [22], which define clusters as areas of high density separated by areas of low density; or the BIRCH method [23] which optimizes the used memory and is efficient for large databases.

A spectral clustering algorithm [24] is a method of graph clustering which requires an affinity (similarity) matrix between items. It first performs a dimensionality reduction, i.e., a low-dimension embedding of the affinity matrix, and then performs clustering of the components of the eigenvectors in the low dimensional space (using e.g. K-Means). The eigenvectors are found by solving the *eigenvalue problem*, using e.g. the AMG solver [25]. For spectral clustering, we used the implementation from the *scikit-learn* library [26].

Most clustering algorithms have been proposed for clustering of numerical data, such as vectors of numerical features. Such data has the advantage of belonging to a vector space where distance metrics are well defined and we can use a distance-based similarity such as Euclidean distance. Also, various distance properties (such as triangle inequality) are true, which is a good ground for the clustering algorithm – e.g., two items that are both very similar to a third item will also be mutually similar. Categorical features, on the other hand, represent data that is divided into a given number of categories with discrete and finite set of feature values, without any clear numerical relations between different categories and their features. Usually, there is no natural order among categorical values (e.g. among different blood types or different professions). In this case, it is more difficult to define similarity or distance measure between data items, and clustering is therefore a more challenging task [27]. The approaches differ from case to case and depend on the nature of the problem and its properties. In this work, one such task (namely, a clustering of *job candidate skills*) was successfully done.

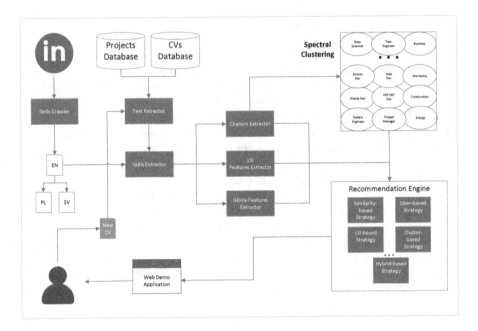

Fig. 1. System overview

3   Methods

By courtesy of the Ework Group AB (a consultant supplier company based in Sweden, https://www.eworkgroup.com/en/contact), we have been provided a large dataset of CV documents and project descriptions. Namely, we have collected around 150 000 CVs and 70 000 project descriptions, used to perform skill clustering and build LSI and GloVe Models.

In our CV recommended system, for each uploaded document, skill extraction is first performed. Then, the extracted skills are converted into numerical vector representations, which are then used to query an index of representations of existing documents to find similar entities. A high-lever overview of the system is depicted in Fig. 1. The following subsections describe the parts of the system which are the subject of this paper.

3.1   Skill Extraction

The basic idea of our CV recommender system was to compare the entities based on their *hard skills* (competences). They can be extracted from the textual (CV) document, and the examples include words/phrases such as "C++", "3G", "Web Design", "Project Management", "Colorimetry", "Welding", etc.

For this purpose, we have implemented a crawler over the Linkedin database of topics and skills[1] and thus obtained a list of more than 20 000 skills which we

---

[1] https://www.linkedin.com/directory/topics/[letter].

manually filtered to exclude irrelevant or erroneous entries. A list of skills for each language was stored as a standard *set* data structure (internally implemented by a variation of a balanced binary search tree), with the ability of quickly answering queries of the form "does string x belong to the set?". The time complexity equals the logarithm of the number of skills.

For each uploaded CV or project description, we perform a single pass over the document words and extract all hards skills that are present. Whether a word (or two/three consecutive words) is a hard skill can be efficiently checked by querying a set of all hard skills as mentioned above.

3.2 Skill Clustering

To be able to detect roles, we decided to perform a clustering of all skills in the system, with the idea that a group of skills which frequently appear together define a role. For clustering purposes, we introduced a notion of *skill similarity* with the meaning of *"how related are skills s_1 and s_2?"*. Using a set of documents D, we defined it follows:

$$similarity(s_1, s_2) = \sum_{\substack{d \in D \text{ s.t.} \\ s_1 \in d, \, s_2 \in d}} \left(\frac{1}{totalCount(s_1)} + \frac{1}{totalCount(s_2)} \right), \quad (1)$$

where skill count (frequency) is the number of documents where the skill appears:

$$totalCount(s) = |\{d \in D \text{ s.t. } s \in d\}|. \quad (2)$$

In other words, for each document where the two skills appear together, their similarity is increased, but the amount of increment depends on their general individual frequency. Namely, if two skills are very frequent anyway, then their joint occurrence does not give a strong indication of their similarity; on the other hand, if two uncommon skills appear together, then it is a strong indication of their similarity. Notice that the normalization of the obtained sums is not necessary because all similarities are calculated over the same set of documents and only the relative relations between similarities are important for clustering. We have discarded the skills with too low frequency ($totalCount(s) < 25$).

Using the defined skill similarity, we performed spectral clustering by viewing the skills as nodes in the graph, and similarities as their weights (affinities). For spectral clustering we used the *scikit-learn* library [26] and the set number of clusters was 120. Because of the nature of our problem, with large variation of skill frequencies and a significant number of skills that are very common, combined with the nature of spectral clustering, the result was one huge cluster and many small clusters. Therefore, we decided to adapt the spectral clustering results. Namely, we have discarded the clusters which were too small (less than 10 skills), and skills from each cluster which was too large (more than 200 skills) were added to other clusters instead. Those skills from large clusters were called *frequent skills* because most of them had high frequencies. For each frequent skill, we calculated its similarity to other clusters (by taking the average similarity to all skills in the cluster), and the frequent skill was added to at most 5 other clusters with the highest obtained similarity, with the requirement that each cluster receives at most 10 frequent skills.

3.3   Candidate Classification

We manually inspected all obtained clusters, gave each cluster a name, and cleaned some skills that seemed false for the corresponding cluster. The final list of cluster names is presented below (there are 66 clusters), in alphabetic order:

Cluster name	Description
.Net Developer	Expert in .NET technologies, C#, Visual Studio, etc.
Architect	Plans, designs and reviews the construction of buildings
Automation Engineer	Designs, programs, simulates and tests automated machinery and processes
Automotive Designer	Develops the appearance of motor vehicles
Automotive Engineer	Develops passenger cars, trucks, buses, motorcycles or off-road vehicles
Brand Manager	Responsible for branding, web content management, internet marketing, etc.
Business Service Manager	Managing service desk, service delivery, etc.
Citrix Administrator	Maintains Citrix applications
Civil Engineer	Design, construction, maintenance of physical and naturally built environment
Clerk	Office tasks, record keeping
Cloud Software Developer	Develops software which runs in a cloud
Computer Hardware Engineer	Development and maintenance of computer hardware
Corporate Trainer	Expert in personal/group/leadership development, conflict management etc.
Data Analyst	Expert in information analysis and data modeling
Data Quality Specialist	Supports quality management systems operation within organization
Data Scientist	Extracts knowledge and insights from data
Database Administrator	Maintains Oracle and other databases
Digital Games Developer	Game development, animation, computer graphics
Digital Marketing Director	Developing, implementing and managing marketing campaigns
Electronic Engineer	Design electronic circuits, devices, VLSI devices and their systems
Embedded Software Engineer	Develops low-level software for various devices
Energy Engineer	Design and develops energy-related projects
Environmental Engineer	Develops solutions to environmental problems
Environmental Health Inspector	Carrying out measures for protecting public health
Environmental Technician	Works on projects to asses, clean up and protect the environment
Finance Consultant	Expert in finance, accounting, tax etc.
Financial Analyst	Makes business recommendations for an organization
Financial Controller	Verifies financial reports, regulatory compliance and analysis of financial data
Frontend Developer	Develops interfaces of websites and applications
Geographic Information Systems Specialist	Expert in systems for storing and accessing geospatial data
Graphic Designer	Creates images, typography, or motion graphics
Human Resources Manager	Coordinates the administrative functions of an organization
IBM BPM Engineer	Specialist in IBM's business process manager (BPM) tools
IT specialist	Computer support and hardware/software troubleshooting

(continued)

(contniued)

Industrial Designer	Expert in mechanical design of manufactured products
Information Security Manager	Protects an organization's computers, networks and data against computer viruses, security breaches and hacker attacks
Java Developer	Expert (programmer) in Java technologies
Javascript Developer	Expert in web programming (Javascirpt and related technologies)
Logistics Analyst	Coordinates and analyzes logistical functions or supply chain of an organization
Machine Learning Engineer	Expert in artificial intelligence, neural networks, predictive modeling...
Marketing Specialist	Develops marketing programs and materials to reach customers
Materials Engineer	Design and discovery of new materials, particularly solids
Mechanical Engineer	Designs, analyzes, manufactures and maintains mechanical systems
Mobile App Developer	Develops applications for mobile devices (Androis, iOS, etc.)
Network Engineer	Plans, constructs and manages computer networks
Offshore Engineer	Technical professional who is actively involved in the offshore oil and gas industry
Oracle Developer	Expert in Oracle applications and technologies
Production Engineer	Oversees the production of goods in industries at factories or plants
Project Manager	Responsible for planning, procurement and execution of a (team) project
Public Relations Manager	Developing and implementing an organisation's PR and media strategy.
Ruby On Rails Developer	Responsible for writing server-side web application logic in Ruby, around the framework Rails
SAP Developer	Writes programs using Advanced Business Application Programming (ABAP)
Scrum Master	Responsible for scrub-based workflow
Security Consultant	Advisor and supervisor for security measures to protect a company or client's assets
SharePoint Administrator	Responsible for overseeing an installation of the Microsoft SharePoint collaboration and content management platform
Solution Architect	Responsible for the design of one or more applications or services within an organization
Storage Manager	Management and administration of data storage systems
Strategic Planning Manager	Responsible for planning and directing an organization's strategic and long-range goals
System Engineer	Creating and maintaining computer systems
Technical Writer	Prepares instruction manuals, journal articles and supporting documents to communicate technical information
Telecommunications Engineer	Designing and overseeing the installation of telecommunications equipment and facilities
Test Engineer	Designing and implementing the tests that ensure quality and functionality of a product
User Experience Designer	Designs user-product interaction to achieve usability, accessibility and desirability
Webmaster	Responsible for maintaining one or more websites
Wireless Networks Engineer	Responsible for setup, maintenance and troubleshooting of a wireless network
iOS Developer	Developing applications for mobile devices with Apple's iOS operating system

We here note that most of the clusters are IT-related because of the nature of our CV dataset.

The candidate classification is done in the following manner. When a candidate uploads a CV, we first extract a list of hard skills from the CV text, and then rank the clusters with respect to how many skills from a cluster are present in the extracted candidate's skills, divided by the total number of skills from that cluster (otherwise, clusters with more skills would have an advantage). In other words, for a cluster C (a set of role skills) and a document CV (a set of candidate's skills):

$$probability_{CV}(C) = \frac{|C \cap CV|}{|C|}. \tag{3}$$

The top 3 clusters from the obtained probability ranking are presented to the user as role recommendations, with the corresponding cluster probabilities normalized so that their sum equals one.

3.4 Skill Recommendation

To recommend missing skills for a given CV, we again used the extracted list of CV skills and applied the following strategies.

Similarity-Based Strategy. For each skill that is not present in the candidate's CV, using a predefined skill similarity (Eq. (1)) we calculate its average similarity to the extracted CV skills. Then, top 15 skills with the highest obtained average similarity are recommended.

LSI-Based Strategy. We calculate the numeric (LSI) representation of the candidate's CV document. Then, using an index of LSI representations of all skills, we find 15 skills which are nearest to the LSI representation of the candidate's CV. This is based on the idea that the numeric representation of a CV will be closer to representations of the skills which are relevant to the candidate, than to the other skills.

Cluster-Based Strategy. We calculate the recommended clusters in candidate classification as in the above section. Then, we recommend 15 most frequent skills from those clusters (ignoring those which are already present in the candidates's CV), with their frequencies normalized by the clusters' probabilities.

User-Based Strategy. We find the 10 most similar candidates to the given candidate using LSI and Glove representations of their extracted skills. Then, we recommend the 15 skills which are most frequent among similar candidates, but not present in the candidate's CV.

Hybrid Strategy. We combine some of the above strategies by merging their results and ranking their recommended skills using weights. We found that the hybrid strategy which uses the user-based strategy (weighting its recommendations by 2) and similarity-based strategy (weighting its recommendations by 1) gives best results.

4 Evaluation

4.1 Candidate Classification

To evaluate candidate classification, we have conducted an empirical study with 80 randomly chosen CV documents and 8 human testers. The documents were divided into 8 chunks of 10 documents. Each chunk was given to two different testers: one tester was performing a manual classification of a candidate (based on the CV document) by selecting the top 3 relevant roles from the cluster list, while the other tester was evaluating results of the candidate classification by our recommender system, labeling each of the top 3 recommended clusters as "relevant" or "irrelevant" to the candidate (based on the CV document). This enabled us to answer the following questions: *(A) Do the roles recommended by the system correspond to the roles obtained by manual classification?* and *(B) Are the roles recommended by the system relevant to the candidate?*

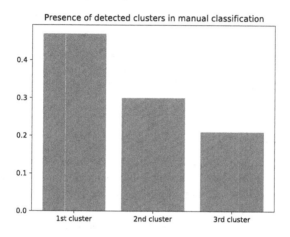

Fig. 2. Candidate classification experiment (A)

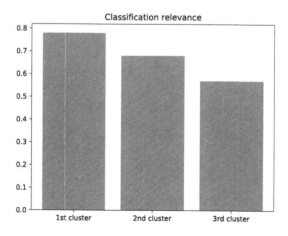

Fig. 3. Candidate classification experiment (B)

The results are depicted in Figs. 2 and 3. We can see that the automatically recommended clusters by our system are judged relevant in 57%–78% cases

(Fig. 3), more often than they are present in the manual classification (21%–47%, Fig. 2). This is explained by the nature of the experiments where a human annotator might miss some roles that are relevant to the candidate. Relevance of ≈70% or more, which corresponds to the first and second recommended clusters, can be considered a very good result.

When comparing the system's role recommendations with manual classification as ground truth, using the standard top-N recommendation metrics, we obtained the following results for top-3 precision (a fraction of ground-truth roles among the recommended roles) and normalized discounted cumulative gain [28]:

Top-3 precision = 32.76%
nDCG = 42.29%

These result are partially affected by human error (of manual classification), but when taking into account the nature of the experiment and problem difficulty (even for human solvers), they still show a significant accuracy of our recommender system.

4.2 Skill Recommendation

To evaluate and compare skill recommendation strategies, we have conducted an experiment on 71321 CV documents. For each document, hard skills were extracted, and a random number of skills (between 8 and 13) was artificially removed. Then, each of the five skill recommendation strategies (described in Sect. 3.4) was used to recommend 15 skills to the candidate. The goal of the experiment was to verify whether the removed skills (which are clearly relevant to the candidate) will be recommended by our system. For this purpose, we compared the skills recommended by each strategy with the artificially removed skills for which the recommendation can be expected.

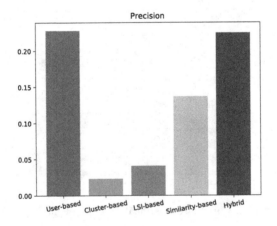

Fig. 4. Skill recommendation experiment - precision

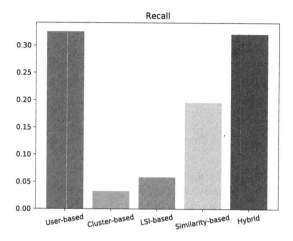

Fig. 5. Skill recommendation experiment - recall

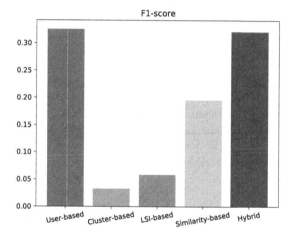

Fig. 6. Skill recommendation experiment - F1 score

We have tested the five skill recommendation strategies from Sect. 3.4: User-based, Cluster-based, LSI-based, Similarity-based and Hybrid strategy. We have evaluated the most commonly used metrics for test accuracy: precision, recall, and F1 score. The *precision* metric gives a fraction of relevant skills among the recommended skills. The *recall* metric gives a fraction of total number of relevant skills that were recommended. The *F1 score* includes both accuracy aspects as a harmonic mean of precision and recall.

The results are depicted in Figs. 4, 5 and 6. We can see that User-based and Hybrid strategies achieve best results, with precision $\approx 22.5\%$, recall $\approx 32.5\%$ and F1 score $\approx 26.5\%$. The obtained accuracy measures are not very high, which is explained by the strict nature of the experiment and the difficulty of skill recommendation problem even by human experts. The removed skills in tested real-world documents are not always the most relevant skills of the candidate, as it is difficult to differentiate between "strong" and "weak" skills of the candidate in this kind of experiment. With an accuracy of about 30%, if five skills out of 15 recommended are relevant to the candidate and able to improve their profile, we consider it to be a very good result.

5   Conclusion

We have presented a CV recommender system capable of efficient candidate classification and skills recommendation for job candidates based on their CV documents. Spectral clustering with additional enhancements provided ground for candidate classification, which was verified by empirical study. The skill similarity definition which was used in clustering turned out to also provide a good ground for the skill recommendation task. The experimental results (for Hybrid strategy) suggest that combining skills recommended by similarity-based strategy (those with highest similarity to the extracted original CV skills) and skills recommended by the user-based strategy (frequent among the candidates with similar numeric representations) give best results for the skill recommendation task.

The presented methods of skill clustering and recommendation were shown effective in a CV recommender system. This shows the benefits of their possible further use in other recommender systems based on textual documents with user/item classification. In our future work, we will focus on extracting other relevant information from the job candidate's textual CV document, such as qualifications, employment history, etc.

Acknowledgment. The dataset for this research has been collected by EWORK (https://www.eworkgroup.com/en/contact). The authors acknowledge the support of the **Croatian Science Foundation** through the *Reliable Composite Applications Based on Web Services* (**IP-01-2018-6423**) research project. The Titan X Pascal used for this research was donated by the NVIDIA Corporation.

References

1. Pazzani, M.J., Billsus, D.: Content-based recommendation systems. In: Brusilovsky, P., Kobsa, A., Nejdl, W. (eds.) The Adaptive Web, pp. 325–341. Springer, Heidelberg (2007). https://doi.org/10.1007/978-3-540-72079-9_10
2. Su, X., Khoshgoftaar, T.M.: A survey of collaborative filtering techniques. In: Advances in Artificial Intelligence 2009, pp. 4:2–4:2, January 2009
3. Felfernig, A., Isak, K., Szabo, K., Zachar, P.: The VITA financial services sales support environment. In: Proceedings of the 19th National Conference on Innovative Applications of Artificial Intelligence, IAAI 2007, vol. 2. AAAI Press, pp. 1692–1699 (2007)

4. Chen, H.H., Gou, L., Zhang, X., Giles, C.L.: CollabSeer: a search engine for collaboration discovery. In: Proceedings of the 11th Annual International ACM/IEEE Joint Conference on Digital Libraries, JCDL 2011, pp. 231–240. Association for Computing Machinery, New York (2011)

5. Chen, H., II, A.G.O., Giles, C.L.: ExpertSeer: a keyphrase based expert recommender for digital libraries. CoRR abs/1511.02058 (2015)

6. Diaby, M., Viennet, E.: Taxonomy-based job recommender systems on Facebook and LinkedIn profiles. In: 2014 IEEE Eighth International Conference on Research Challenges in Information Science (RCIS), pp. 1–6. IEEE (2014)

7. Hong, W., Zheng, S., Wang, H., Shi, J.: A job recommender system based on user clustering. JCP 8(8), 1960–1967 (2013)

8. Gupta, A., Garg, D.: Applying data mining techniques in job recommender system for considering candidate job preferences. In: 2014 International Conference on Advances in Computing, Communications and Informatics (ICACCI), pp. 1458–1465. IEEE (2014)

9. Hong, W., Zheng, S., Wang, H.: Dynamic user profile-based job recommender system. In: 2013 8th International Conference on Computer Science & Education, pp. 1499–1503. IEEE (2013)

10. Hutterer, M.: Enhancing a job recommender with implicit user feedback. Citeseer (2011)

11. Abel, F., Benczúr, A., Kohlsdorf, D., Larson, M., Pálovics, R.: RecSys challenge 2016: job recommendations. In: Proceedings of the 10th ACM Conference on Recommender Systems, pp. 425–426. ACM (2016)

12. Siting, Z., Wenxing, H., Ning, Z., Fan, Y.: Job recommender systems: a survey. In: 2012 7th International Conference on Computer Science & Education (ICCSE), pp. 920–924. IEEE (2012)

13. Al-Otaibi, S.T., Ykhlef, M.: A survey of job recommender systems. Int. J. Phys. Sci. 7(29), 5127–5142 (2012)

14. Deerwester, S., Dumais, S., Furnas, G., Landauer, T., Harshman, R.: Indexing by latent semantic analysis. J. Am. Soc. Inform. Sci. Technol. 41, 391–407 (1990)

15. Pennington, J., Socher, R., Manning, C.D.: GloVe: global vectors for word representation. In: Empirical Methods in Natural Language Processing (EMNLP), pp. 1532–1543 (2014)

16. Malkov, Y.A., Yashunin, D.A.: Efficient and robust approximate nearest neighbor search using hierarchical navigable small world graphs. CoRR abs/1603.09320 (2016)

17. Boytsov, L., Naidan, B.: Engineering efficient and effective non-metric space library. In: Brisaboa, N., Pedreira, O., Zezula, P. (eds.) SISAP 2013. LNCS, vol. 8199, pp. 280–293. Springer, Heidelberg (2013). https://doi.org/10.1007/978-3-642-41062-8_28

18. Arthur, D., Vassilvitskii, S.: K-means++: the advantages of careful seeding. In: Proceedings of the Eighteenth Annual ACM-SIAM Symposium on Discrete Algorithms, SODA 2007, USA, Society for Industrial and Applied Mathematics, pp. 1027–1035 (2007)

19. Johnson, S.C.: Hierarchical clustering schemes. Psychometrika 32(3), 241–254 (1967)

20. Comaniciu, D., Meer, P.: Mean shift: a robust approach toward feature space analysis. IEEE Trans. Pattern Anal. Mach. Intell. 24(5), 603–619 (2002)

21. Ester, M., Kriegel, H.P., Sander, J., Xu, X.: A density-based algorithm for discovering clusters a density-based algorithm for discovering clusters in large spatial databases with noise. In: Proceedings of the Second International Conference on Knowledge Discovery and Data Mining, KDD 1996, pp. 226–231. AAAI Press (1996)
22. Ankerst, M., Breunig, M.M., Kriegel, H.P., Sander, J.: OPTICS: ordering points to identify the clustering structure. In: Proceedings of the 1999 ACM SIGMOD International Conference on Management of Data. SIGMOD 1999, pp. 49–60. Association for Computing Machinery, New York (1999)
23. Zhang, T., Ramakrishnan, R., Livny, M.: BIRCH: an efficient data clustering method for very large databases. SIGMOD Rec. **25**(2), 103–114 (1996)
24. Ng, A.Y., Jordan, M.I., Weiss, Y.: On spectral clustering: analysis and an algorithm. In: Advances in Neural Information Processing Systems, pp. 849–856 (2002)
25. Olson, L.N., Schroder, J.B.: PyAMG: algebraic multigrid solvers in Python v4.0. Release 4.0 (2018)
26. Pedregosa, F., et al.: Scikit-learn: machine learning in Python. J. Mach. Learn. Res. **12**, 2825–2830 (2011)
27. Ahmad, A., Khan, S.S.: Survey of state-of-the-art mixed data clustering algorithms. IEEE Access **7**, 31883–31902 (2019)
28. Valizadegan, H., Jin, R., Zhang, R., Mao, J.: Learning to rank by optimizing NDCG measure. In: Proceedings of the 22nd International Conference on Neural Information Processing Systems. NIPS 2009, pp. 1883–1891. Curran Associates Inc., Red Hook (2009)
29. Kurdija, A.S., et al.: Building vector representations for candidates and projects in a CV recommender system. In: Xu, R., De, W., Zhong, W., Tian, L., Bai, Y., Zhang, L.-J. (eds.) AIMS 2020. LNCS, vol. 12401, pp. 17–29. Springer, Cham (2020)

A Novel Method to Estimate Students' Knowledge Assessment

Phuoc Hung Pham and Javed I. Khan[✉]

Kent State University, Kent, OH, USA
hung205a2@gmail.com, javed@kent.edu

Abstract. Performance of learning can be enriched with proper and timely feedback. This paper proposes a solution based on a Bayesian network in machine learning that can examine and judge students' written response to identify evidences that students fully comprehend concepts being considered in a certain knowledge domain. In particular, it can estimate probabilities that a student has known concepts in computer science at different cognitive ability levels in a sense. Thus, the method can offer learners personalized feedbacks on their strengths and shortcomings, as well as advising them and instructors of supplementary education action actions that may help students to resolve any lacks to improve their knowledge and exam score.

Keywords: Concept · Knowledge · Assessment · Learning · Machine learning

1 Introduction

In a learning process, an assessment is essential to help instructors to evaluate if learners' activities or performances get along with the academic community's expectations, understand dimensions of studies to improve learners' achievement, design course materials and learning activities. Educators have often tried to design an sufficient assessment to cover broader objectives of their courses [22]. Its purpose is to arrange a superlative educational process to inspire students to learn both skills directly related to their specialty and additional knowledge domains in the professional working environment. Knowing what and how students learn is important for judging the appropriateness of learning objectives and deciding how to improve instructions [9]. In an education circumstance, instructors usually want their learners by themselves to discover connections between concepts they study in their major and materials they study across other courses in their curriculum from a basic understanding of concepts to asking more complex questions via assessments. For the time being, Concept Mapping (*CM*) [1] and Bloom's Taxonomy (*BT*) [2] have been becoming common assessment techniques in science education. Concept mapping is one of the most powerful graphical tools for the knowledge acquisition [10, 11], showing what learners see as important concepts and how they relate these concepts. Valery et al. in [9] delineates how the concept mapping technology is utilized in engineering education in the field of electronics to help learners to see what they have

© Springer Nature Switzerland AG 2020
R. Xu et al. (Eds.): AIMS 2020, LNCS 12401, pp. 45–59, 2020.
https://doi.org/10.1007/978-3-030-59605-7_4

acquired from lessons. Nevertheless, cognitive ability levels of students are not well-thought-out. The studies [3–5] research the problem in evaluation by using semantic network ontology and do not come up with understandable estimation for students. *BT* is to organize higher forms of knowledge in education from simple to more complex levels [15]. To reach a higher level, the previous level must be mastered. The authors in [21] using *BT* levels to validate learners' concept states by using analysis methods without taking relationships between concepts at multiple cognitive bloom levels, or "lucky guess" and "careless mistake" reliance, as well as fairly considered academic concepts in a dimension into account. "Lucky guess" is a case that a student doesn't know an answer, but he/she can guess it correctly while "careless mistake" is a case that a student knows an answer, but he/she answers it incorrectly. From this perspective, we utilize the two techniques to simply present a concept based assessment method by using Cognitive Ability Levels, which are in reference to *BT* [2, 3]. In this paper, we introduce a novel model called Cognitive Ability Level Concept based Graphs which maps entire concepts in computer sciences into one concept domain space used for checking students' knowledge. A concept domain space is a knowledge space along with relationships between concepts of an assessed domain, and multi Cognitive Ability Levels (*CALs*) indicate levels of "Remember", "Understand", "Apply", "Analyze", "Evaluate", "Create" that students have achieved. In addition, we propose a Bayesian network based technique to deeply estimate students' knowledge at different ability levels in an assessment with respect to concepts and their multiple *CAL* relationship in a sense while taking into account "Lucky guess" and "careless mistake" reliance, fair pedagogical concepts consideration. As a result, it can give learners feedbacks on their strengths and shortcomings, along with advising learners and instructors of additional learning exertions that may help learners to resolve any weakness. Besides, it can also assist instructors to verify exactly the covered knowledge of a course objective and answer a question of whether an assessment model can be constructed properly and build a new prototype of learning analytics such as course and learning activity design, knowledge based test design, assessment of learning activity design, building a learning map of curriculum areas from this point forward. Moreover, to validate the cognitive ability levels and concept states which inform if a student has already learned, is ready to learn, or is not ready to learn knowledge at a certain ability level, the approach is experimentally conducted and the experiment results can show the efficiency and usability of our method.

Further sections of the study are organized as follows: Sect. 2 provides information about related work, Sect. 3 discusses the knowledge representation, Sect. 4 details the problem statement and its corresponding solution approach, Sect. 5 describes experiments and results. Section 6 concludes the paper and outlines future work.

2 Related Studies and Background

Various researches have been done to solve related problems to develop the knowledge assessment theory as adaptive assessment [8, 10, 19]. Yusuf Kavurucu et al. in [12] presents an approach where data is symbolized in graph structures and graph mining techniques are used for knowledge detection. Concept detection in multi-relational data mining is to find relational policies that best define a relation, called target relation, with regard to other relations in a database, called background knowledge. The proposed method, namely G-CDS (Graph-based Concept Discovery System), utilizes methods both from substructure-based and path-finding based approaches, hence it can be considered as a hybrid method. G-CDS generates disconnected graph structures for each target relation and its related background knowledge, which are initially stored in a relational database, and utilizes them to guide generation of a summary graph. The summary graph is traversed to find concept descriptors. In [6], Falmagne et al. introduced the knowledge state assessment theory. This theory was derived from the Knowledge Space Theory earlier proposed by Falmagne, Doignon and Thiery [7]. Many research works tried to develop the knowledge assessment theory as adaptive assessment [8, 10, 19]. The work in [6] is in reality accomplished by establishing an Assessment and Learning in Knowledge Spaces (ALEKS). Much research work has been done for ALEKS such as [11, 12]. Systems like ALEKS, which are applications of Flamagne's theory, so far have only been applied to mathematics and chemistry. It does not recognize finer distinctions of concepts. Although, such coarse definition of competency generates useful results in some disciplines, finer distinctions of skill levels, for example given links of verbs describing the skills required to attain the concepts, are very important for giving accurate results in applied disciplines such as all the branches of engineering education as well as computer science and technology education. During 1990's, Anderson [2] revised the Bloom category to ponder the levels as verbs rather than nouns. His efforts were to use verbs to create sufficient understanding of learning results and student performance. Using revised Bloom Taxonomy [2] for educational assessment has been an extremely rich and interesting research area. Some scientists try to apply pedagogical taxonomy in a learning space of a learning subject such as [16–18]. In the most related work [16], they used the ideas of Competence-based Knowledge Space Theory. They propose a skill characterized as a pair consisting of a concept and an activity. Some other researchers try to use the revised Bloom Taxonomy for assessment and present new assessment approaches such as the work of [19–21]. None of them used the verbs of revised Bloom's Taxonomy to identify the relation between the concepts in the assessed domain and the assessment. However, Rania Aboalela et al. [18] assumed that those cognitive Bloom's taxonomy levels (understanding, applying, analyzing, evaluating,

Table 1. Existing methods and ours.

Methods	Relationships between concepts at CALs	Fairly consideration	Dependency
Falmagne et al. [6]	No	No	No
Valery Vodovozov et al. [9]	No	No	No
J. C. Shieh et al. [10]	No	No	No
R. Rudraraju et al. [11]	No	No	No
Yusuf Kavurucu et al. [12]	Yes	No	No
Rania Aboalela et al. [18]	Yes	No	No
Fatema Nafa et al. [19]	Yes	Yes	Yes

creating) are given then testing can be done based on Bayesian inference to determine student's proficiency levels (specific to only a cognitive domain level) from student test results with an assumption that there is no relation between "lucky guess" and "careless mistake" and no fair consideration among concepts. Moreover, a major unsolved problem in the new paradigm of learning analytics is the automatic inference of cognitive domain relationship between domain-concepts in a particular context (sense) and the link between two concepts are only at a specific cognitive ability level. Fatema Nafa et al. [19] proposes a platform that can infer cognitive relationship (Cognitive Skill Dependencies) among domain concepts as they appear in the text in either phrase or single word form by identifying the link between the concepts as the skill required to learn the concepts at a certain skill level, which identifies the prerequisite relations between the concepts. For ease of understanding, we present an overview of common related approaches along with ours in Table 1.

As shown in Table 1, our study considers all of the three factors comprising:

- Concept relationships at multiple cognitive ability levels at a sense.
- Dependency of "Lucky guess" and "careless mistake".
- In a dimension, fair pedagogical concept consideration.

Moreover, it focuses on more precisely Bayesian estimating ability levels of student knowledge in an assessment in order to offer students feedbacks on strengths and shortcomings, as well as advising students and instructors of additional learning activities that may help students to resolve any shortages.

3 Representation

In this section, some terms, notations used in the paper are defined and some assumptions are delivered.

Content skill knowledge representation here is visualized by graphs in a dimension and used natural language to represent concepts and propositions, i.e. to represent semantic knowledge and its conceptual organization (structure).

Pedagocal Knowledge Dimesional Lattice (PKDL) (e.g., as in Fig. 1) is an arrangement which is a combination of pedagogical knowledge unit concept nodes and their relationships in three dimensions (or perspectives): Collection dimension (*CoD*), Cognitive Ability Level (CAL) dimension and Ontology dimension (*OnD*) defined together with related definitions as follows:

- Pedagogical knowledge unit concept (*C*): Basic elements of this lattice are Pedagogical knowledge unit concepts *C* and their relationships. *C* is the smallest unit in knowledge representation [17], means mental representations, abstract objects or abilities that make up the fundamental building blocks of thoughts and beliefs. They play an important role in all aspects of cognition in pedagogy. A concept can have one sense or many senses (called sense set). A sense of a concept is like a meaning of a concept based on the context of the concept's usage in a sentence. In the composition graph at the Fig. 1, concepts are enclosed in ovals such as the concept "State", which has 4 senses $s1, s2, s3, s4$.

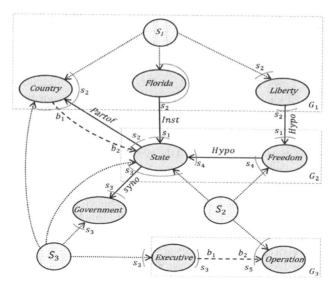

Fig. 1. Composition graph

- Pedagogical Knowledge Concept Graph (*PKCG*): *PKCG* is a graph including all elementary concepts covered in a knowledge domain in a collection dimension. A *PKCG* contains Pedagogical knowledge unit concepts nodes, collection nodes and their links. A textbook provides an organization of concepts in a tree hierarchy. A *PKCG* tries to capture a book's presentation or organization. Thus, leaves of *PKCG* are concepts either in single words or phrase words. The location of a node in *PKCG* indicates the concept occurs in the textbook. For example: collection area. book title. author. publisher. ISBN. date of publication. chapter. section. subsection. sentence. word location. A concept can appear in sentences of multiple paragraphs. The role of concept graph is to support personal learning, thus, help instructors or students to find errors in knowledge acquisition. For instance, the part *G*1 of the Fig. 1 represents a fragment of concept graph built for a science domain. The graph developed includes nodes with key concepts enclosed in ovals, connecting to other collection nodes in circles.

In *PKDL*, each dimension provides additional classifications of knowledge units and their relationships.

Collection Dimension

Collection Dimension classifies the nodes into following types. Collection nodes: a collection includes atomic concepts, and higher level aggregations of atomic concepts used in pedagogy. These can be chapters, sections, subsections, sentences of book, or learning materials such as syllabus, test, questions, etc. Collection nodes are the nodes $S1$, $S2$, $S3$ in circles as shown in the Fig. 1. Besides *CoD* includes the link type 'Collection' which is a directed round dot link representing 'member of' relationship between sink node and source nodes at specific senses. For example, the link in the part *G*1 of the

Fig. 1 represents that the concepts "Country" at the sense s2, "Florida" at the sense s2, and "Liberty" at the sense s2 are members of the sentence node $S1$.

Cognitive Ability Level Dimension (CAL)

Cognitive Ability Level Dimension (*CAL*): *CAL* Dimension presents relationships between pedagogical knowledge unit concepts regarding ability supports needed from a source concept $C_s^{L_s}$ $\forall s \in N$ at a certain cognitive ability level L_i at a sense set element s_s, to a target concept $C_t^{L_t}$ at a specific cognitive ability level L_t at a sense set element s_t, $\forall t \in N$. When there is a directed link from the source concept $C_s^{L_s}$ to the target concept $C_t^{L_t}$, it means that knowing $C_t^{L_t}$ correctly at a cognitive ability level L_t at the sense s_t is dependent on knowing $C_s^{L_s}$ correctly at a cognitive ability level L_s at the sense s_s. The cognitive ability levels refer to 6 levels such as "Remember", "Understand", "Apply", "Analyze", "Evaluate", "Create" [2] which are equal to $\{b_1, b_2, b_3, b_4, b_5, b_6\}$ with the same order. The part G_3 of the Fig. 1 illustrates that a direct dash link from the concept "Executive" to the concept "Operation" means that to know the concept "Operation" at the cognitive ability level b_2 at the sense s_5 $\forall b_2 \in BTS = \{b_1, b_2, b_3, b_4, b_5, b_6\}$, the concept "Executive" must be known at the level b_1 at the sense s_3 in advance. A defined concept is described by a particular entry while earlier entries used to explain the defined concept are called parents.

Ontology Dimension

Ontology is the philosophical study of being. More broadly, it studies concepts that directly relate to being, in particular becoming, existence, reality, as well as the basic categories of being and their relations [16]. An ontology link presents the ontological relationship between concepts. We identified the ontological relationship between concepts based on WordNet [19]. There are 10 types of links of ontological relationships between concepts including: Synonym (Syno), Antonym (Anto), Hyponym (Hypo), Subpart (Subp), Subclass (Subc), Instance (Inst), Attribute (Attr), Functional Property (FPro), Environment (Envi), and Measure (Meas). In a graph, ontological relationships are characterized as directed links from a source to a target. E.g. if A is, Subpart, Subclass, Instance of, or Synonym of concept B then the concept A is represented as a source node at a sense and the concept B is represented as a target node at another sense. In the part $G2$ of the Fig. 1, the ontological relationship shows that the concept "State" at the sense $s4$ is a hyponym of the concept "Freedom" at the sense $s4$.

4 Problem Definition and Solution

This section discusses some terms used, and then we are going to describe the problem statement.

- Evidence Set (ES) [18]: in an assessment, a test is introduced to students in a class. A test normally is composed of a set of questions. Answering a question qi with a response Qi requires knowledge about a set of concepts. A set of responses is called an evidence set. When a student successfully answers a question, we can conclude that he has learned the concept set at a certain skill level, which is asked by the question. After the test, an examiner can evaluate and grade for the test.

- Confirmed Ability set (CA): CA [6] is defined as where there is a direct evidence that an individual knowing or not knowing a concept C_y at a cognitive ability level L_y at a sense s_y. The concept is considered a part of Confirmed Ability set at a cognitive ability level L_y if C_y is a correct concept at the cognitive ability level L_y at a sense s_y. We denote $C_y^{L_y} \in CA(L_y, s_y) \forall C_y, s_y$. The collection answer node denoted by Q_i in squares and the concept node C_y at a cognitive ability level L_y denoted by $C_y^{L_y} \forall_{i,y} \in N$ at the sense $s_y \forall y \in N$ in ovals. When there is a directed link from the collection node Q_i to the concept node $C_y^{L_y}$ (indicated by a dash arrow) it means that the ability to have the answer Q_i correctly is dependent on knowing the concept $C_y^{L_y}$ correctly. In other words, to answer the question q_i correctly, a student should know the concept C_y at the level L_y at the sense s_y as an example presented in Fig. 2.

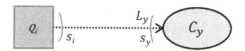

Fig. 2. Confirmed Ability illustration

- Derived Ability set (DA): DA indicates there is an indirect evidence that learners know a specific concept at a certain ability level at a specific sense. Thus, DA is an essential set of confirmed concepts at a certain ability level, but they have never been directly tested. In Fig. 3, there is an indirect evidence that the concept node Cw at Cognitive Ability Level Lw can be understood by learners, then the concept Cw belongs to DA set.

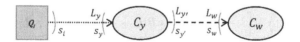

Fig. 3. Derived Ability

Let a learner answer a question q_r with an answer Q_r, which gives evidence of his/her state of prior knowledge about a set of concepts $S = \{C_u^{L_u}, \ldots, C_z^{L_z}\}, S \in CG$, including children nodes of Q_r and $L_u, L_z \in BTS$. A correct answer is denoted by Q_r, and an incorrect answer is denoted by $\bar{Q}_r$. We are going to define other terms as follows.

- Apriority probability (non-evidence based probability): Without evidences, unconditional probability of knowing the concept $C_i^{L_i}$ is $P(C_i^{L_i}) = k$ and unconditional probability of giving the correct answer Q_r is $P(Q_r) = a$.
- Evidence based probability: Supposing parent of a concept $C_i^{L_i}$ is unknown, a conditional probability of knowing concept $C_i^{L_i}$ based on its unknown parents is $P\left(C_i^{L_i} \mid \overline{C_{i-x}^{L_i}}\right) = u^{1/h}$ with h being the number of parent's children nodes, $\forall x < i, x \in N$.

- Lucky guess: In case a response's dependence concepts are not known, it is still correct. That is a "lucky guess". Assumed the response is correct, the probability of not knowing the dependence concepts $S = \{C_u^{L_u}, \ldots, C_z^{L_z}\}$, is $P\left(\overline{C_u^{L_u} \ldots C_z^{L_z}} \Big| Q_r\right) = l_r$ $\forall l_r \in [0, 1)$ (called "lucky guess" probability), then probability of not knowing the concept $C_i \in S$ is $P\left(\overline{C_i^{L_i}} \Big| Q_r\right) = l_r^{1/y}$ with y being the number of concepts of the set S because according to the conditional independence probability [20] $P\left(\overline{C_u^{L_u} \ldots C_z^{L_z}} \Big| Q_r\right) = P\left(\overline{C_u^{L_u}} \Big| Q_r\right) \ldots P\left(\overline{C_z^{L_z}} \Big| Q_r\right)$. The subscript r indicates an index of the question number. This can lead us to consider concepts in a dimension fairly.
- Careless mistake: Oppositely, in the event of known dependence concepts of a response, the response is incorrect. That is a "careless mistake". If the response Q_r to a question q_r is incorrect, the probability of knowing the dependence concept $S = \{C_u^{L_u} \ldots C_z^{L_z}\}$, which has been asked by the question q_r. is $P\left(C_u^{L_u} \ldots C_z^{L_z} \Big| \bar{Q}_r\right) = m_r$ (called "careless mistake" probability), then probability of knowing the concept C_i $\in S$ $P\left(C_i^{L_i} \Big| \bar{Q}_r\right) = m_r^{1/y} \forall m_r \in [0, 1)$.

In addition, there is a constraint between m_r and l_r as follows:

$$l_r^{\frac{1}{y}} = P\left(\bar{C}_i^{L_i} | Q_r\right) = \frac{P\left(Q_r | \bar{C}_i^{L_i}\right).P\left(\bar{C}_i^{L_i}\right)}{P(Q_r)} = \frac{\left[1 - P\left(\bar{Q}_r | \bar{C}_i^{L_i}\right)\right].P\left(\bar{C}_i^{L_i}\right)}{P(Q_r)}$$

$$= \left[1 - \frac{P\left(\bar{C}_i^{L_i} | \bar{Q}_r\right).P\left(\bar{Q}_r\right)}{P\left(\bar{C}_i^{L_i}\right)}\right] \frac{P\left(\bar{C}_i^{L_i}\right)}{P(Q_r)} = \frac{P\left(\bar{C}_i^{L_i}\right) - P\left(\bar{C}_i^{L_i} | \bar{Q}_r\right).P\left(\bar{Q}_r\right)}{P(Q_r)}$$

$$= \frac{P\left(\bar{C}_i^{L_i}\right) - \left[1 - P\left(C_i^{L_i} | \bar{Q}_r\right)\right].P\left(\bar{Q}_r\right)}{P(Q_r)} = \frac{k - \left(1 - m_r^{\frac{1}{y}}\right)(1 - a)}{a}$$

4.1 Problem Statement

Given a set of questions $q = \{q_1, q_2, q_3, \ldots q_n\}$ with their corresponding evaluated answers $R_j = \{Q_1, Q_2, Q_3, \ldots Q_n\}$. Let aprioriprobability $P\left(C_i^{L_i}\right) = k$ and $P(Q_r) = a$, evidence based probability $P\left(C_i^{L_i} \Big| \overline{C_{i-x}^{L_i}}\right) = u^{1/h}$. Our purpose is to find any $P(C_i^{L_i} | R_j)$ which is the conditional probability of knowing a concept C_i at a cognitive ability L_i with the observing set of responses R_j at a sense.

Next, we explain how a Bayesian based method calculated for learning assessment to solve the above problem.

4.2 Solution

This section explains how to build a formula to estimate probability of knowing pedagogical concepts of students [6, 21]. Intuitively, it is suggested Bayes' Theorem [13] and Bayesian networks could be used to compute the probability of knowing a concept even though the concept is evaluated based on reflected evaluations of the concept. It could also be used to calculate the probability of knowing the concept even in the existence of complex connections between concepts in a concept space. Bayesian networks are a sort of probabilistic graphical model that uses Bayesian inference for probability calculations. Bayesian networks aim to model conditional dependence, and therefore causation, by representing conditional dependence by edges in a directed graph. Via these connections, we can competently carry out inference on the random variables in the graph through the use of factors. It is first useful for us to review probability theory before going into precisely what a Bayesian network is.

First, recall that the joint probability distribution of random variables $C_1^{L_1}, \ldots, C_n^{L_n}$, denoted as $P(C_1^{L_1}, \ldots, C_n^{L_n})$, is equal to $P(C_1^{L_1} | C_2^{L_2}, \ldots, C_n^{L_n}) * P(C_2^{L_2} | C_3^{L_3}, \ldots, C_n^{L_n}) * \ldots * P(C_n^{L_n})$ by the chain rule of probability [15]. We can consider this a factorized representation of the distribution, since it is a product of n factors that are localized probabilities.

$$P\left(\bigcap_{k=1}^{n} C_k^{L_k}\right) = \prod_{k=1}^{n} P(C_k^{L_k} \bigcap_{i=1}^{k-1} |C_i^{L_i}) \tag{4.1}$$

Next, remember that conditional independence [20] between two random variables, A and B, given another random variable, C, is equivalent to satisfying the following property: $P(A, B | C) = P(A | C) * P(B | C)$. That is to say, as long as the value of C is known and fixed, A and B are independent. Another way of stating this is that $P(A | B, C) = P(A | C)$. If n random variables $A_1, A_2, \ldots, A_n$ are independent, then

$$P\left(\bigcap_{k=1}^{n} A_k | C\right) = \prod_{k=1}^{n} P(A_k | C) \tag{4.2}$$

At that point, we describe a Bayesian network as follows:
A Bayesian network is a directed acyclic graph [14] in which each edge corresponds to a conditional dependency, and each node corresponds to a unique random variable as shown in the Fig. 3. In a Bayesian networks, a node is conditionally independent of its non-descendants given its parents. Its parents are incoming nodes linking to the node. In the above example in the Fig. 4, $P(C_3 | C_1, C_4)$ is equal to $P(C_3 | C_1)$ since C_3 is conditionally independent of its non-descendant, C_4, given its parents C_1. This property allows us to simplify the joint distribution, obtained in the previous section using the chain rule, to a smaller form. After simplification, the joint distribution for a Bayesian network is equal to the product of $P(node | Parents$ (node)) for all nodes, stated below:

$$P\left(C_1^{L_1} \ldots C_n^{L_n}\right) = \prod_{i=1}^{n} P\left(C_i^{L_i} | C_1^{L_1}, \ldots, C_{i-1}^{L_{i-1}}\right) = \prod_{i=1}^{n} P\left(C_i^{L_i} | Parents\left(C_i^{L_i}\right)\right) \tag{4.3}$$

where $Parents(C_i^{L_i})$ is a set of concepts connecting directly to the node $C_i^{L_i}$ then

$$P(C_1^{L_1} \ldots C_n^{L_n} | R_j) = \prod_{i=1}^{n} P\left(C_i^{L_i} | R_j . Parents\left(C_i^{L_i}\right)\right) \tag{4.4}$$

In a larger concept graph, this property lets us significantly decrease the amount of required computation, since generally, most nodes will have few parents relative to the overall size of the graph. In order to calculate $P(C_i^{L_i}|R_j)$, we must marginalize the joint probability distribution over the variables that do not appear in $C = \{C_1^{L_1}, \ldots, C_n^{L_n}\}$. Therefore,

$$P(C_k^{L_k}|R_j) = \sum_{dom\left(C_n^{L_n}\right)} \cdots \sum_{dom\left(C_i^{L_i}\right)} P(C_k^{L_k} C_i^{L_i} \ldots C_n^{L_n}|R_j) \qquad (4.5)$$

where dom is a domain consisting of all possible value of the concepts $C_i^{L_i}, \ldots, C_n^{L_n}$..

From (4.4), (4.5), we can calculate the probability of knowing a concept C_k given knowing the response R_j based on the relations of all concepts as follows:

$$P(C_k^{L_k}|R_j) = \sum_{dom\left(C_n^{L_n}\right)} \cdots \sum_{dom\left(C_i^{L_i}\right)} \prod_{i=k}^{n} P\left(C_i^{L_i}|R_j.Parents\left(C_i^{L_i}\right)\right) \qquad (4.6)$$

5 Implementation and Validation

5.1 Experiment Overview

We organize an experiment to validate the pedagogical knowledge unit concept states proposed in the assessment. With the intention of proving the efficient estimation of our proposal in a concept space, we have conducted an experiment while considering relationships between concepts at multiple cognitive ability levels at a sense, dependency of "Lucky guess" and "careless mistake" as well as fairly considered pedagogical concepts in a CAL dimension according to the formula (4.6). In this experiment, an assessment includes a set of questions. The questions are designed to test students' knowledge related to thinkable concept sets at cognitive ability level. Instructors prepare any questions, which specifies skill levels of concepts. There are two types of questions: Implicit Questions and Direct Questions. The Implicit Question (IQ) is prepared by instructors to implicitly test ability levels of students while the Direct Question (DQ) is used to directly test ability levels of students. When IQ is examined, we can determine which ability level was included in that IQ. Consequently, for each detected concept Ci at a certain cognitive ability level, either CA set or DA set, DQ are planned for directly verifying the matching of related skills between OQ and DQ based on the relation within the sets of concept states CA, DA. If a student answers a question correctly, we can conclude that he/she has known concepts required to answer the question.

The simulations are developed on Java with jdk-8u161, Eclipse Jee 2019-06. In our experiment at this current step, number of concepts increase from 5 to 30. All parameters are reflected in Table 2. A particular CAL graph input is in the Fig. 4.

5.2 Validation Test and Analysis Results

The following figures show the measured results of the experimentation. It is understandable to see that there are some changes between the simulated results. This is chiefly caused by the partial order instability combination of the input questions.

The Fig. 5, 6, 7, 8, 9 provides a summary of the conditional probability values of knowing the concept C_i at a cognitive ability L_i given the observing set of responses

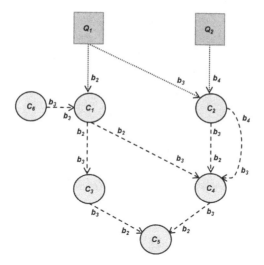

Fig. 4. Input CAL graph

Table 2. Parameter table

Parameter	Meaning
Operating system	Window 7 professional
Number of concepts	[5, 100]
Number of questions	[1, 12]
Number of students	48
Probability of a lucky guess	[0, 1]
Probability of a careless mistake	[0, 1]
Apriority probability	[0,2–0,5]
CAL graph	8 nodes

R_j of students. Let $\alpha(R_j)$, $\alpha(R_t)$ be the number of correct answers in responses $R_j = \{\bar{Q}_1, Q_2, Q_3, \ldots Q_n\}$, $R_t = \{\bar{Q}_1, \bar{Q}_1, Q_3, \ldots, Q_n\}$, respectively. Intuitively, if $\alpha(R_j) \geq \alpha(R_t)$ then $P\left(C_k^{L_k}|R_j\right) \geq P\left(C_k^{L_k}|R_t\right)$. This is still correct for our particular cases whose results presented in the Fig. 5, 6, 7, 8, 9. The Figures indicates that $P(C_i^{L_i}|R_1) >= P(C_i^{L_i}|R_2)$, $P(C_i^{L_i}|R_1) >= P(C_i^{L_i}|R_3)$ and $P(C_i^{L_i}|R_2) >= P(C_i^{L_i}|R_4)$, $P(C_i^{L_i}|R_3) >= P(C_i^{L_i}|R_4)$ with $R_1 = Q_1Q_2$, $R_2 = \bar{Q}_1, Q_2$, $R_3 = Q_1, \bar{Q}_2$, $R_4 = \bar{Q}_1, \bar{Q}_2$. This means the more accuracy response at cognitive ability levels, the higher probability of knowing the concepts students can get. Probabilities $P(C_2^{L_i}|R_i) >= P(C_1^{L_i}|R_i)$ and $P(C_4^{L_i}|R_i) >= P(C_3^{L_i}|R_i)$ in the Fig. 5, 6, 7, 8, 9 are because $C_2^{L_i}$, $C_4^{L_i}$ have more related incoming evidences than $C_1^{L_i}$, $C_3^{L_i}$.

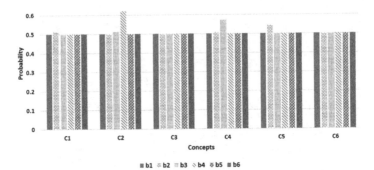

Fig. 5. Concept probabilities with Q_1, Q_2 combination

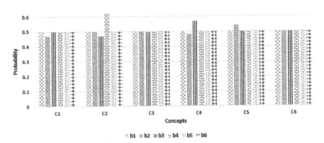

Fig. 6. Concept probabilities with $\bar{Q}_1, Q_2$ combination

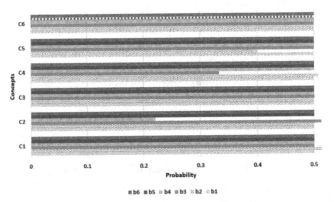

Fig. 7. Concept probabilities with $Q_1, \bar{Q}_2$ combination

In addition, the graph in the Fig. 5, which shows probabilities of knowing concepts given a $Q1, Q2$ combination evidence at six Bloom levels, displays variety of students' knowledge while the Fig. 10 illustrates how deep students' knowledge is at different Bloom levels. According to this, an instructor can decide whether he/she needs to teach concepts again or not. The instructor can clearly build questions that assess precise expertise of students. If majority of students find it tough to understand the concept, then

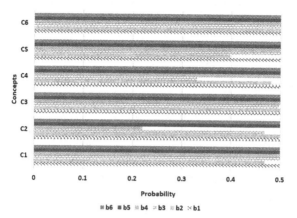

Fig. 8. Concept probabilities with $\bar{Q}_1$, $\bar{Q}_2$ combination

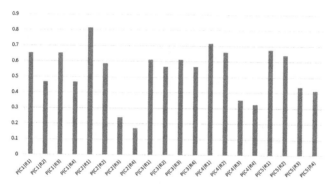

Fig. 9. Concept probabilities at different Bloom levels

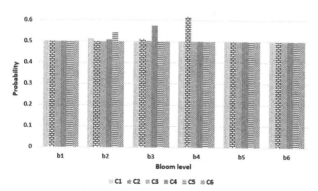

Fig. 10. Concept probabilities at different Bloom levels

the instructor can take on another instruction style and the institution can offer support for the teacher.

6 Conclusion

This paper proposed a Bayesian network based technique to estimate probabilities of knowing concepts at different Bloom levels given responses of students to evaluate students' knowledge. The composition graph of the method can also make simpler building questions that measure precise skills of students. Besides, the proposed method can maximize the quality of estimations of students' knowledge by giving students feedbacks on strong points and weaknesses, along with advising instructors to design appropriate assessments that accurately measure the required skills of students to achieve course goals. Moreover, we conducted simulations to evaluate our approach. Through the implementation, it has been seen that our solution is usable and efficient to measure an assessment properly. Hereafter, we will spread out our approach in diverse environments to achieve higher trustworthiness and better performance.

References

1. Novak, J.D., Cañas, A.J.: The theory underlying concept maps and how to construct and use them, Technical report IHMC CmapTools 2006-01 Rev 2008-01, Florida Institute for Human and Machine Cognition, USA, February 2008
2. Anderson, L.W., et al.: A taxonomy for learning, teaching, and assessing: a revision of Bloom's taxonomy of educational objectives, USA (2001)
3. Khan, J.I., Hardas, M.S, Ma, Y.: A study of problem difficulty evaluation for semantic network ontology based intelligent courseware sharing. In: IEEE/WIC/ACM International Conference on Web Intelligence, pp. 426–429 (2005)
4. Khan, J.I., Hardas, M.S.: Does sequence of presentation matter in reading comprehension? A model based analysis of semantic concept network growth during reading. In: IEEE Seventh International Conference on Semantic Computing (ICSC), 16–18 September 2013, pp. 444–452 (2013)
5. Khan J.I., Yongbin M., Hardas M.: Course composition based on semantic topical dependency. In: International Conference on Web Intelligence, pp. 502–505, December 2006
6. Falmagne, J.C., Cosyn, E., Doignon, J.-P., Thiery, N.: The assessment of knowledge, in theory and in practice. In: International Conference on Integration of Knowledge Intensive Multi-Agent Systems, pp. 609–615 (2003)
7. Falmagne, J.C., Doignon, J.P.: Knowledge Spaces. Springer, Berlin (1999). https://doi.org/10.1007/978-3-642-58625-5
8. Dowling, C.E., Hockemeyer, C., Ludwig, A.H.: Adaptive assessment and training using the neighbourhood of knowledge states. In: Frasson, C., Gauthier, G., Lesgold, A. (eds.) ITS 1996. LNCS, vol. 1086, pp. 578–586. Springer, Heidelberg (1996). https://doi.org/10.1007/3-540-61327-7_157
9. Vodovozov, V., Raud, Z.: Concept maps for teaching, learning, and assessment in electronics. Educ. Res. Int. J. **2015** (2015)
10. Shieh, J.C., Yang, Y.T.: Concept maps construction based on student-problem chart. In: Proceedings of the IIAI 3rd International Conference on Advanced Applied Informatics (IIAIAAI 2014), Kokura Kita-ku, Japan 2014, pp. 324–327 (2014)
11. Rudraraju, R., Najim, L., Gurupur, V.P., Tanik, M.M.: A learning environment based on knowledge storage and retrieval using concept maps. In: Proceedings of the IEEE Southeastcon 2014, Lexington, Ky, USA, March 2014, pp. 1–6 (2014)

12. Yusuf, K., Alev, M., Tolga, E.: Graph-based concept discovery in multi relational data. In: 6th International Conference - Cloud System and Big Data Engineering, India (2016)
13. Bayes network. http://homepages.wmich.edu/~mcgrew/Bayes8.pdf
14. Directed acyclic graph. https://en.wikipedia.org/wiki/Directed_acyclic_graph
15. Chain rule. https://en.wikipedia.org/wiki/Chain_rule_%28probability%29
16. Ontology. https://en.wikipedia.org/wiki/Ontology
17. Fatema, N., Khan Javed, I.: Discovering hidden cognitive skill dependencies between knowledge units using Markov cognitive knowledge state network (MCKSN). PhD dissertation (2018)
18. Rania, A., Khan, J.: Model of learning assessment to measure student learning: inferring of concept state of cognitive skill level in concept space. In: 3rd International Conference on Soft Computing & Machine Intelligence (ISCMI) (2016)
19. Wordnet. https://en.wikipedia.org/wiki/WordNet
20. Conditional probability. https://en.wikipedia.org/wiki/Independence_(probability_theory)
21. Rania, A., Khan, J.: Computation of assessing the knowledge in one domain by using cognitive skills levels. Int. J. Comput. Appl. **180**(12) (2018)
22. Rania, A., Khan, J.: Are we asking the right questions to grade our students in a knowledge-state space analysis. In: IEEE 8th International Conference on Technology for Education (2016)

Answer Selection Based on Mixed Embedding and Composite Features

Mingli Wu[✉], Xianwei Cui, Jiale Li, and Jianyong Duan

North China University of Technology, Beijing 100144, China
wuml@ncut.edu.cn, cuixw1227@163.com, lijiale.korn@gmail.com,
duan_jianyong@163.com

Abstract. With the rapid growth of text information, intelligent question answering has gained more attention than ever. In this paper, we focus on answer selection, one kind of question answering tasks. In this field, deep neural networks and attention mechanism have brought encouraging results. To improve the performance further, we investigate mixed embedding (word embedding and character embedding) representation for sentences to encode rich meaning. At the same time, we introduce a convolutional neural network (CNN) to compensate the loss of the max pooling layer in our attention based bidirectional Long Short-Term Memory (biLSTM) model. CNN features and the features from max pooling form final composite features, which are employed to select correct answers. Experimental results show that we can obviously improve the Mean Reciprocal Rank (MRR) performance by 6.0% with the help of mixed embedding and composite features. The MRR and ACC@1 score are 79.63% and 69.60% respectively.

Keywords: Answer selection · Question answering · Mixed embedding · Composite features · Attention

1 Introduction

With the rapid growth of the Internet, a lot of text data are provided. How to quickly obtain valuable information has become a problem. Therefore, intelligent question answering (QA) has gained more attention than ever. In this paper, we focus on Chinese answer selection, one kind of automatic question answering tasks. It can be described as follows: given a question sentence q and a set of candidate answer sentences {a1, a2, ..., an}, the goal is to find correct answer sentences from this set. The main challenge is that correct answers may not directly share lexical units with the corresponding question, and candidate answers contain much irrelevant information.

Shallow learning methods are mainly based on typical machine learning model, such as Bayesian classifier and support vector machine. Morphology, grammar and syntax features are designed with much effort. However, deep semantic information is not well learned and these methods are not well adaptive. Recently, deep learning technologies have brought encouraging results in the fields of machine translation, reading comprehension and question answering [1, 2].

© Springer Nature Switzerland AG 2020
R. Xu et al. (Eds.): AIMS 2020, LNCS 12401, pp. 60–73, 2020.
https://doi.org/10.1007/978-3-030-59605-7_5

In this work, we employ bidirectional Long Short-Term Memory (biLSTM) network as our basic deep learning QA model, which does not require feature engineering and language tools. Cosine similarities are used to evaluate the relationships between questions and answers. In addition, we also adopt attention mechanism between question and answer, which is reported effective [3].

To improve the performance of the basic model further, we investigate mixed embedding. In Chinese documents, not only words convey meaningful information, but also Chinese characters. Inspired by Wang et al. [4], we exploit word embedding and character embedding representation to form rich meaning vector representation for deep neural networks.

To reduce possible feature loss caused by the max pooling layer in the basic model, we construct a convolutional neural network to provide compensatory features [5]. They are concatenated with the features that come from max pooling, to form the final composite features. Finally, we propose a comprehensive model based on mixed embedding and composite features.

Experimental results on NLPCC-ICCPOL 2016 document-based QA dataset show that the proposed two techniques obviously improve the performance. Compared with the attention based biLSTM model, the comprehensive model has improved the MRR performance of QA by 6.0%. The MRR and ACC@1 score are 79.63% and 69.60% respectively. It can be seen that mixed embedding and composite features are effective for answer selection.

The rest of the paper is organized as follows: in Sect. 2 we describe the research works related to answer selection. In Sect. 3 we present the details of the proposed models. The experimental results and data set are discussed in Sect. 4. Finally, we conclude our work and describe the future plan in Sect. 5.

2 Related Work

Shallow models of machine learning were used for answer selection in the past. However, sematic information conveyed by sentences was not well exploited. Recently deep learning models have achieved encouraging results in the field of question answering. One approach is to construct a joint feature vector based on the question and answer, and transform the task into a classification or ranking problem. Wang and Nyberg [6] transformed answer selection to classification by building joint feature vectors of question and answer for Long Short-Term Memory (LSTM) network. Feng et al. [7] calculated similarity between question and answer vector representation to evaluate candidate answers. CNN networks were investigated to retrieve meanings of sentences. Yin et al. [8] proposed a multi-layer CNN model based on attention mechanism to model semantic representation of sentences, and reported positive effect on the performance of answer matching. Wang et al. [9] proposed a compare-aggregate model for answer selection, including multiple different methods to calculate similarity, and achieved promising results on all four data sets.

Another approach is to learn and match the expressions of questions and answers through specific similarity measures. Liu et al. [3] built SAN model to simulate the multi-step reasoning process and integrate multiple features, such as part-of-speech tags and named entities. Wang et al. [4] studied gated self-matching bi-directional RNN and character level embedding for reading comprehension. Hu et al. [10] proposed a re-attention mechanism that can solve the problem of redundant or insufficient attention. Lin et al. [11] reported a self-attention approach for sentences embedding. They reported promising performance based on deep neural models. Gu et al. [12] used multi-head attention to promote neural machine translation by calculating multiple attentions in different subspaces, and used a refined network to combine information from multiple attention points. Clustering similar information to keep unique information, the performance is obviously improved.

3   Methodology

A biLSTM model is employed to match questions and candidate answers. Attention mechanism is exploited to assign different weights to each part of candidate answers according to corresponding questions. To improve the performance of the basic model further, mixed embedding and CNN compensatory features are exploited. Finally, we propose a comprehensive model based on the two techniques.

3.1   Attention Based BiLSTM Model

After Dzmitry et al. [13] proposed attention mechanism, it has been applied to various NLP tasks, such as reading comprehension and question answering. We build our basic model based on a biLSTM network with attention. It is shown in Fig. 1. Word embedding is obtained by word2vec training after Chinese word segmentation. Then word embedding vectors of question sentences and answer sentences are fed into two

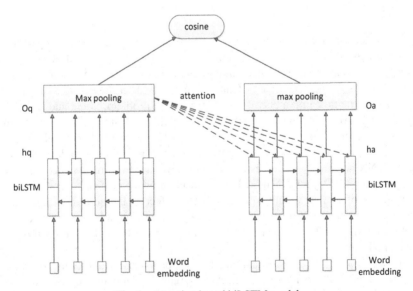

Fig. 1. Attention based biLSTM model

biLSTM networks respectively. After attention calculation and max pooling, cosine similarities of vectors are used to find correct answers.

Given an input sequence x = $\{x_1, x_2, \ldots, x_n\}$, where x_t is a word embedding vector, the output h_t of a hidden layer at time step t of a LSTM will be updated as follows:

$$i_t = sigmoid(W_i h_{t-1} + U_i x_t + b_i) \tag{1}$$

$$f_t = sigmoid\left(W_f h_{t-1} + U_f x_t + b_f\right) \tag{2}$$

$$\tilde{c_t} = \tanh(W_c h_{t-1} + U_c x_t + b_c) \tag{3}$$

$$c_t = f_t * c_{t-1} + i_t * \tilde{c_t} \tag{4}$$

$$o_t = sigmoid(W_o h_{t-1} + U_o x_t + b_o) \tag{5}$$

$$h_t = o_t * tanh(c_t) \tag{6}$$

Here W_i, W_f, W_c, W_o, U_i, U_f, U_c and U_o are weight parameters, and b_i, b_f, b_c and b_o are bias values. To explore the context beside a word, a bi-directional LSTM (biLSTM) model is employed. At each time step, the output representation is the concatenation of the two vectors from two directions.

Attention mechanism is described as follows. At time step t, question representation o_q is obtained after biLSTM and the pooling layer. Answer representation h_a is obtained after biLSTM, and the updated representation $\tilde{h_a}$ can be obtained by:

$$s_{a,q}(t) = softmax\left(W_{ms}^T \tanh\left(W_{am} h_a(t) + W_{qm} o_q\right)\right) \tag{7}$$

$$\tilde{h_a}(t) = h_a(t) s_{a,q}(t) \tag{8}$$

Here $S_{a,q}(t)$ is the attention weight of $h_a(t)$, and $\tilde{h_a}(t)$ is the updated value of $h_a(t)$. W_{am}, W_{qm} and W_{ms} are weight parameters.

3.2 Mixed Embedding

To encode rich meaning information of Chinese sentences, we introduce mixed embedding vectors into the attention based biLSTM model, which is described in the Sect. 3.1. Given a Chinese sentence, for example, "天安门场位于北京/Tiananmen Square is located at Beijing", we get the word token list "[天安门场/Tiananmen Square] [位于/is located] [北京/Beijing]" after word segmentation. Word embedding vectors and character embedding vectors are obtained by training based on word and character unit respectively. After our previous study, we find that directly concatenating the word embedding vector and the character embedding vector does not work very well for answer selection. We propose a vectorized representation method based on mixed embedding. The two vectorization generation methods are compared as follows:

$$E_w = E\_list_w(word) \tag{9}$$

$$mixed\_E_w = f_{concat}(E_w, f_{ch}(word)) \tag{10}$$

Formula (9) is a commonly used traditional vectorization method, and word obtains its embedding vectors through E_listw; and formula (10) is the mixed embedding vectorization method proposed in this article: the character vector feature is introduced based on the traditional method. The specific implementation of the character vector feature is shown in formula (11), (12).

$$E_{ch} = E\_list_{ch}(ch_{word}) \tag{11}$$

$$f_{ch}(word) = f_{softmax}\left(f_{concat}\left(f_{pool}\left(f_{conv}(E_{ch})\right)\right)\right) \tag{12}$$

As can be seen from the above, the vector feature acquisition process of character is: (1) Obtain the character vector matrix representation corresponding to the word through the word vector word list E_listch; (2) Extract the features with different word spacing by convolution and pooling operations; (3) Connect and activate the obtained features.

A CNN network is employed to process original character embedding vectors and obtain character representation vectors. For each word in the previous sentence, for example, "[天安门广场/Tiananmen Square]", this procedure is shown in Fig. 2.

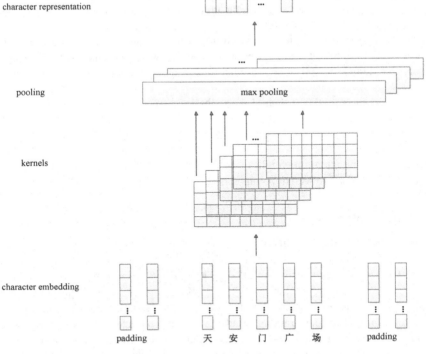

Fig. 2. Character representation vector

After padding character embedding vectors of this word, we have a matrix with fixed size for convolution operation. Different convolution kernels and corresponding max pooling operations are exploited for feature extraction. Then we concatenate the results of pooling together to get the character representation vector. Finally, we concatenate the word embedding vector and character representation vector of " 天安丁场/Tiananmen Square" to get the final mixed embedding vector for this word. The mixed embedding vector of each word will be feed into a biLSTM network.

3.3 Composite Features

We propose an extension of the CNN convolutional neural network for the answer selection model. In the attention based biLSTM model, the max pooling layer usually selects the most important features. A convolutional neural network is employed along with the max pooling layer. The purpose is to make up for the max pooling layer feature loss, and make full use of the hidden layer output of biLSTM at each time step. The structure of this CNN is shown in Fig. 3 and the usage is shown in Fig. 4.

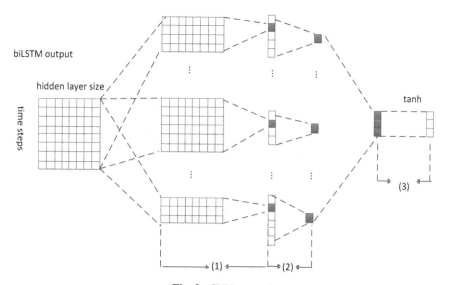

Fig. 3. CNN network

This CNN network includes the following three parts. (1) convolution layer and activation layer: multiple convolution kernels are applied to biLSTM output, and then an activation function is applied to each convolution vector; (2) max pooling layer: max pooling strategy is employed to obtain the maximum value of each vector; (3) full connection layer: there are only input layer and output layer. After combining the results of each max pooling layer and applying *tanh* function, the CNN compensatory features are generated. After combining the supplementary feature vector of the question and answer with the output vector of the max pooling layer according to a certain weight, a more composite feature vector is obtained, which can compensate for the feature loss caused by the max pooling layer to a certain extent.

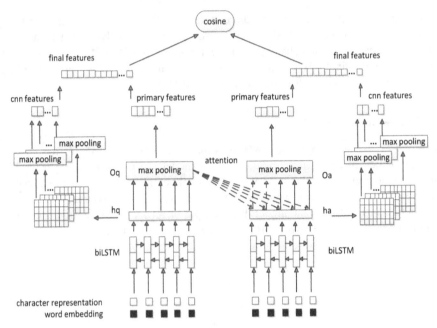

Fig. 4. The comprehensive model

3.4 The Comprehensive Model

To extend the attention based biLSTM model in Sect. 3.1, we propose a comprehensive model to incorporate mixed embedding representation and composite features, which is shown in Fig. 4. Vector representations of questions and answers are obtained based on word and character unit. Then, vectors of questions and answers are fed into two biLSTM networks respectively. Attention mechanism is adopted to modify candidate answer representations by question representation. In addition to the primary features given by attention guided biLSTM, a convolutional neural network is also employed to further extract features for the hidden layer output. Then the primary features and CNN compensatory features are combined as final composite features. Cosine similarities are used to measure distance of questions and answers. Each pair of question and true/false answer in training data is used train the model. Finally the trained model can be used to tell whether a candidate answer is true or not.

4   Experiments and Discussion

4.1   Dataset

NLPCC-ICCPOL 2016 document-based QA (DBQA) dataset is employed to train and test our models. It includes a Chinese training set and a Chinese testing set. The numbers of QA pairs and questions are shown in Table 1. In the training set, questions, document sentences (candidate answers), and labels are provided. If a sentence is a correct answer of the corresponding question, then the label is 1. Otherwise, the label is 0. In the testing set, only questions and candidate answers are provided. Some typical training samples are shown in Table 2.

Table 1. Numbers of QA pairs and questions

Dataset	QA pairs	Questions
Training Set	181882	8772
Testing Set	122531	5997

Table 2. Training samples

Question	Candidate Answer	Label
瑞安公主是谁的妹妹？ Whose sister is Princess Rui'an?	万历十三年下嫁万炜。 She married Wan Wei at the 13th year of Wanli.	0
瑞安公主是谁的妹妹？ Whose sister is Princess Rui'an?	崇祯时，主累加大长公主。 Chongzhen named her Great Princess.	0
瑞安公主是谁的妹妹？ Whose sister is Princess Rui'an?	瑞安公主朱尧媛，明神宗的同母妹妹。 Princess Rui'an Zhu Yaoyuan is a sister of one emperor of the Ming dynasty.	1
瑞安公主是谁的妹妹？ Whose sister is Princess Rui'an?	炜官至太傅，管宗人府印。 Wei is the teacher of the emperor, charging of the Royal Court.	0
瑞安公主是谁的妹妹？ Whose sister is Princess Rui'an?	所产子及庶子长祚、弘祚皆官都督。 Her sons, Changzuo and Hongzuo, are both generals.	0

4.2 Experimental Setup

In our experiments, Chinese Wikipedia documents are used to train a Word2Vec model and generate word embedding and character embedding vectors. The dimensions of word embedding and character embedding vectors are 50 and 100 respectively. As the number of words in a Chinese sentence may be different, we normalize the sentence length as 100. If a sentence contains more words, then it will be truncated. If a sentence contains fewer words, padding operation will be adopted.

The number of nodes in a hidden layer of biLSTM is important. If it is too small, the performance may be poor. If it is too large, the training procedure is time consuming.

After preliminary experiments, we set it as 300. When calculating character representation vector (see Fig. 2), we evaluate different convolution kernels. Then the kernels $1 \times 50, 2 \times 50, 3 \times 50, 4 \times 50$ and 5×50 are selected. The length of character representation is set as 7 experimentally. In the compensative convolutional neural network, the convolutional layer is made up of $5 \times 600, 10 \times 600, 15 \times 600, 20 \times 600, 25 \times 600, 30 \times 600, 35 \times 600, 40 \times 600, 45 \times 600$ and 50×600 convolution kernels.

We define a hinge loss function as the following equation. Here a+ denotes a correct answer, and a− denotes a wrong answer. M is a constant parameter to optimize the objective function.

$$L = max\{0, M - cosine(q, a+) + cosine(q, a-)\} \qquad (13)$$

The constant threshold M is a sensitive parameter. When training our models, we try to reduce the distance between right answers and the question, and extend the distance between wrong answers and the question. If M is too small, then correct answer sentences and wrong answer sentences are difficult to discriminate. If it is too large, models are difficult to training for convergence. It is set as 0.1 in our experiments. The learning rate is initialized as 0.2. In training procedure, it will decay exponentially. Our training strategy is mini-batch gradient descent method, and there are 20 questions in each batch.

4.3 Experimental Result

According to NLPCC-ICCPOL 2016 QA task guideline, we employ Mean Reciprocal Rank (MRR) and ACC@1 to evaluate proposed models. MRR is average all correct answers. The score is calculated by taking the inverse of the position of the first correct answer in the candidate answer list. It is shown in the following formula:

$$MRR = \frac{1}{|Q|} \sum_{i=1}^{|Q|} \frac{1}{rank_i} \qquad (14)$$

For each question, the models may generate multiple correct answers with different scores. Here $|Q|$ denotes the number of questions and $rank_i$ denotes the position of the first correct answer in the generated answer set for the question Q_i. In contrast, to compute ACC@1, we just consider whether the first generated answer is correct.

Table 3. Experimental results of our models

Model	MRR	ACC@1
Att-biLSTM	75.12%	65.28%
Att-biLSTM + Mix	78.58%	68.82%
Att-biLSTM + Mix + Comp	79.63%	69.60%

In Table 3, we record the experimental results of our three models. The first model is attention based biLSTM. The second model is attention based biLSTM with mixed embedding. The third model is attention based biLSTM with mixed embedding and composite features. The parameters of biLSTM in the three models are similar. According to Table 3, we find that mixed embedding and composite features improve MRR performance by 4.6% and 1.3% respectively. Compared with the Attention based biLSTM model, our comprehensive model improves MRR performance by 6.0%. To train the comprehensive model to convergence, we consume about 95 h.

Learning curves of these three models on MRR and ACC@1 are shown in Fig. 5 and Fig. 6 respectively. It can be seen that the performance of each model is improved when the number of training epochs is increased. After same training epochs, normally the MRR scores and ACC@1 scores of attention based biLSTM model with mixed embedding and composite features are the best ones. We conclude that mixed embedding and composite features are effective for answer selection.

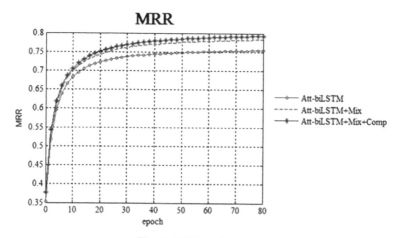

Fig. 5. MRR performance

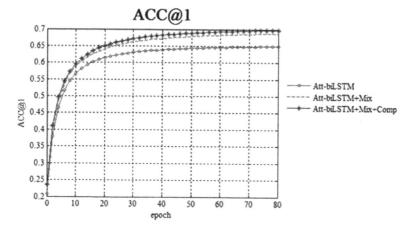

Fig. 6. ACC@1 performance

We list the performance of previous typical models in Table 4 [14, 15]. It can be seen that biLSTM and attention mechanism are effective. At the same time, the performance of our comprehensive model is similar with that of the best model B, which incorporates much feature engineering effort.

Table 4. Experimental results of previous typical models

Model	Method	MRR
Model A	TFIDF SVM	45.31%
	Re-estimate query likelihood	69.36%
	BLSTM	66.34%
Model B	Word overlap	51.54%
	Average word embedding	46.10%
	Embedding-based features	74.70%
	All features	80.08%

4.4 Discussion

We analyze wrong answer sentences generated by our model. Typical wrong answers are listed in Table 5. The annotated correct answers are also recorded in this table. We can see that actually wrong answers are about certain parts of questions, but they do not satisfy the requirement exactly. The question Q1 is about "when is more precipitation". In the sentence WA1, rain, type and season are mentioned. Here rain and season are relevant to the question, but type is not. In the sentence CA1, rain, amount and season are given. Therefore it is the correct answer. The word "mainly" in CA1 and the word "more" in Q1 are closely related. In the sentence WA2, course names are given. The question Q2 is about research field. The question Q3 is interesting. Q3 is about the ranking of Chinese national men's football team in the world. CA3 gives the words "world" and "ranking", while WA3 gives the words "Asian" and "ranking". Maybe the reason is that the team is active in Asia, not the world.

After analyzing these wrong samples, we find that fine grained concept relations should be focused, such "more" and "mainly", "study" and "research", "look like" and "on the head". These relationships may not be learned from training data, as the data size is limited. To further improve the performance, a large training corpus is helpful. On the other hand, knowledge is another source to retrieve these relationships. How to incorporate extra knowledge into deep learning models is a key point.

Table 5. Error analysis

Question (Q)	Correct Answer (CA)	Wrong Answer (WA)
Q1: 佛罗伦萨什么时候降水比较多？ Q1: When is more precipitation in Florence?	CA1: 降水主要集中在冬季。 CA1: Precipitation is mainly in winter.	WA1: 在夏季的少量降雨属于对流雨类型。 WA1: A small amount of rain in summer is a type of convective rain.
Q2: 陈红研究什么的？ Q2: What does Chen Hong study?	CA2: 研究方向：战略管理、知识与技术管理。 CA2: Research direction: strategic management, knowledge and technology management.	WA2: 主要讲授《现代管理学》《西方经济学》《人力资源管理》《市场营销》《战略管理》等课程。 WA2: Mainly teaches courses such as Modern Management, Western Economics, Human Resource Management, Marketing, and Strategic Management.
Q3: 中国国家男子足球队在世界的最新排名是多少？ Q3: What is the latest ranking of the Chinese national men's football team in the world?	CA3: 最新世界排名：88（2014年10月） CA3: Latest World Ranking: 88 (October 2014)	WA3: 最新亚洲排名：9（2014年10月） WA3: Latest Asian rankings: 9 (October 2014)
Q4: 大荒十大凶兽中珊瑚独角兽长什么样子？ Q4: What do Coral Unicorns look like among the ten great wild beasts in the Great Wilderness?	CA4: 头顶上一支弯月般的珊瑚角傲然而立，神威凛凛，大有君临天下，唯我独尊之势。 CA4: A crescent coral horn stands proudly and imposingly on its head, making it look like a king.	WA4: 大荒十大凶兽：在远古大荒时代，传说有十大凶兽。 WA4: The ten wild beasts of the wilderness: in the ancient times of the Great Wilderness, there was a legend that ten great wild beasts existed.
Q5: 李刚什么时候毕业的？ Q5: When did Li Gang graduate?	CA5: 李刚，1991年毕业于安顺二中，后考入北京大学历史系，并任北京市学联主席，1999年获历史学硕士学位。 CA5: Li Gang, graduated from Anshun No. 2 Middle School in 1991, was admitted to the Department of History of Peking University, and served as the chairman of the Beijing students' Federation. In 1999, he obtained a master's degree in history.	WA5: 出生日期：1975.12.14 WA5: Date of birth: 1975.12.14

5 Conclusions

In this paper, we investigate the function of word embedding and character embedding representation for answer selection. Mixed embedding incorporates more meaningful information than word embedding. Experimental results show that it improves the performance obviously. The MRR score is improved by 4.6%. We also study the function of a convolutional neural network to compensate for the loss of max pooling. The MRR score is improved by 1.3%. Finally, mixed embedding and composite features improve the performance by 6.0%. The MRR and ACC@1 score are 79.63% and 69.60% respectively. It can be seen that they are effective for answer selection when applied with biLSTM model. In the future, we plan to combine the BERT pre-trained model, and study answer selection based on fine-tuning BERT.

Acknowledgement. This work is partially supported by the National Natural Science Foundation of China (61672040).

References

1. Ding, M., Zhou, C., Chen, Q., Yang, H., Tang, J.: Cognitive graph for multi-hop reading comprehension at scale. In: Proceedings of the 57th Annual Meeting of the Association for Computational Linguistics (ACL), Florence, pp. 2694–2703 (2019)
2. Yang, R., Zhang, J., Gao, X., Ji, F., Chen, H.: Simple and effective text matching with richer alignment features. In: Proceedings of the 57th Annual Meeting of the Association for Computational Linguistics (ACL), Florence, pp. 4699–4709 (2019)
3. Liu, X., Shen, Y., Duh, K., Gao, J.: Stochastic answer networks for machine reading comprehension. In: Proceedings of 56th Annual Meeting of the Association for Computational Linguistics (ACL), Melbourne, pp. 1694–1704 (2018)
4. Wang, W., Yang, N., Wei, F., Chang, B., Zhou, M.: Gated self-matching networks for reading comprehension and question answering. In: Proceedings of 55th Annual Meeting of the Association for Computational Linguistics (ACL), Vancouver, pp. 189–198 (2017)
5. Collobert, R., Weston, J., Bottou, L., Karlen, M., Kavukcuoglu, K., Kuksa, P.: Natural language processing (almost) from scratch. J. Mach. Learn. Res. **12**, 2493–2537 (2011)
6. Wang, D., Nyberg, E.: A long short-term memory model for answer sentence selection in question answering. In: Proceedings of 53rd Annual Meeting of the Association for Computational Linguistics and the 7th International Joint Conference on Natural Language Processing (ACL), Beijing, pp. 707–712 (2015)
7. Feng, M., Xiang, B., Glass, M.R., Wang, L., Zhou, B.: Applying deep learning to answer selection: a study and an open task. In: Proceedings of 2015 IEEE Workshop on Automatic Speech Recognition and Understanding (ASRU), Scottsdale, pp. 813–820 (2015)
8. Yin, W., Schütze, H., Xiang, B., Zhou, B.: ABCNN: attention-based convolutional neural network for modeling sentence pairs. Trans. Assoc. Comput. Linguist. **4**, 259–272 (2016)
9. Wang, S., Jiang, J.: A compare-aggregate model for matching text sequences. In: Proceeding of International Conference on Learning Representations (ICLR), Toulon, pp. 1–15 (2017)
10. Hu, M., Peng, Y., Huang, Z., Qiu, X., Wei, F., Zhou, M.: Reinforced mnemonic reader for machine reading comprehension. In: Proceedings of 27th International Joint Conference on Artificial Intelligence, Stockholm, pp. 4099–4106 (2018)

11. Lin, Z., Feng, M., Santos, C.N.D., Yu, M.: A structured self-attentive sentence embedding. In: Proceedings of 5th International Conference on Learning Representations (ICLR), Toulon (2017)

12. Gu, S., Feng, Y.: Improving multi-head attention with capsule networks. In: Tang, J., Kan, M.-Y., Zhao, D., Li, S., Zan, H. (eds.) NLPCC 2019. LNCS (LNAI), vol. 11838, pp. 314–326. Springer, Cham (2019). https://doi.org/10.1007/978-3-030-32233-5_25

13. Dzmitry, B., Cho, K., Bengio Y.: Neural machine translation by jointly learning to align and translate. In: Proceedings of International Conference of Learning Representation (ICLR), San Diego (2015)

14. Wu, F., Yang, M., Zhao, T., Han, Z., Zheng, D., Zhao, S.: A hybrid approach to DBQA. In: Lin, C.-Y., Xue, N., Zhao, D., Huang, X., Feng, Y. (eds.) ICCPOL/NLPCC -2016. LNCS (LNAI), vol. 10102, pp. 926–933. Springer, Cham (2016). https://doi.org/10.1007/978-3-319-50496-4_87

15. Wang, B., et al.: A Chinese question answering approach integrating count-based and embedding-based features. In: Lin, C.-Y., Xue, N., Zhao, D., Huang, X., Feng, Y. (eds.) ICCPOL/NLPCC -2016. LNCS (LNAI), vol. 10102, pp. 934–941. Springer, Cham (2016). https://doi.org/10.1007/978-3-319-50496-4_88

A Neural Framework for Chinese Medical Named Entity Recognition

Zhengyi Zhao, Ziya Zhou, Weichuan Xing, Junlin Wu, Yuan Chang,
and Binyang Li[✉]

School of Information Science and Technology, University of International Relations,
Beijing, China
byli@uir.edu.cn

Abstract. Named Entity Recognition (NER) in the medical field targets to extract names of disease, surgery, and the organ location from medical texts, which is considered as the fundamental work for medical robots and intelligent diagnosis systems. It is very challenging to recognize the named entities in Chinese medical texts, because (a) one single Chinese medical named entity is usually expressed with more characters/words than other languages, i.e. 3.2 words and 7.3 characters in average; (b) different types of medical named entities are usually nested together. To address the above issue, this paper presents a neural framework that is constructed by two modules: a pre-trained module to distinguish each individual entity from the nested expressions, while a modified Bi-LSTM module to effectively identify long entities. We conducted the experiments based on the CCKS2019 dataset, our proposed method can identify the medical entity in Chinese, especially for those nested entities embodied in long expressions, and 95.83% was achieved in terms of F1-score, and 18.64% improvement was achieved compared to the baseline models.

Keywords: Named Entity Recognition · Chinese electronic medical records

1 Introduction

Named Entity Recognition (NER) aims at identifying the named entities mentioned in the text, such as the name of persons, locations, and organizations, and classifying them into the predefined categories. To ensure the accuracy of extraction and classification, most of the current research work focuses on recognize the named entity in specific domain, including finance, medical, legal, and political field.

With the rapid development of electronic medical records and medical texts, NER in the medical field has received much attention from both academics and industry. Medical named entity recognition is to identify the names of disease, drug, surgery, afflicted organ, and classify them into predefined types [1]. e.g., CCKS has organized medical named entity recognition open challenge for Chinese electronic medical records (CEMRs) in 2019. These open challenges cannot only provide a batch of high-quality annotated datasets for subsequent research, but also boom many products, medical intelligent diagnosis robot, medical decision support system, and so on.

© Springer Nature Switzerland AG 2020
R. Xu et al. (Eds.): AIMS 2020, LNCS 12401, pp. 74–83, 2020.
https://doi.org/10.1007/978-3-030-59605-7_6

For this purpose, there are some study on the medical NER for English. Based on the compiled English medical text data set and the entity extraction model, the target entity can be extracted well from unstructured text. However, due to the expression style of medical texts and the morphological characters of Chinese, it is very challenging in Chinese medical named entity recognition. In Chinese, a medical named entity is usually constituted by several characters or words, and to express the same meaning, more Chinese characters/words will be required than that of English in most medical named entity expression. Figure 1 illustrates an example from CCKS 2019 dataset. There is only three English words "ulcerative rectal adenocarcinoma" to describe the type of cancer, but in the Chinese expression 浸润溃疡型直肠腺癌(ulcerative rectal adenocarcinoma), it consists of 3 words (9 characters) in total. According to our statistics on CCKS 2019 dataset, 3.2 words and 7.3 characters in average are required to form a Chinese medical entity.

Example: 患者术后病理示为浸润溃疡型直肠腺癌。

Translation: The ulcerative rectal adenocarcinoma was shown by postoperative pathology. showed.

Fig. 1. An example of medical NER from CCKS 2019 datasets.

More importantly, it is frequently occurring that one complex entity may cover multiple entities, and different types of medical named entities are nested together. In Fig. 1, for the entity 直肠腺癌(rectal adenocarcinoma), only part of its Chinese expressions, i.e. 直肠腺(rectal gland), 直肠(rectum), are also medical entities without any morphological changes. But the corresponding English expressions can be easily identified because different morphological structures are used in the entity.

To address the above issue, this paper presents a neural framework of BERT + Bi-LSTM + CRF, named BBC, that is constructed by two modules: a Bi-LSTM module that can capture the dependency with long distance within a sentence and extract the medical entities with multiple words or characters; a pre-trained model that can better express the rich semantics of medical texts and represent the relations between sentences [2]. The explements were conducted based on CCKS 2019 datasets, experiments show that BBC can identify the medical entity in Chinese, especially for those nested entities embodied in long expressions, and 95.83% was achieved in terms of F1-score, and 18.64% improvement was achieved compared to the baseline models.

2 Related Works

As a classic task of NLP, there are many studies on NER. The previous work can be generally divided into the following categories: rule-based, unsupervised learning, supervised learning, and deep learning based method. Since this paper is focusing on medical area, we also review some corpus as well as the techniques on medical NER.

(1) Traditional Methods

The rule-based NER methods relied on handcrafted rules, which performed well when the dictionary (such as WordNet [3]) was well constructed, but it could not be easily transferred to other domains, which would achieve the result with high precision and low recall. For those domains without resources, unsupervised learning is used to extract named entities from clustering groups based on contextual word similarity, calculate lexical resources, lexical patterns, and statistics on a large corpus and use them to predict the phrases of named entities. Huang et al. [4] applied unsupervised entity linking to link entity mentions to a domain-specific knowledge base. The framework learned the entity distribution through the global contexts, and a specific representation of entities from the knowledge base, and then identified the entity as well as the types.

In the supervised learning method, NER is generally regarded as a classification or sequence labeling task. Many existing machine learning algorithms were applied, which include Hidden Markov Models (HMM), maximum entropy Markov models (MEMMs), Support Vector Machines (SVM), and Conditional Random Fields (CRF). Li et al. describe an SVM model that used an uneven parameter to improve the performance for document classification [5].

(2) Deep Learning-Based Methods

In recent years, Huang et al. [6] first applied a BI-LSTM-CRF model to NLP benchmark sequence labeling datasets, that captured the features by Bi-LSTM effectively, and output the tag information through the CRF module Rei Maiek [7] uses the attention mechanism to dynamically use word vector and character vector information based on the RNN-CRF model structure. Akash Bharadwaj [8] later added phonological features to the original Bi-LSTM-CRF model and used the attention mechanism on character vectors to learn to focus on more efficient characters.

(3) Medical NER Corpus

Early NER tasks for medical texts were mostly rule-based and dictionary-based methods. Some corpus were constructed and widely used, such as MedLEE [9] 和GENIES [10]. Recently, Wang [11] annotated a corpus of medical progress notes with more than 15,000 medical named entities in 11 entity types and proposed a system combining CRF, SVM and maximum entropy models to reduce the misclassification. The corpus was used on the i2b2 challenge 2010 [12, 13] has also been applied to the medical text NER. In China, there are far fewer data sets based on Chinese medical texts than on English medical texts. More typical are the Chinese medical text evaluation dataset provided by the CCKS conference and the Q&A data of the medical online forum. The follow-up experiments in this paper are based on the CCKS 2019 dataset [14].

3 Methodology

3.1 Problem Definition

To better understand the task of medical named entity recognition, we firstly give the definition and the type of medical entity, and then introduce our model.

In this paper, we follow the definition of medical NER in CCKS 2019 evaluation [14], where the medical entities can be divided into 6 types: *disease, imaging test, laboratory testing, operation, medicine, and anatomic site.*

Without the loss of generality, we assume that we define that the input Chinese medical text is composed of a set of words, represented as $s = \{w_1, w_2 \cdots, w_n\}$. The objective of medical NER is to identify a successive sequence of m words $\{w_{i-m}, w_{i-m+1} \cdots, w_i\}$ as the medical named entity and classify it into one of the above types.

3.2 Model

Recall that the Chinese medical NER faces two challenges, the long entity recognition and nested structure. The former one will result in the incomplete identification of medical entity, while the latter one will classify the entity into an incorrect type, which will in turn affect the performance.

To solve the above problems, this paper presents a neural framework constructed by *BERT+Bi-LSTM+CRF* (BBC) modules. The overall structure of BBC is shown in Fig. 2. Unlike word2vec model [15], BERT is designed to pre-train the representation to further increase the generalization ability of the word2vec model and describe the rich features of character-level, word-level, sentence-level, and even inter-sentence relationships. So, the pre-trained module can well represent the inter-sentence contextual information to and accurately learn the characteristics of complex entities, thereby improving the accuracy of complex entity recognition [16].

Moreover, Bi-LSTM is able to solve the long-distance dependency of the medical text and make use of contextual features. Therefore, in this task, Bi-LSTM is trained to perform category prediction based on each word in the long entity, so as to express the actual meaning of the word more accurately in the long entity of the whole text.

In summary, our framework uses BERT as the model of the embedding layer and use the Bi-LSTM-CRF model to predict the label of each word in the medical text. This combination of model effectively increases the accuracy of the long entity recognition as well as complex entity recognition.

Pre-trained Module
In order to identify the nested entity, we should capture the relation between sentence, i.e. inter-sentence semantics. So, we design a pre-trained module in our model. On one hand, the pre-trained embedding can well represent the context semantics between sentences; on the other hand, the domain-dependent semantics can also be well represented. More detailly, in our pre-trained module, we employ the BERT-based Chinese model provided by Google [16]. The outputs generated by the last layer of BERT are the input of the subsequent neural network model.

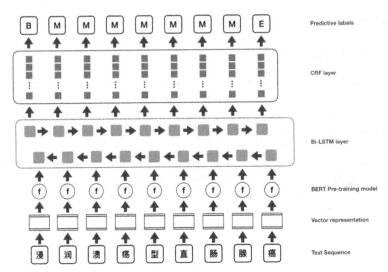

Fig. 2. Model architecture.

The BERT model follows the structure of GPU model and uses transformer encoder as the main model structure. Transformer abandons RNN circular network structure and models a text entirely based on attention mechanism [17].

Bi-LSTM Module

After the pre-trained module, the embedding layer is to convert the text into a set of corresponding word vectors, $x = \{x_1, x_2 \cdots, x_n\}$. We then attempt to capture the intra-sentence contextual information to identify the entity from the nested structure. Inspired by the excellent performance of [16], we also adopt Bi-LSTM. The structure of the Bi-LSTM neural network is shown in Fig. 3. Assume that there are input vector x_t, cell state C_t, temporary cell state $\tilde{C}_t$, hidden layer state h_t, forget gate f_t, memory gate i_t, output gate o_t at time t. We have access to calculate and pass on useful information for subsequent time by memorizing new information in the current unit state, while useless information is discarded, and the hidden state h_t is output at each time step.

Given the hidden state h_{t-1} at the last moment and input word vector x_t, we compute $i_t, f_t, \tilde{C}_t$, previous cell state C_{t-1} as follows:

$$f_t = \sigma\left(W_f \cdot [h_{t-1}, x_t] + b_f\right)$$

$$i_t = \sigma\left(W_i \cdot [h_{t-1}, x_t] + b_i\right)$$

$$\tilde{C}_t = \tanh\left(W_C \cdot [h_{t-1}, x_t] + b_C\right)$$

The current cell state C_t and hidden layer state h_t can be calculated as follows:

$$C_t = f_t * C_{t-1} + i_t * \tilde{C}_t$$

$$h_t = \sigma\left(W_o \cdot [h_{t-1}, x_t] + b_o\right) * \tanh(C_t)$$

Therefore, we obtain the hidden vector $h = \{h_0, h_{01}, \cdots, h_{n-1}\}$.

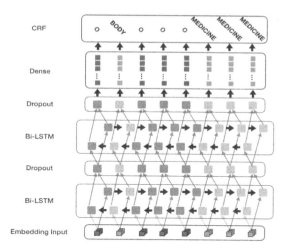

Fig. 3. Bi-LSTM-CRF structure.

Bi-LSTM-CRF

With the forward and backward passes over the network, the model has access to both past and future features. For the long entity 浸润溃疡型直肠腺癌, it can be maintained as a whole in the Bi-LSTM neural network. Due to the multi-dimensional vector expression of the pre-trained model, the entity features can be well represented, and the " 浸润溃疡型直肠腺癌" can be identified as an entire entity instead of the composition of other short entities. In addition, a dense layer is connected after the probability output to perform the possible splicing of all labels such that the layer can be sufficiently achieving local optimum.

CRF. In our model, we also adopt CRF for the labeling output, where the training is based on MLE and optimization algorithm [18]. For the training datasets, the parameters of the model can be adaptively obtained by maximizing the log-likelihood function of the data, where the log-likelihood function is:

$$L(w) = L_{\tilde{P}}(P_w) = \log \prod_{x,y} P_w(y|w)^{\tilde{P}(x,y)} = \sum_{x,y} \tilde{P}(x, y) \log P_w(y|x)$$

where $P(X, Y)$ is the empirical probability distribution.

After that, we utilize the improved iterative scaling method to continuously update the lower bound of the variable to maximize the log-likelihood function. For the case that the classification probability of each word in "invasive ulcerative rectal adenocarcinoma" is different, CRF can well identify the " 浸润溃疡型直肠腺癌" corresponding to the "*disease*" label by probabilistic labeling of long entities.

4 Experiment

4.1 Experiment Setup

Datasets

To investigate the performance of our BBC model, we conduct a set of experiments based on the CCKS 2019 dataset [14]. CCKS 2019 dataset is consisted of 1,000 real Chinese electronic medical records, and the entities were manually labeled and classified into six predefined categories: *disease, imaging test, laboratory testing, operation, medicine, and anatomic site*. Some statistics on the dataset were shown in Table 1, including the number and the proportion of long entity and complex entity in the six categories.

We argue that the performance of Chinese medical NER was usually affected by the nested entities or the long entities. For ease of comparison, we further classify them from two angles: the character amount and entity structure. The overall medical entity can be divided into simple entity and complex entity, where the structure of simple entity is relatively fixed without nested entities, such as "左附件", "奥沙利铂", etc. On the contrary, the complex entity is with more complicated structure, and some entities are nested together, such as "直肠腺癌" includes "肠", "直肠", "直肠腺" and "腺癌".

We also classify the Chinese medical entities into long entity and short entity. The short entity is constituted by five or fewer Chinese characters, such as "腹", "胃癌", while the long entity contain more than five Chinese characters that may involve some complex entities, such as "左侧盆腔淋巴结", "转移性低分化腺癌".

Table 1. Statistics on the CCKS 2019 dataset.

Categories	#Long entities	Proportion (%)	#Complex entities	Proportion (%)
anatomic site	534	36.08	522	35.27
operation	683	89.40	269	35.21
disease	1,516	72.09	1,210	57.54
medicine	71	15.74	35	7.76
imaging test	81	36.82	70	31.82
lab test	89	56.04	42	14.53
total	2,974	54.49	2,148	40.48

It is obviously that the proportion of the long entity and complex entity is relatively big, which proved the motivation of our work.

Metrics

Similar with other NER tasks, we adopt *Precision, Recall*, and *F1-score* to evaluate the performance of our model. Let $S = \{s_1, s_2, \cdots s_m\}$ denote the output, while $G = \{g_1, g_2, \cdots g_m\}$ denote the correct result, the metrics can be computed as follows.

$$P = \frac{|S \bigcap_r G|}{|S|}, \quad R = \frac{|S \bigcap_r G|}{|R|}, \quad F - 1 = \frac{2PR}{P + R}$$

where $\cap_r$ represents the intersection of .. and G.

Compared Methods

Since there was no method for Chinese medical NER, we redesigned a conventional CRF model [19] as our baseline model. We then compared our model with the baseline model and Huang's model [6]. To better demonstrate the effectiveness of BERT and Bi-LSTM, we also removed some modules of BBC and got the results.

4.2 Results

Table 2 showed the experimental results based on the CCKS 2019 dataset.

Table 2. Experimental results on CCKS 2019.

Types	Precision (%)	Recall (%)	F1-score (%)
Baseline model	79.94	74.63	77.19
Huang's model	76.92	85.07	79.13
Word2Vec+Bi-LSTM+CRF	85.62	84.66	83.90
BBC	**94.88**	**96.80**	**95.83**

In Table 2, BBC model achieved the best run on all the metrics, and 18.64% and 16.7% improvement were reached against the Baseline model and Huang's model in terms of F1-score. *Word2Vec+Bi-LSTM +CRF* performed better than *Huang's model*, it was because that Huang's model adopted a universal word embedding, while the *Word2Vec+Bi-LSTM +CRF* model used a medical domain-dependent word embedding. BBC incorporated pre-trained model outperformed the above two, it proved that domain-dependent information was very useful in medical NER. *Word2Vec+Bi-LSTM +CRF* outperformed Baseline model, and *Huang's model* beat the Baseline model, it proved that the Bi-LSTM module could well represent the intra-sentence semantics.

Table 3 and Table 4 provided the insights of each individual type of medical NER. We could find that the BBC could achieve 99.48% and 96.83% of F1-score in average on long entity and complex entity, respectively. As to the largest amount of long entity and complex entity, i.e. *disease* type, it could achieve 93.11% and 98.37% of F1-score, which was comparable with short entity and simple entity, respectively. That means our BBC model could effectively identify the long entity and the complex entity. Recall the example in Fig. 1, it could be successfully recognized by BBC model.

Table 3. Insights on the performance of long entity for each individual type.

Types	Long entity			Short entity		
	PRE	REC	F−1	PRE	REC	F−1
disease	94.69	91.58	93.11	94.99	98.96	96.93
operation	100.00	100.00	100.00	100.00	100.00	100.00
anatomic site	97.76	98.20	97.98	100.00	100.00	100.00
lab test	16.67	9.41	12.03	38.42	45.36	41.61
imaging test	94.44	97.14	95.77	100.00	100.00	100.00
medicine	100.00	94.44	97.14	95.21	95.47	95.34
total	99.17	99.79	99.48	93.36	95.71	95.42

Table 4. Insights on the performance of complex entity for each individual type

Types	Complex entity			Simple entity		
	PRE	REC	F−1	PRE	REC	F−1
disease	96.79	100.00	98.37	93.55	91.64	92.58
operation	100.00	100.00	100.00	100.00	100.00	100.00
anatomic site	99.05	99.52	99.29	99.55	99.55	99.55
lab test	9.38	100.00	17.14	36.73	32.60	34.54
imaging test	96.67	100.00	98.30	100.00	99.38	99.69
medicine	100.00	100.00	100.00	95.30	95.30	95.30
total	93.98	99.85	96.83	92.80	91.49	92.14

5 Conclusion

This paper targets on medical named entity recognition from Chinese medical records. To tackle with the challenges of long entity and nested structure in Chinese medical texts, this paper presents a neural framework by incorporating pre-trained module and Bi-LSTM module. Beneficial from the modules, both of intra-sentence semantics and inter-sentence semantics can be well captured so as to significantly improve the performance on Chinese medical NER. Based on the CCKS2019 evaluation dataset, those entities hidden in the nested structures and the entity with multiple words can be successfully identified. 95.83% was achieved in terms of F1-score, and 18.64% improvement was achieved compared to the baseline models.

Acknowledgements. This research is supported by the Natural Science Foundation of China (61976066, 61502115, U1636103), the Fundamental Research Fund for the Central Universities (3262019T29), the Joint funding (SKX182010023, 2019GA35) and Students' Academic Training Program of UIR (3262019SXK15).

References

1. Hopfield, J.: Neural networks and physical systems with emergent collective computational abilities. https://doi.org/10.1142/9789812799371_0043
2. de Benito-Gorron, D., Lozano-Diez, A., Toledano, D.T., Gonzalez Rodriguez, J.: Exploring convolutional, recurrent, and hybrid deep neural networks for speech and music detection in a large audio dataset. EURASIP J. Audio Speech Music Process. **2019**(1). https://doi.org/10.1186/s13636-019-0152-1
3. Fellbaum, C.: WordNet. In: Poli, R., Healy, M., Kameas, A. (eds.) Theory and Applications of Ontology: Computer Applications, pp. 231–243. Springer, Dordrecht (2010). https://doi.org/10.1007/978-90-481-8847-5_10
4. Huang, L., May, J., Pan, X., Ji, H.: Building a fine-grained entity typing system overnight for a new X(X = Language, Domain, Genre), 10 March 2016. arXiv:1603.03112v1
5. Li, Y., Bontcheva, K., Cunningham, H.: SVM based learning system for information extraction. In: Winkler, J., Niranjan, M., Lawrence, N. (eds.) DSMML 2004. LNCS (LNAI), vol. 3635, pp. 319–339. Springer, Heidelberg (2005). https://doi.org/10.1007/11559887_19
6. Huang, Z., Xu, W., Yu, K.: Bidirectional LSTM-CRF models for sequence tagging, 9 August 2015. arXiv:1508.01991
7. Marek, R., Crichton, G.K.O., Pyysalo, S.: Attending to characters in neural sequence labeling models, 14 November 2016. arXiv:1611.04361
8. Bharadwaj, A., Mortensen, D., Dyer, C., Carbonell, J.: Phonologically aware neural model for named entity recognition in low resource transfer settings. https://doi.org/10.18653/v1/d16-1153
9. Friedman, C., Alderson, P., Austin, J., Cimino, J., Johnson, S.: A general natural-language text processor for clinical radiology. J. Am. Med. Inform. Assoc. **1**(2), 161–174 (1994)
10. Friedman, C., Kra, P., Yu, H., Krauthammer, M., Rzhetsky, A.: GENIES: a natural-language processing system for the extraction of molecular pathways from journal articles. Bioinformatics **17**(Suppl. 1), S74–S82 (2001)
11. Wang, Y.: Annotating and recognising named entities in clinical notes. https://doi.org/10.3115/1667884.1667888
12. Uzuner, O., South, B., Shen, S., Duvall, S.: 2010 i2b2/VA challenge on concepts, assertions, and relations in clinical text. J. Am. Med. Inform. Assoc. **18**(5), 552–556 (2011)
13. Kiritchenko, S., de Bruijn, B., Cherry, C.: NRC at i2b2: one challenge, three practical tasks, nine statistical systems, hundreds of clinical records, millions of useful features. In: Proceedings of the 2010 i2b2/VA workshop on challenges in natural language processing for clinical data (2010)
14. CCKS 2019 NER of CEMR. https://www.biendata.com/competition/ccks_2019_1/
15. Rong, X.: word2vec parameter learning explained, 11 November 2014. arXiv:1411.2738v4
16. Devlin, J., Chang, M.-W., Lee, K., Toutanova, K.: BERT: Pre-training of deep bidirectional transformers for language understanding, 11 October 2018. arXiv:1810.04805
17. Gong, C., Tang, J., Zhou, S., Hao, Z., Wang, J.: Chinese named entity recognition with Bert. ISBN: 978-1-60595-651-0 (2019)
18. Xishuang, D., Shanta, C., Lijun, Q.: Deep learning for named entity recognition on Chinese electronic medical records: Combining deep transfer learning with multitask bi-directional LSTM RNN. PLoS ONE (2019). https://doi.org/10.1371/journal.pone.0216046
19. Konkol, M., Konopík, M.: CRF-Based Czech named entity recognizer and consolidation of Czech NER research. In: Habernal, I., Matoušek, V. (eds.) TSD 2013. LNCS (LNAI), vol. 8082, pp. 153–160. Springer, Heidelberg (2013). https://doi.org/10.1007/978-3-642-40585-3_20

An Annotated Chinese Corpus for Rumor Veracity Detection

Bo Yan[1,2], Yan Gao[1], Shubo Zhang[1], Yi Zhang[1], Yan Du[1], Xurui Sun[1], and Binyang Li[1(✉)]

[1] University of International Relations, Beijing, China
byli@uir.edu.cn
[2] The 54th Research Institute of China Electronics Technology Group Corporation, Shijiazhuang, China

Abstract. With the popularity of social media, Twitter, Facebook, and Weibo etc. platforms have become an indispensable part of people's life, where users can freely release and spread information. Meanwhile, the information credibility cannot be guaranteed and there exist a great amount of rumors in social media. These information will usually bring negative impact, and even affect the real society. To solve this problem, there are some work on the rumor corpora construction for automatic rumor detection. However, existing work focused on political domain and most of them were limited in English texts. As a result, these corpora cannot be well applied into other domains with resource-poor languages. This paper proposes a Chinese rumor detection corpus, named CRDC. This corpus consists of 10,000 rumors and 14,472 non-rumors from Weibo. Moreover, other information including language-independent features are also acquired, including rumors' retweet and like information, which can effectively help rumor detection and rumor propagation research in other languages. To better demonstrate the corpus, we also conducted some initial experiments to show details and statistics of our corpus.

Keywords: Rumor detection · Social media · Veracity · CRDC

1 Introduction

With the emergence of the Internet and especially the popularity of mobile Internet, Online Social Networks (OSN) has become an important information dissemination platform, which has become an indispensable part of people's life, such as Sina Weibo, Twitter, etc. In OSN, people are no longer merely receivers of information, but also play the role of creator of information [1]. Especially, with the development of social media, information is released and received more quickly, and it can be quickly spread and interacted between the users. At the meanwhile, online information is mixed up with the rumors or fake news, and these information will generate negative impact on society with the quick spread on social media [2]. For example, in 2011, a rumor that Obama was shot while on the campaign trail was posted on Twitter and received a lot of attention and retweets. The news generated sell-off on Wall Street. Another well-known example

R. Xu et al. (Eds.): AIMS 2020, LNCS 12401, pp. 84–92, 2020.
https://doi.org/10.1007/978-3-030-59605-7_7

came on Weibo. After the Fukushima nuclear power plant leaked in 2011, a post said that iodized salt can protect against radiation. This rumor caused people to scramble for iodized salt, and drove up the price of salt [3]. Thus it can be seen that rumors have great harmfulness, which even affect the real-world society. Therefore, there is an urgent need to study a method for detecting and identifying rumors automatically. This has also prompted researchers to devote their energies to rumor detection, authenticity assessment and other work.

To automatically detect rumors, the first step is to construct an annotated corpus, as we all know, a good corpus is particularly important for model training. According to our knowledge, most of the methods mainly focus on the direct acquisition from social media such as Twitter or Weibo. In addition, some researchers collected rumors through rumor refuting websites. However, current corpora mainly focused on some specific topics, e.g. political domain. So, the models constructed on this corpus cannot be well applied into other domains. Moreover, most existing corpora consisted of the rumors in English, while the corpus in other languages, e.g. Chinese is very limited.

This paper proposes a Chinese rumor detection corpus, named CRDC. This corpus consists of 10,000 rumors and 14,472 non-rumors from Weibo. To better support the task, other information including language-independent features are also acquired, including rumors' forwarding and like information, which can effectively help rumor detection and rumor propagation research in other languages.

Compared with other corpora, our Chinese rumor corpus has the following characteristics. First of all, the time span is longer. We collected all the rumors that appeared on Weibo from 2013 to 2018. So, the number of rumors is much larger and the coverage of the topics is more wide other than only politics. Secondly, our rumor corpus contains *comments, retweets, likes*. It can facilitate the researchers to capture the features of rumor from different dimensions. In order to assess the quality of our corpus, this paper also conducted some baseline tests including machine learning and deep learning on the corpus.

To sum up, our contributions are as follows:

- A high-quality corpus for Chinese rumor detection has been created and it can be freely accessed, named CRDC.
- Detailed description on CRDC has been introduced, including the information sources, the annotation schema, the statistics, etc.
- Some baseline tests are performed to give the fundamental study on the CRDC corpus.

The remainder of this paper is organized as follows: Sect. 2 introduces the related work. Section 3 details the annotation schema and the data acquisition. Section 4 describes our baseline methods, and Sect. 4 presents the initial experimental results and some important statistics of the corpus. Section 5 concludes this work.

2 Related Work

Nowadays, social media like twitter or microblog are more and more popular with the public, because these social media provide a simple way for people to express their personal opinions on any events. At the same time, the dissemination of information also becomes faster with the development of social media. However, social media have also become hotbeds for rumors to spread, because people can publish information anytime and anywhere without restriction. Therefore, rumors in recent years are mainly concentrated on social media. Thus, the rumor data is mainly obtained from twitter, microblog and rumor-debunking websites, Therefore, this section mainly introduces the acquisition method of rumor data.

2.1   English Data Collection

In English social platforms, twitter has a large number of users. so many authors collect rumor data through twitter for analysis. The first large-scale publicly available rumor data set published by [4] is collected by Twitter search API. This API is the only API that returns results from the entire public Twitter stream. The author uses the twitter API to search keywords to obtain the text of relevant events, and then annotate. They have annotated of more than 10,400 tweets based on five different controversial topics (Obama, air France, cellphone, Michelle, Palin). Among these rumors, 3,643 are non-rumors, while the remaining 6,774 are rumors. Among these rumors, 3,803 users express denial, doubt or neutrality while 2,971 show their belief. This corpus also uses the kappa coefficient to calculate the accuracy of labeling. These datasets open a new dimension in analyzing online misinformation. In [5], the authors focus on time-sensitive information, in particular on current news events. They use Twitter Monitor to detect Twitter events during a period of 2 months. Those twitter data is divided into two categories, news and conversation according to their topic. The final dataset contains 10,000 tweets. [6] obtained 6 high impact crisis events of 2013 which include Boston Marathon Blasts, Typhoon Haiyan, cyclone phailin, Washington navy yard shooting, polar vortex cold wave and Oklahoma tornadoe. Those events contain about 10,074,150 tweets. The annotations data were obtained through crowdsourcing provider CrowdFlower.4. In [7] the authors present a method that can be used to collect, identify and annotate a dataset, which was constructed by 330 rumor threads and involve 4,842 tweets associated with 9 newsworthy events. Those data can be analyzed to understand how users spread, support, or deny rumors. A typical example of event-based public datasets is the large-scale datasets collected by [8] from the Twitter data, the confirmed rumors and non-rumors from www.snopes.com, an online rumor debunking service, in which 992 events have been collected in all.

2.2   Chinese Data Collection

In [8], a set of Chinese rumor dataset was also collected. A set of known rumors were firstly collected from the Sina community management center, which reports various misinformation. They also gather a similar number of non-rumor events by crawling the posts of general threads that are verified to be non-rumors. The dataset consists of 2,313 rumors in political domain and 2,351 non-rumors. In [9], some keywords were considered to be the seed for searching, and the microblogs published by the rumor busting account were crawled. Then those microblogs posts irrelevant to the rumors were removed. Note that these rumors were verified by Sina Weibo official rumor-busting account from March

1, 2010 to February 2, 2012. Finally, about 5100 microblogs posts have been collected. Topic information has been used confirm a post to be a false rumor in [10, 11] also collected 400 rumors published on microblogs in 2013 and 2014 through Sina Weibo's official rumor debunking website.

3   Corpus Construction

As far as we know, there are mainly three ways to collect rumor data from microblogs. The first is to obtain rumor events through some accounts that refute rumors and then search the keywords of each event through microblogs, and then manually select the useful information. The second way is to collect the original text and comments of specific hot events, and then label the data. The third way is to get the specific content of certain rumors through the API of microblogs. For rumor detection task, however, the primary goal is how to determine whether the post is a rumor, and the determination of rumor will directly affect the quality of the corpus.

To do this, we use the microblogs rumor reporting platform to obtain rumors, where the rumors are reported by users and confirmed by the parts with high authority. That is a easy and credible way to obtain the rumors. In other words, the posts have been confirmed as a rumor officially. First of all, we have obtained all the microblogs URL from 2013 to 2019 whose contents are judged as rumors by the microblogs reporting platform. To fill the gap generated by the language issue, we cannot only obtain the content itself, and additional information are also required. Therefore, we obtain many other important information through the microblog API, including the *nickname, ID, release time, comment, retweets* and *like* information, and so on. To enrich our corpus, we manually selected the keywords, and then search for relevant microblogs to get the non-rumor documents. Finally, the total number of these rumor microblogs is 24,472, including 10,000 rumors and 14,472 non-rumors.

More detailedly, different parts in our corpus have the following structure:

Rumor. Arumor is usually containing the contents of the original post, the URL of *repost, comments, attitude*. It also includes the user *ID*, the *publish time*, and so on (Fig. 1).

Fig. 1. The information structure of a rumor.

Comment. The rumor comments contain the comments from different users towards the original post, and including the user nickname and homepage URL, the number of like of individual comment, the date, and the time (Fig. 2).

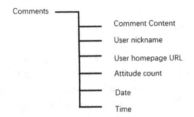

Fig. 2. The information structure of a comment.

Repost. Reposts part contains the user nickname who retweet, the homepage URL, the content of the retweet, and the date and time of the retweet (Fig. 3).

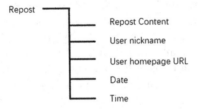

Fig. 3. The structure of Repost.

Like. Like contains the user nickname, the home page URL, and the date and time (Fig. 4).

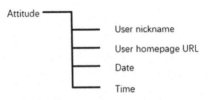

Fig. 4. The structure of like information.

Table 1 shows some statistics of the corpus. The corpus contains a total of 24,472 microblogs, involving 25,545,511 *users*, a total of 175,505 *comments*, 5,778,150 *reposts* and 1,043,434 *likes*. For each rumor, there is an average of 70 comments to ensure that the training data is not sparse.

Table 1. Statistics of CDRC corpus.

Statistic	Weibo
Users	2,554,511
Rumors	24,472
Comments	1,705,505
Reposts	578,150
Attitudes	1,043,434
Avg. of comments/rumors	70
Max of comments/event	75,276

4 Baseline Methods

To investigate the characteristics of our corpus, we developed SVM model [13], LSTM [12] model and HAN [14] model as the baseline to compare its accuracy, recall and F1-measure.

SVM Methods. SVM is one of the classical machine learning classification algorithms, which is easy to be implemented [15]. In order to evaluate the performance of our corpus, we trained an SVM classifier for rumor detection. Specifically, we took *n-gram* of the rumor text and the corresponding comments as the features.

LSTM Methods. SVM is one of the classical machine learning classification. In the process of rumor detection, it is not enough to only depend on the expression of the event itself. Due to the simplicity of the event expression, it is difficult to directly distinguish whether it is a false rumor or not. In social media, each individual message is not static, but it will propagate through the network. In the cycle of rumor dissemination, people often express different opinions by posting their comments towards the event. These posts on the event can help us identify the veracity of the event.

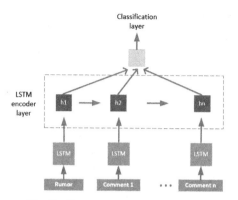

Fig. 5. The structure of LSTM model.

Without the loss of generality, we use LSTM network as the encoder, as shown in Fig. 5. The word embedding e_{ij} has been randomly initialized as the input, and after a layer of LSTM encoding, we get a rumor or comment representation h_{ij}. The average value of each LSTM hidden layer state as the output. Then each post has been encoded by another LSTM layer using Eq. 2. Then we get the encoding of the rumor event h_i. The full connection layer (Eq. 3) and *softmax* layer (Eq. 4) are used for classification. The cross entropy (Eq. 5) is used as the loss function.

HAN Methods. HAN is hierarchical attention network for document classification [15]. This network has two levels of attention mechanisms applied at the word and sentence-level. HAN network is used to encode posts and events. The full connection layer and *softmax* layer are also used for classification.

We implement our SVM model by using LibSVM, while construct LSTM and HAN model with Tensorflow. We used the same amount of microblog data as a positive sample. The corpus are split with a ratio of 4:1 for training and test. We use the classic evaluation metrics, including accuracy, precision, recall and F-measure. Table 2 shows the performance of two methods.

Table 2. Results of the baseline models for rumor detection.

Method	Class	Accuracy	Precision	Recall	F1
SVM	R	0.712	0.836	0.532	0.650
	N		0.625	0.892	0.735
LSTM	R	0.857	0.855	0.860	0.857
	N		0.833	0.812	0.822
HAN	R	0.876	0.890	0.840	0.864
	N		0.843	0.885	0.863

In Table 2, the performance of the HAN model is significantly better than that of the SVM and LSTM method, both in terms of accuracy and F-measure. We found that using longer sentences and attention mechanism improves the performance of the model. Because the model is able to capture more information from the comments.

$$h_{io} : h_{ij} = LSTM(e_{i0} \cdots e_{ij}) \quad j \in [0, l_{word}] \tag{1}$$

$$h_0 : h_i = LSTM(h_{i0} \cdots h_{ij}) \quad j \in [0, l_{word}] \tag{2}$$

$$h_{final} = W^T * (mean(h_0 : h_i)) + b \tag{3}$$

$$Prediction = softmax(h_{final}) \tag{4}$$

$$loss = -\sum_{i=1}^{n} y_{predict}(y_{truth}) \tag{5}$$

5 Conclusion

In this paper, we constructed a Chinese annotated corpus for rumor detection, which is obtained from Weibo. This corpus consists of 10,000 rumors and 14,472 non-rumors. Different from the existing corpora, this corpus covers more topics, including political field, medical field, financial field, and other fields. Moreover, to reduce the language dependency, this corpus also obtained more information, such as the number of retweet, like, comment, that are language-independent features, which is very helpful for those non-Chinese researchers.

Moreover, to investigate the characteristics of our corpus, we also developed SVM model, LSTM model and HAN model as the baseline to compare its accuracy, recall and F1-measure. This will facilitate the follower to understand our corpus and design a more effective model.

Acknowledgements. We would like to thank the anonymous reviewers for their valuable comments. This research is supported by the Natural Science Foundation of China (61976066, 61502115, U1636103), the Fundamental Research Fund for the Central Universities (3262019T29), the Joint funding (SKX182010023, 2019GA35).

References

1. O'reilly, T.: What is web 2.0: design patterns and business models for the next generation of software. Soc. Sci. Electron. Publ. **97**(7), 253–259 (2007)
2. Moreno, Y., Nekovee, M., Pacheco, A.F.: Dynamics of rumor spreading in complex networks. Phys. Rev. E Stat. Nonlinear Soft Matter Phys. **69**(6 Pt 2), 066130 (2004)
3. Takayasu, M., Sato, K., Sano, Y., Yamada, K., Miura, W., Takayasu, H.: Rumor diffusion and convergence during the 3.11 earthquake: a Twitter case study. PLoS ONE 10, e0121443 (2015)
4. Qazvinian, V., Rosengren, E., Radev, D.R., et al.: Rumor has it: identifying misinformation in microblogs. In: Proceedings of the Conference on Empirical Methods in Natural Language Processing, EMNLP 2011, Stroudsburg, PA, USA. Association for Computational Linguistics (2011)
5. Castillo, C., Mendoza, M., Poblete, B.: Information credibility on Twitter. In: Proceedings of the 20th International Conference on World Wide Web, WWW 2011, Hyderabad, India, 28 March– 1 April 2011. DBLP (2011)
6. Gupta, A., Kumaraguru, P., Castillo, C., et al.: TweetCred: a real-time web-based system for assessing credibility of content on Twitter. Eprint Arxiv (2014)
7. Zubiaga, A., Hoi, G.W.S., Liakata, M., et al.: Analysing how people orient to and spread rumours in social media by looking at conversational threads. PLoS ONE **11**(3), e0150989 (2015)
8. Ma, J., Gao, W., Mitra, P., et al.: Detecting rumors from microblogs with recurrent neural networks. In: The 25th International Joint Conference on Artificial Intelligence (IJCAI 2016) (2016)
9. Yang, F., Yu, X., Liu, Y., et al.: Automatic detection of rumor on Sina Weibo. ACM (2012)
10. Cai, G., Wu, H., Lv, R.: Rumors detection in Chinese via crowd responses. In: 2014 IEEE/ACM International Conference on Advances in Social Networks Analysis and Mining (ASONAM). ACM (2014)

11. Liu, Y., Xu, S.: Detecting rumors through modeling information propagation networks in a social media environment. IEEE Trans. Comput. Soc. Syst., 1–17 (2016)
12. Hochreiter, S., Schmidhuber, J.: Long short-term memory. Neural Comput. **9**(8), 1735–1780 (1997)
13. Burges, C.J.C.: A tutorial on support vector machines for pattern recognition. Data Min. Knowl. Discov. **2**(2), 121–167 (1998)
14. Yang, Z., Yang, D., Dyer, C., et al.: Hierarchical attention networks for document classification. In: Proceedings of the 2016 Conference of the North American Chapter of the Association for Computational Linguistics: Human Language Technologies (2016)
15. Lilleberg, J., Zhu, Y., Zhang, Y.: Support vector machines and Word2vec for text classification with semantic features. In: 2015 IEEE 14th International Conference on Cognitive Informatics & Cognitive Computing. IEEE (2015)

Attention-Based Asymmetric Fusion Network for Saliency Prediction in 3D Images

Xinyue Zhang and Ting Jin[✉]

School of Computer Science and Cyberspace Security, Hainan University,
Haikou 570228, Hainan, China
tingj@fudan.edu.cn

Abstract. Nowadays the visual saliency prediction has become a fundamental problem in 3D imaging area. In this paper, we proposed a saliency prediction model from the perspective of addressing three aspects of challenges. First, to adequately extract features of RGB and depth information, we designed an asymmetric encoder structure on the base of U-shape architecture. Second, to prevent the semantic information between salient objects and corresponding contexts from diluting in cross-modal distillation stream, we devised a global guidance module to capture high-level feature maps and deliver them into feature maps in shallower layers. Third, to locate and emphasize salient objects, we introduced a channel-wise attention model. Finally we built the refinement stream with integrated fusion strategy, gradually refining the saliency maps from coarse to fine-grained. Experiments on two widely-used datasets demonstrate the effectiveness of the proposed architecture, and the results show that our model outperforms six selective state-of-the-art models.

Keywords: Saliency prediction · RGB-D images · Global guidance module · Channel attention module

1 Introduction

When finding the interest objects in an image, human can automatically capture the semantic information between objects and their contexts, paying much attention to the prominent objects, and selectively suppress unimportant factors. This precise visual attention mechanism has already been explained in various of biologically plausible model [1, 2]. Saliency prediction aims to automatically predict the most informative and attractive parts in images. Rather than concentrating on the whole image, noticing salient objects can not only reduce the calculational cost but also improve the performance of saliency models in many imaging applications, including quality assessment [3, 4], segmentation [5–7], recognition [8, 9], to name a few. Existing saliency models mainly utilize two strategies to localize salient objects: bottom-up strategy and top-down strategy. Bottom-up strategy is driven by external stimuli. By exploiting low-level features, such as brightness, color and orientation, the bottom-up strategy outputs final saliency maps in an unsupervised manner. However, only using bottom-up strategy cannot recognize sufficient high-level semantic information. Conversely, the top-down strategy is

© Springer Nature Switzerland AG 2020
R. Xu et al. (Eds.): AIMS 2020, LNCS 12401, pp. 93–105, 2020.
https://doi.org/10.1007/978-3-030-59605-7_8

driven by tasks. It can learn high-level features in a supervised manner with labeled ground truth data, which is beneficial to discriminate salient objects and surrounding pixels.

The recent trend is to extract multi-scale and multi-level features in high-level with deep neural networks (DNNs). We have witnessed an unprecedented explosion in the availability of and access to the saliency models focus on RGB images and videos [10, 14, 36]. Although saliency models in 2D images have achieved remarkable performance, most of them are not available in 3D applications. With the recent advent of widely-used RGB-D sensing technologies, RGB-D sensors now have the ability to intelligently capture depth images, which can provide complementary spatial information over RGB information to mimic human visual attention mechanism, as well as improve the performance of saliency models. Therefore, how to make full use of the cross-modal and cross-level information becomes a challenge. Among a variety of DNNs based RGB-D saliency models [40, 41], U-shape based structures [42, 43] attract most attention since their bottom-up pathways can extract low-level feature information while top-down pathways can generate rich and informative high-level features, which can take advantage of cross-modal complementarity and cross-level continuity of RGB-D information. However, in the top-down pathways of U-shape network, while high-level information is transmitting to shallower stages, semantic information is gradually diluting. We remedy this drawback by designing a global guidance module following by a series of global guidance flows. Global guidance flows deliver high-level semantic information to feature maps in shallower layers as complementarity after dilution. And we introduce a channel-wise attention module, which helps to strengthen the feature representation.

What is more, we observed that the current RGB-D visual saliency models are essentially a symmetric dual-stream input encoder structure (both RGB stream and depth stream have the same encoder structure). Although the same encoder structure improves the accuracy of the results, it also imposes a bottleneck on RGB-D saliency prediction. Therefore, the depth stream does not need to use the same deep level encoder structure as the RGB stream. Through the analysis of the asymmetric encoder structure, and inspired by the above studies, we exploit an asymmetric U-shape based network to make full leverage of high-level semantic information with global guidance module. In refinement processing, we build fusion models, which embedding with global guidance flows and channel-wise attention modules, to gradually refine the saliency maps and finally obtain high-quality fine-grained saliency maps. Overall, the main three contributions of our architecture are as follows:

1. Instead of using the symmetric encoder structure, we proposed an asymmetric encoder structure for RGB-D saliency (VGG-16 for RGB stream and ResNet-50 for depth stream), which can extract the RGB-D features effectively.
2. We designed a global guidance module at the top of encoder stream, which links strongly with the top-down stream, to deal with the problem of high-level information diluting in U-shape architecture.
3. We innovatively introduced a channel-wise self-attention model in the cross-modal distillation stream, to emphasize salient objects and suppress unimportant surroundings, thus improves the feature representation.

2 Related Work

Recently, the capability of DNNs attracts more and more attention, which is helpful to extract significant features. Numerous DNN based models have proposed in 2D saliency prediction. For instance, Yang et al. [11] proposed a salient object predicted network for RGB images by using parallel dilated convolutions in different sizes, and providing a set of loss functions to optimize the network. Cordel et al. [12] proposed a DNN-based model, embedding with the improved evaluation metric, to deal with the problem of measure the saliency prediction for 2D images. Cornia et al. [13] proposed an RGB saliency attentive model by combining the dilated convolutions, attention models and learned prior maps. Wang et al. [14] trained an end-to-end architecture with deep supervision manner, to obtain final saliency maps of RGB images. Liu et al. [15] aimed at improving saliency prediction in three aspects, and thus proposed a saliency prediction model to capture multiple contexts. Liu et al. [16] aiming at predicting human eye-fixations in RGB images, hence proposed a computation network. Although these methods achieve great success, they ignore the generalization in 3D scenarios.

To overcome this problem, Zhang et al. [17] proposed a deep learning feature based RGBD visual saliency detection model. Yang et al. [18] proposed a two-stage clustering-based RGBD visual saliency model for human visual fixation prediction in dynamic scenarios. Nguyen et al. [19] investigated a Deep Visual Saliency (DeepVS) model to achieve a more accurate and reliable saliency predictor even in the presence of distortions. Liu et al. [20] first proposed a cluster-contrast saliency prediction model for depth maps, and then obtained the human fixation prediction with the centroid of the largest clusters of each depth super-pixel. Sun et al. [21] proposed a real-time video saliency prediction model in an end-to-end manner, via 3D residual convolutional neural network (3D-ResNet). Despite they emphasize the importance of auxiliary spatial information, there is still a larger room to improve. To fully utilize cross-modal features, we adopt a U-shaped based architecture in light of its cross-modal and cross-level ability.

Considering that different spatial and channel information of features return different salient responses, some works introduce the attention mechanism in saliency models, so as to enhance the discrimination of salient regions and background. Liu et al. [22] on the base of previous studies, but went further, they proposed an attention-guided RGB-D salient object network, the attention model consists of spatial and channel attention mechanism, which provides the better feature representation. Noori et al. [10] employed a multi-scale attention guided model in the RGB-D saliency model, to intelligently pay more attention to salient regions. Li et al. [23] developed an RGB-D object model, embedding with a cross-modal attention model, to enhance the salient objects. Jiang et al. [24] properly exploit the attention model in the RGB-D tracking model to assign larger weights to salient features of two modalities. Therefore, the model obtains the more fined salient features. Different from above attention mechanism, our attention module focuses on channel features, and can model the interdependencies of high-level features. The proposed attention mechanism can be embedded in any network seamlessly and improve the performance of saliency prediction models.

3   The Proposed Method

3.1   Overall Architecture

The proposed RGB-D saliency model comprises five primary parts on the base of the U-shape architectures: the encoder structures, the cross-model distillation streams, the global guidance module, the channel attention module, and the fusion modules for refinement. Figure 1 shows the overall framework of the proposed model. Concretely, we adopt the VGG-16 network [27] as the backbone of encoder structure for depth information, and the ResNet-50 network [28] as the backbone of encoder structure for RGB information. In order to meet the need of saliency prediction, we remain five basic convolution blocks of VGG-16 and ResNet-50 network, and eliminate their last pooling layers and full connection layers. We build the global guidance module inspired by the Atrous Spatial Pyramid Pooling [29]. More specifically, our global guidance module is placed on the top of RGB and depth bottom-up streams to capture high-level semantic information. The refinement stream mainly consists of fusion modules, gradually refining the coarse saliency maps to high-quality predicted saliency maps.

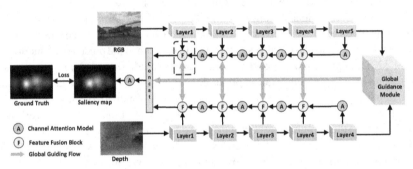

Fig. 1. The overall architecture of proposed saliency prediction model: dotted box here represents the fusion processing in refinement stream, which is explained in Sect. 3.5. (Colour figure online)

3.2   Hierarchical RGB-D Feature Extraction

The main functionality of the RGB and depth streams is to extract the multi-scale and multi-level RGB-D feature information at different levels of abstraction. In proposed U-shape based architecture, we use ImageNet [30] pre-trained VGG-16 network and pre-trained ResNet-50 network as backbone of the bottom-up stream for RGB and depth images, respectively. Since depth information cannot input into backbone network directly, we transform depth image into three-channel HHA image [31]. We resize the input resolution $W \times H$ (W represents the width and H represents the height) of RGB image and paired depth image to size 288×288, and then feed into backbone networks. Meanwhile, considering that the size of RGB feature maps and depth feature maps in backbone can both denote as $\left(\frac{W}{2^{n-1}}, \frac{H}{2^{n-1}} \right)$, (n = 1, 2, 3, 4, 5), we utilize RGB feature maps and depth feature maps to learn the multi-scale and multi-level feature maps (F_M).

3.3 Global Guidance Module

We utilize U-shape based architecture due to its ability to build affluent feature information with top-down flows. In light of that U-shape network will lead a problem that the high-level features gradually dilutes when transmitting to shallower layers, inspired by introducing dilated convolutions in saliency prediction networks to capture multi-scale high-level semantic information in the top layers [32, 33], we provide an individual module with a set of global guiding flows (GFs) (shown in Fig. 1 as a series of green arrows) to explicitly make high-level feature maps be aware of the locations of the salient targets. To be more specific, the global guidance module (GM) is constructed upon the top of the bottom-up pathways. GM consists of four branches to capture the context information of high-level feature maps (G$_{FM}$). We design the first branch by using a traditional convolution with kernel size as 1×1. And we use 2, 6, 12 dilation convolutions for other branches with kernel size as 2×2, 6×6, 12×12, respectively. All the strides are set to 1. To deal with the diluting issues, we introduce a set of GFs, which deliver G$_{FM}$ to and merge with feature maps in shallower layers. Following this way, we effectively supplement the high-level feature information to lower layers when transmitting, and prevent the salient information from diluting when refining the saliency maps.

3.4 Channel Attention Module

In top-down streams we introduce attention mechanism to enhance the feature representation, which is beneficial for discriminating salient details and background. The proposed channel-wise attention module (CWAM) is illustrated in Fig. 2.

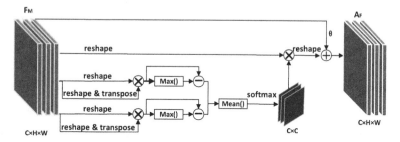

Fig. 2. Illustration of proposed channel-wise attention module: symbol $\otimes$ denotes the matrix multiplication, $\oplus$ denotes the addition operation, $\ominus$ denotes the subtract operation.

Specifically, from the origin hierarchical feature maps $F_M \in \mathbb{R}^{C \times H \times W}$, we calculate the channel attention map $A_M \in \mathbb{R}^{C \times N}$ through reshaping the $H \times W$ dimension into N dimensions. Then use a matrix multiplication between A_M and transpose of A_M, which denotes as R_A. Next, for the purpose of distinguishing salient targets and background, we import Max() function to determine the maximum between the value and -1, and then utilize multiplication results subtract the maximum. Then we adopt Mean() function to obtain an average result, which is denoted as A_B, to suppress useless targets and emphasize significant pixels. The operation is shown in Eq. (1).

$$A_B = \frac{1}{c} \sum_{i=1}^{C} \left\{ Max\left[\left(R_A \otimes (R_A)^T \right), -1 \right] - R_A \right\} \tag{1}$$

where $\otimes$ denotes the matrix multiplication operation. Then input A_B into the Softmax layer to obtain channel-wise attention maps. In addition, we adopt another matrix multiplication and reshape into origin dimension. The formula of final output is shown as Eq. (2).

$$A_F = R(A_B \otimes R_A) \oplus (\theta \times F_M) \tag{2}$$

where $\oplus$ denotes the addition operation, θ represents a scale parameter learnt gradually from zero.

3.5 Refinement

We improve the quality of feature maps in refinement stream. Although attention mechanism can reinforce feature representation, this leads to unsatisfactory salient constructions. Aiming to obtain subtle and accurate saliency prediction, we employ integrated fusion modules (IFM) in the refinement stream. Specifically, four IFMs linking with four CWAMs make up of one top-down stream, and two top-down streams combines with global features G_{FM} transmitting with GFs comprise the refinement stream. Figure 3 illustrates the details in refinement stream.

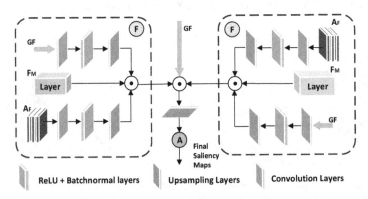

Fig. 3. Illustration of the details in refinement stream: as shown in the dotted box in Fig. 1, at end of our network, the global guidance flow (the green thick arrow) compromises IFM of RGB information (right dotted boxes) and IFM of depth information (left dotted boxes); Two IFMs concatenate with high-level global features, then expand their size with an up-sampling layer to obtain the final saliency maps. (Colour figure online)

For each IFM_m (m = 1, 2, 3, ..., 8), its input contains three parts:

i) F_M of the RGB encoder stream (shown as a red cuboid in Fig. 3), or the depth encoder stream (shown as a pale blue cuboid in Fig. 3).

ii) A_F output by CWAM in corresponding top-down stream, following by traditional convolution layers, nonlinear activation function ReLU and Batchnormal layers, and up-sampling layers.

iii) G_{FM} following by traditional convolution layers, nonlinear activation function ReLU, Batchnormal layers, and up-sampling layers.

We set all the size of convolution kernels to 3×3, and the stride set to 1. We formulate the output of IFM as Eq. (4).

$$O(IFM_m) = \sum_{i=1}^{2} \lambda(\gamma(u_i(c_i(A_F, G_{FM})))) \odot F_M \qquad (4)$$

Where $\gamma()$ denotes the ReLU function, and $\lambda()$ denotes the Batchnormal layer. c_i, u_i (i = 1, 2) represents traditional convolution layers and upsampling layers of A_F and G_{FM}, respectively. Symbol $\odot$ denotes the concatenate operation.

At last, we combine two types metric, including MSE and modified Pearsons Linear Correlation Coefficient (CC) metric as the loss function, to compare the final saliency prediction map and the ground truth. We use the standard deviation $\sigma()$ here, and the loss function is shown as Eq. (3).

$$LOSS = \frac{1}{M} \sum_{m=1}^{M} \left\| T - \hat{T} \right\|^2 + 1 - \frac{\sigma\left(T, \hat{T}\right)}{\sigma(T) \times \sigma\left(\hat{T}\right)} \qquad (3)$$

Where T denotes the real value, and $\hat{T}$ denotes the predicted value. $\sigma()$ denotes the function of correlation coefficient.

4 Experiments

4.1 Implementation Details

The entire experiments were implemented on the PyTorch 1.1.0 [34] framework. The training and testing processes were equipped with a TITAN Xp GPU with 8 GB memory workspace. Our backbone, including VGG-16 network and ResNet-50 network, their parameters are initialized on the ImageNet dataset. We use 288×288 resolution images to train the network in an end-to-end manner. The batch size was set to one image in every iteration, and we initiate the learning rate to 10^{-5}. We trained the proposed network for 70 epochs altogether.

4.2 Datasets

We conduct experiments on two popular public saliency prediction datasets, including NUS dataset [25] and NCTU dataset [26], to evaluate the performance of our proposed network. The NUS dataset is comprised of 600 images, including 3D images and corresponding color stimuli, fixation maps, smooth depth maps, as well as paired depth images. The NCTU dataset is comprised of 475 images with 1920×1080 resolution, including 3D images, corresponding left and right view maps, fixation maps, disparity maps, and paired depth images.

4.3 Evaluation Criteria

To evaluate our approach performance, we use four widely-agreed and evaluation metrics: Pearsons Linear Correlation Coefficient (CC), Area Under Curve (AUC), Normalized Scanpath Saliency (NSS), and Kullback-Leibler Divergence (KL-Div).

CC is a statistical index, which reflects the linear correlation between our model (T) and predicted human fixation (G). The bigger the CC value is, the more relevant two variables are. Equation (5) represents the calculation of CC.

$$CC = \frac{cov(T, G)}{\sqrt{cov(T)}\sqrt{cov(G)}} \tag{5}$$

where cov means the covariance between the final output T and the round truth G.

AUC is defined as the area under the ROC curve. We use AUC as the evaluation criteria since a single ROC curve cannot assess the performance of the model adequately. The larger the AUC value is, the better the model performance is. Equation (6) shows the formulation of AUC.

$$AUC = \frac{\sum_{pos} k - \frac{NUM_{pos}(NUM_{pos}+1)}{2}}{NUM_{pos}NUM_{neg}} \tag{6}$$

where the $\sum_{pos} k$ in the nominator is a fixed value, and only relevant with the amount of positive instances. $\sum_{pos}$ represents the sum of positive instances, and k is the ranking. NUM_{pos} and NUM_{neg} denote the number of positive and negative instances, respectively.

NSS mainly evaluates the average of M human fixations in a normalized map. The bigger the NSS value is, the better the performance of model is. We utilize the standard deviation $\sigma()$ to calculate NSS with Eq. (7).

$$NSS = \frac{1}{M} \sum_{i=1}^{M} \frac{T(x_G^i, y_G^i) - \mu_T}{\sigma_T} \tag{7}$$

KLDiv measure is used for saliency prediction model evaluation. The smaller the KLDiv value is, the better the saliency model performance is. Given two probability distribution for x, which are denoted as c(x) and d(x), the KLDiv can be calculated with Eq. (8).

$$KLDiv = \sum_{i=1}^{n} c(x) log \frac{c(x)}{d(x)} \tag{8}$$

4.4 Ablation Studies and Analysis

In order to thoroughly investigate the effectiveness of different components in proposed network, we conduct a series of ablation studies on NCTU and NUS datasets. The comparison results are demonstrated in Table 1. We remove GM and CWAMs of proposed network, what is more, we denote the backbone as B in the Table 1. Figure 4 shows a visual comparison of different model components on NCTU dataset. To explore the effectiveness of GM, we remove them from the network, which is denoted as $B + A$ in

Table 1. Ablation studies of different components

Dataset		CC	KLDiv	AUC	NSS
NUS	**B**	0.5441	1.8344	0.8325	2.2608
	B + A	0.5495	2.1210	0.8302	2.2777
	B + G	0.5652	2.0676	0.8503	2.3134
	B + A + G	**0.5694**	**1.1402**	**0.8600**	**2.3494**
NCTU	**B**	0.8301	1.6001	0.8715	1.9392
	B + A	0.8251	0.6270	0.8784	1.9282
	B + G	0.8392	0.6036	**0.8802**	1.9441
	B + A + G	**0.8419**	**0.5935**	0.8798	**1.9572**

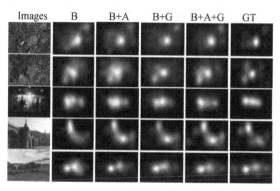

Fig. 4. Visual comparison of ablation studies.

Table 1. We can find that GM contributes to the proposed network. To prove the positive effects of CWAMs, we take away them from the proposed network, which is denoted as $B + G$ in Table 1.

In Fig. 4, we can see clearly that B trained with GM (see column 3), learns more elaborate salient region. And B trained with CWAMs (see column 4) can enhance prominent regions, learn more certain and less blurry salient objects. Thus, taking the advantages of adopting above modules in our network, our model (see column 5) can generate more accurate saliency maps, which are much closer to the ground truth (see column 6) compared to other six methods.

4.5 Comparison with Other Saliency Prediction Models

We compared our proposed model on the two benchmark datasets against with six other state-of-the-art models, namely, Qi's [39], Fang's [35], DeepFix [36], ML-net [37], DVA [14], and iSEEL [38]. Note that all the saliency maps of above models are obtained by running source codes with recommended parameters. For fair comparison, we trained all models on NCTU and NUS datasets. Table 2 presents the quantitative results of

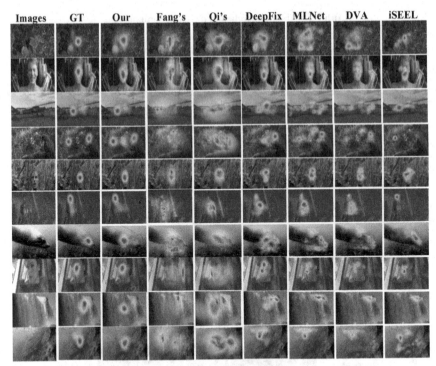

Fig. 5. Visual comparison between selective six models and our proposed model: we comparing with six saliency prediction models; column 1 shows origin left images, column 2 represents the ground truth, column 3 is our proposed method, and column 4 to 9 represents the saliency prediction models from [14, 35–39].

different models, and we show a visual comparison between selective six models and our proposed model in Fig. 5.

Table 2. CC, KLDiv, AUC and NSS comparisons of different models

Dataset	Metric	Fang's	Qi's	DeepFix	MLNet	DVA	iSEEL	Our
NUS	**CC**	0.333	0.371	0.4322	0.446	0.4549	0.5195	**0.5694**
	KLDiv	1.560	1.505	1.8138	1.780	2.4349	1.2479	**1.1402**
	AUC	0.795	0.806	0.7699	0.766	0.7236	0.8273	**0.8600**
	NSS	1.209	1.357	1.6608	1.821	1.7962	2.1250	**2.3494**
NCTU	**CC**	0.542	0.595	0.7974	0.696	0.6834	0.7578	**0.8429**
	KLDiv	0.674	0.616	1.3083	0.900	1.1045	**0.3985**	0.4846
	AUC	0.806	0.816	0.8650	0.835	0.8023	0.8315	**0.8820**
	NSS	1.264	1.373	1.8575	1.588	1.5546	1.7187	**1.9669**

For stimuli-driven scenes, no matter the discrimination between targets and background is explicit (see row 1, 3), or implicit (see row 4, 7), our model can handle effectively. For task-driven scenes, our model can predict faces (see row 2, 5, 8) and people in complex background (see row 6). As for the scenes are influenced by light (see row 9, 10), our attention mechanism locates the salient objects appropriately. It can be seen that our method is capable of ignoring disturbed background and highlighting salient objects in various scenes.

5 Conclusion

In this paper, we proposed an asymmetric attention-based network. Concretely, in bottom-up streams, we capture multi-scale and multi-level features of RGB and paired depth images. In top-down streams for cross-modal features, incorporating with global guidance information and features from parallel layers, we introduce a channel-wise attention model to enhance salient feature representation. Experimental results show that our model out-performs six state-of-the-art models. For the future work, we expect the proposed model can be applied in other 3D scenarios including video object detection and object tracking.

Acknowledgement. This paper is supported by Hainan Provincial Natural Science Foundation of China (618QN217) and National Nature Science Foundation of China (61862021).

References

1. Itti, L., Koch, C.: Computational modelling of visual attention. Nat. Rev. Neurosci. **2**(3), 194–203 (2001)
2. Moon, J., Choe, S., Lee, S., Kwon, O.S.: Temporal dynamics of visual attention allocation. Sci. Rep. **9**(1), 1–11 (2019)
3. Bosse, S., Maniry, D., Müller, K.R., Wiegand, T., Samek, W.: Deep neural networks for no-reference and full-reference image quality assessment. IEEE Trans. Image Process. **27**(1), 206–219 (2017)
4. Po, L.M., et al.: A novel patch variance biased convolutional neural network for no-reference image quality assessment. IEEE Trans. Circuits Syst. Video Technol. **29**(4), 1223–1229 (2019)
5. Liu, C., et al.: Auto-DeepLab: hierarchical neural architecture search for semantic image segmentation. In: 2019 IEEE/CVF Conference on Computer Vision and Pattern Recognition (CVPR), Long Beach, CA, USA, pp. 82–92. IEEE (2019)
6. Lei, X., Ouyang, H.: Image segmentation algorithm based on improved fuzzy clustering. Cluster Comput. **22**(6), 13911–13921 (2018). https://doi.org/10.1007/s10586-018-2128-9
7. Huang, H., Meng, F., Zhou, S., Jiang, F., Manogaran, G.: Brain image segmentation based on FCM clustering algorithm and rough set. IEEE Access **7**, 12386–12396 (2019)
8. Chen, Z., Wei, X., Wang, P., Guo, Y.: Multi-label image recognition with graph convolutional networks. In: 2019 IEEE/CVF Conference on Computer Vision and Pattern Recognition (CVPR), Long Beach, CA, USA, pp. 5172–5181. IEEE (2019)
9. He, K., Zhang, X., Ren, S., Sun, J.: Deep residual learning for image recognition. In: 2016 IEEE Conference on Computer Vision and Pattern Recognition, pp. 770–778, Las Vegas, NV. IEEE (2016)

10. Noori, M., Mohammadi, S., Majelan, S.G., Bahri, A., Havaei, M.: DFNet: discriminative feature extraction and integration network for salient object detection. Eng. Appl. Artif. Intell. **89**, 103419 (2020)
11. Yang, S., Lin, G., Jiang, Q., Lin, W.: A dilated inception network for visual saliency prediction. IEEE Trans. Multimed. **22**, 2163–2176 (2019)
12. Cordel, M.O., Fan, S., Shen, Z., Kankanhalli, M.S.: Emotion-aware human attention prediction. In: 2019 IEEE/CVF Conference on Computer Vision and Pattern Recognition, Long Beach, CA, USA, pp. 4021–4030. IEEE (2019)
13. Cornia, M., Baraldi, L., Serra, G., Cucchiara, R.: SAM: pushing the limits of saliency prediction models. In: 2018 IEEE/CVF Conference on Computer Vision and Pattern Recognition Workshops, Salt Lake City, UT, pp. 1971–19712. IEEE (2018)
14. Wang, W., Shen, J.: Deep visual attention prediction. IEEE Trans. Image Process. **27**(5), 2368–2378 (2017)
15. Liu, W., Sui, Y., Meng, L., Cheng, Z., Zhao, S.: Multiscope contextual information for saliency prediction. In: 2019 IEEE 3rd Information Technology, Networking, Electronic and Automation Control Conference (ITNEC), Chengdu, China, pp. 495–499, IEEE (2019)
16. Liu, N., Han, J., Liu, T., Li, X.: Learning to predict eye fixations via multiresolution convolutional neural networks. IEEE Trans. Neural Networks Learn. Systems **29**(2), 392–404 (2016)
17. Tao, X., Xu, C., Gong, Y., Wang, J.: A deep CNN with focused attention objective for integrated object recognition and localization. In: Chen, E., Gong, Y., Tie, Y. (eds.) PCM 2016. LNCS, vol. 9917, pp. 43–53. Springer, Cham (2016). https://doi.org/10.1007/978-3-319-48896-7_5
18. Yang, Y., Li, B., Li, P., Liu, Q.: A two-stage clustering based 3D visual saliency model for dynamic scenarios. IEEE Trans. Multimedia **21**(4), 809–820 (2019)
19. Nguyen, A., Kim, J., Oh, H., Kim, H., Lin, W., Lee, S.: Deep visual saliency on stereoscopic images. IEEE Trans. Image Process. **28**(4), 1939–1953 (2019)
20. Piao, Y., Ji, W., Li, J., Zhang, M., Lu, H.: Depth-induced multi-scale recurrent attention network for saliency detection. In: 2019 IEEE/CVF International Conference on Computer Vision, Seoul, Korea (South), pp. 7253–7262. IEEE (2019)
21. Sun, Z., Wang, X., Zhang, Q., Jiang, J.: Real-time video saliency prediction via 3D residual convolutional neural network. IEEE Access **7**, 147743–147754 (2019)
22. Liu, Z., Duan, Q., Shi, S., Zhao, P.: Multi-level progressive parallel attention guided salient object detection for RGB-D images. Vis. Comput. (2020). https://doi.org/10.1007/s00371-020-01821-9
23. Li, G., Gan, Y., Wu, H., Xiao, N., Lin, L.: Cross-modal attentional context learning for RGB-D object detection. IEEE Trans. Image Process. **28**(4), 1591–1601 (2018)
24. Jiang, M.X., Deng, C., Shan, J.S., Wang, Y.Y., Jia, Y.J., Sun, X.: Hierarchical multi-modal fusion FCN with attention model for RGB-D tracking. Inf. Fusion **50**, 1–8 (2019)
25. Lang, C., Nguyen, T.V., Katti, H., Yadati, K., Kankanhalli, M., Yan, S.: Depth matters: influence of depth cues on visual saliency. In: Fitzgibbon, A., Lazebnik, S., Perona, P., Sato, Y., Schmid, C. (eds.) ECCV 2012. LNCS, vol. 7573, pp. 101–115. Springer, Heidelberg (2012). https://doi.org/10.1007/978-3-642-33709-3_8
26. Ma, C.Y., Hang, H.M.: Learning-based saliency model with depth information. J. Vis. **15**(6), 19 (2015)
27. Simonyan, K., Zisserman, A.: Very deep convolutional networks for large-scale image recognition. arXiv preprint. arXiv:1409.1556 (2014)
28. He, K., Zhang, X., Ren, S., Sun, J.: Deep residual learning for image recognition. In: 2016 IEEE Conference on Computer Vision and Pattern Recognition, Las Vegas, NV, pp. 770–778. IEEE (2016)
29. Chen, L.C., Papandreou, G., Schroff, F., Adam, H.: Rethinking atrous convolution for semantic image segmentation. arXiv preprint arXiv:1706.05587 (2017)

30. Krizhevsky, A., Sutskever, I., Hinton, G.E.: ImageNet classification with deep convolutional neural networks. In: 2012 Advances in Neural Information Processing Systems, NIPS, Lake Tahoe, Nevada, US, pp. 1097–1105 (2012)

31. Gupta, S., Girshick, R., Arbeláez, P., Malik, J.: Learning rich features from RGB-D images for object detection and segmentation. In: Fleet, D., Pajdla, T., Schiele, B., Tuytelaars, T. (eds.) ECCV 2014. LNCS, vol. 8695, pp. 345–360. Springer, Cham (2014). https://doi.org/10.1007/978-3-319-10584-0_23

32. Song, H., Wang, W., Zhao, S., Shen, J., Lam, K.-M.: Pyramid dilated deeper ConvLSTM for video salient object detection. In: Ferrari, V., Hebert, M., Sminchisescu, C., Weiss, Y. (eds.) ECCV 2018. LNCS, vol. 11215, pp. 744–760. Springer, Cham (2018). https://doi.org/10.1007/978-3-030-01252-6_44

33. Huang, M., Liu, Z., Ye, L., Zhou, X., Wang, Y.: Saliency detection via multi-level integration and multi-scale fusion neural networks. Neurocomputing **364**, 310–321 (2019)

34. Paszke, A., et al.: Automatic differentiation in PyTorch. In: NIPS 2017 Workshop Autodiff Decision Program Chairs. NIPS, Long Beach, US (2017)

35. Fang, Y., Wang, J., Narwaria, M., Le Callet, P., Lin, W.: Saliency detection for stereoscopic images. IEEE Trans. Image Process. **23**(6), 2625–2636 (2014)

36. Kruthiventi, S.S., Ayush, K., Babu, R.V.: DeepFix: a fully convolutional neural network for predicting human eye fixations. IEEE Trans. Image Process. **26**(9), 4446–4456 (2017)

37. Cornia, M., Baraldi, L., Serra, G., Cucchiara, R.: A deep multi-level network for saliency prediction. In: 23rd International Conference on Pattern Recognition, Cancun, Mexico, pp. 3488–3493. IEEE (2017)

38. Tavakoli, H.R., Borji, A., Laaksonen, J., Rahtu, E.: Exploiting inter-image similarity and ensemble of extreme learners for fixation prediction using deep features. Neurocomputing **244**, 10–18 (2017)

39. Qi, F., Zhao, D., Liu, S., Fan, X.: 3D visual saliency detection model with generated disparity map. Multimedia Tools Appl. **76**(2), 3087–3103 (2016). https://doi.org/10.1007/s11042-015-3229-6

40. Hou, Q., Cheng, M.M., Hu, X., Borji, A., Tu, Z., Torr, P.H.: Deeply supervised salient object detection with short connections. IEEE Trans. Pattern Anal. Mach. Intell. **41**(4), 815–828 (2017)

41. Wang, T., Borji, A., Zhang, L., Zhang, P., Lu, H.: A stagewise refinement model for detecting salient objects in images. In: 2017 IEEE International Conference on Computer Vision, Venice, pp. 4039–4048. IEEE (2017)

42. Liang, Y., et al.: TFPN: twin feature pyramid networks for object detection. In: 2019 IEEE 31st International Conference on Tools with Artificial Intelligence, Portland, OR, USA, pp. 1702–1707. IEEE (2019)

43. Zhao, B., Zhao, B., Tang, L., Wang, W., Chen, W.: Multi-scale object detection by top-down and bottom-up feature pyramid network. J. Syst. Eng. Electron. **30**(1), 1–12 (2019)

Review Spam Detection Based on Multi-dimensional Features

Liming Deng[1,2,3], Jingjing Wei[4], Shaobin Liang[1,2,3], Yuhan Wen[1,2,3], and Xiangwen Liao[1,2,3(✉)]

[1] College of Mathematics and Computer Science, Fuzhou University, Fuzhou 350116, China
liaoxw@fzu.edu.cn
[2] Fujian Provincial Key Laboratory of Networking Computing and Intelligent Information Processing, Fuzhou University, Fuzhou 350116, China
[3] Digital Fujian Institute of Financial Big Data, Fuzhou 350116, China
[4] College of Electronics and Information Science, Fujian Jiangxia University, Fuzhou 350108, China

Abstract. Review spam detection aims to detect the reviews with false information posted by the spammers on social media. The existing methods of review spam detection ignore the importance of the information hidden in the user interactive behaviors and fail to extract the indistinct contextual features caused by irregular writing style of reviews. In this paper, a new review spam detection method based on multi-dimensional features is proposed. The method utilizes the principal component analysis to get low-dimensional features to characterize the user-product relationship. Then, a neural network constructed with nested LSTM and capsule network is trained to extract textual context features and spatial structure features. Finally, the model combines the text and user behavioral features as the overall features, which are used as the input to the classification module to detect spam reviews. Experimental results show that the F1 value of our proposed method is 1.6%~3.5% higher than the existing methods, indicating the efficiency and effectiveness of our model, especially on the natural distribution datasets.

Keywords: Review spam detection · Feature extraction · NLSTM

1 Introduction

With the rapid development of the Internet, people can post their opinions and reviews on various platforms such as e-commerce, social networking sites, etc. These online reviews act as a reference for consumers and enterprises to purchase, design products, and develop marketing strategies, while the existence of spam reviews brings obstacles. The term spam reviews refer to reviews that maliciously disseminate deceptive information or devalue products and services [1]. The example of a comparison of real review and spam review is shown in Fig. 1. The online spam reviews detection task aims to detect the tendentious false reviews [2] posted by the spammers on the Internet platforms and improve the utilization rate of Internet information. It can be widely used in marketing event analysis, user stickiness analysis, and other application fields [3].

© Springer Nature Switzerland AG 2020
R. Xu et al. (Eds.): AIMS 2020, LNCS 12401, pp. 106–123, 2020.
https://doi.org/10.1007/978-3-030-59605-7_9

Review 1: *Great hotel in heart of Chicago for business or pleasure. Rooms are recently upgraded and very modern and large. Flat screen TVs, marble baths, all rooms are suites, great desk, kitchenette, comfortable bed, free wireless Internet... everything you could ask for. Location is easy walk to Magnificent Mile and lots of great restaurants. Staff is friendly and helpful. Short cab ride to Loop.*

Review 2: *Late night hours and great share plates. It's great to have restaurants like purple pig, long man & eagle and gilt bar opening up in Chicago. The more the better!*

Review3: *It was good, but it can be better, and 24 courses is just too long.*

Review4: *It was good, but it wasn't better than Trotter's, unless you are into the gadgets. And 24 courses is just too long.*

Fig. 1. Comparison of real review and spam review. Review 1 is a real review that try to appraise and evaluate the service from different aspects. Review 2 is a spam review with advertisements. Review 3 and 4 are also spam reviews that use the same template.

The real reviewers and spammers share different witting style and comment behaviors. The real reviewers tend to write comprehensive and pertinent reviews from different aspects based on their real experience, while the spammers always give extreme, intensive, and similar reviews fabricated from a template. Existing research has proposed various methods for review spam detection [4, 7–12]. Linguistic features of reviews are the first thing to be considered in review spam detection [5, 6]. Linguistic features, such as text similarity or feature words, are extracted from the review text for detection. These methods utilize traditional machine learning classifiers to detect spam reviews. The second type of method focuses on the utilization of user behavioral features, which are usually extracted by tensor decomposition [8], Markov algorithm [9], and time-series features [10]. Nevertheless, user behavioral features are extracted through laborious observation and analysis, making it hard to implement and may bring about poor performance in the case of small datasets. The third type of method takes into account both user behavioral features and content features. These features are extracted from the relationship between users and target products by using TransE [11] in the knowledge graph, semi-supervised model [12], etc. However, the time complexity of these methods is too large in terms of big datasets.

In this study, we propose a new review spam detection framework based on multidimensional features to address the issues mentioned above. Under this framework, we firstly utilize the principal component analysis algorithm to obtain user-product relationship feature representations. Then, a text feature extraction module constructed with nested long-term memory network and capsule network is trained to extract textual content features and spatial structure features. By using this method, it can solve the problem that the above methods do not take into account the information hidden in user interaction, and do not fully consider the spatial structure information of review, word position relationship, and other features. We also consider the interactive information which is extracted by a user interactive behavioral features extraction module. Then, we fuse the above feature representations as the input to a classification module. In this way, we can make up for the information loss caused by feature dimensionality reduction. Finally, to endow the model with better detection performance under a natural distribution datasets condition, we construct a double-stack classifier through the integrated learning method to get the output.

The remainder of the paper is organized as follows: Sect. 2 discusses related work on review spam detection. Review spam detection based on multi-dimensional features is proposed in Sect. 3. Section 4 presents the experiments used to evaluate the proposed methods. Finally, the conclusions of our study are given in Sect. 5.

2 Related Work

Existing studies have explored a variety of different review spam detection methods to detect spam reviews. This study reviews the literature from the following three perspectives:

- Methods based on text features. This kind of method designs hand-crafted rules to extract features from reviews as the input to a classifier that detects review spam. Kim et al. [13] proposed an analysis method that contains deep semantic such as viewpoint features and context information, but failed to express complex semantic rules. Feng et al. [14] analyzed the deeper grammatical structure of the reviews from the writing style to extract the features that are irrelevant to the context and grammar, this method can't get all the grammatical structures either and result in losing the spatial structure features of the reviews. Ren et al. [15] used a convolution neural network to learn sentence representations, these representations are latter assembled through gating recurrent neural network with the attention mechanism. Chen et al. [16] proposed a sequence model, which divides the review sentences into different groups and then takes each group as the input to a one-dimensional convolutional neural network for classification. However, the complex parameter tuning process and poor interpretability of the methods based on neural networks make it difficult to apply when the features of reviews are indistinct.
- Methods based on user behavioral features. Such methods analyze and summarized the behavioral features of spam users, from which the user behavior similarity is computed to detect review spam. Santosh et al. [17] performed the random walk algorithm to characterize the structure of the network, which can maximize the possibility of obtaining similar nodes near the network. The model then combines the behavioral features with the underlying network structure features to detect the spam review, but fails to learn good representations when the number of user nodes is small. Mukherjee et al. [7] proposed to define the suspicious behavioral features of users, but only considered the writing behavior of users, lacking the consideration of the interactive behavior of users. Hai et al. [18] introduced the Laplace factor to improve the detection performance of the spam review, but this method gets high time complexity and poor performance when it comes to large datasets. Anyway, when the text features are indistinct, extracting user behavioral features are helpful to improve the performance of review spam detection. However, this kind of methods need human involved features and consumes numerous resources.

- Methods based on combining text features and user behavioral features. This kind of method considered both the information of reviews and user behaviors. Usually, the features of reviews were extracted and fused with the user behavioral features as the input to a classification model. Wang et al. [8] constructed relationship metrics with the information of users, reviews, and corresponding target products, and then used the tensor decomposition technique to learn the embeddings of users and products in the vector space. However, tensor decomposition takes a long time and has poor practicability. Shehnepoor et al. [19] extracted meta-path features to detect review spam and concluded that comment behavioral features were the most effective, but this method ignored the importance of products. Fakhraei et al. [20] modeled the social network as a time-stamped multi-relational graph, and then used the mixed probability model of the k-gram features and probabilistic modeling with a mixture of Markov models to obtain the relational sequence information. However, the user browsing behavior records used in this method are difficult to obtain.

Based on the related work, it has been observed that most of the existing studies did not fully consider the information hidden in the user interactions and the features of reviews are indistinct. We use nested LSTM and capsule network to extract the text features. Then, we integrate the text features with the user interactive features to fully excavate the deep-seated relationship between users and products in order to further improve the accurate prediction of review spam.

3 Model

In this section, we will introduce the review spam detection method based on multi-dimensional features in detail. Firstly, we will introduce the formal definition and symbol representation of the spam review detection task, and then introduce the model in detail.

3.1 Formal Definition of Problem

The purpose of the spam review detection is to learn a classifier, which can take the reviews as inputs and map it into corresponding categories. Here we treat review spam detection task as a binary classification problem. The formal definition of the problem in this paper is as follows: Given the review set $V = \{v_1, v_2, \ldots, v_n\}$ and the category set $Y = \{y_1, y_2\}$, the task of spam review detection is to take each review as an input and map it into corresponding categories by the classifier: $f : v_i \rightarrow y_i$. The category set Y is expressed as spam reviews and non-spam reviews.

3.2 Method

As shown in Fig. 2, the four components of our model are: (1) User-product relationship features extraction module based on dimensionality reduction algorithm, which learns the feature representations of each user-product relationship based on PCA; (2) User interactive behavioral features extraction module, which uses interactive information between users and metadata of reviews to extract behavioral features; (3) Text feature extraction module based on nested LSTM and capsule network, which extracts the feature representations of review texts using nested LSTM and capsule network; (4) Classifier module based on integrated learning, which takes the fusion of all feature representations as the input to the cascade classification model and outputs the corresponding category of the input reviews.

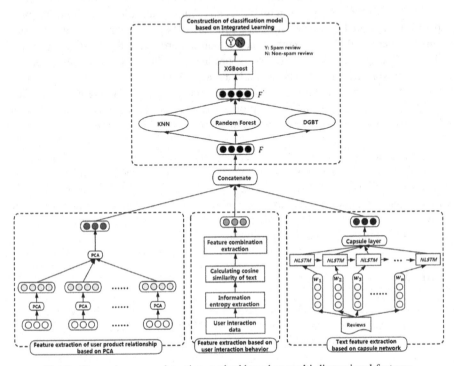

Fig. 2. The review spam detection method based on multi-dimensional features.

User-Product Relationship Features Extraction Module. In this paper, 11 user behavior difference relationships selected by Wang et al. [8] are used, on this basis, the PCA algorithm is used to extract user-product relationship features, which maps high-dimensional feature relationship triples into low-dimensional ones. In this paper, there are K triples with different relationship dimensions, where contain N users, and M target products.

Firstly, the calculated user-product relationship triplet is normalized to reduce the error, and then we use the PCA algorithm to extract the principal components of each user-product relationship triplet. To get the feature vector W with the largest variance of the projected sample points, we set the target dimension of the first reduction as λ_1, and calculate the feature vector covariance of the user-product relationship matrix as the following formula:

$$\frac{1}{M+N}\sum_{i=1}^{m}(x^{(i)T}\omega)^2 = \frac{1}{M+N}\sum_{i=1}^{m}\omega^T x^{(i)}x^{(i)T}\omega = \sum_{i=1}^{m}\omega^T\left(\frac{1}{M+N}x^i x^{(i)T}\right)\omega \qquad (1)$$

where m is the number of feature vectors to be reduced, $x^{(i)}$ is the i-th sample, ω is the feature vector of the projection direction, we denote $A = \frac{1}{n} \sum_{i=1}^{n} \left(x^{(i)T} \omega \right)$, where $\sum = \frac{1}{m} x^{(i)} x^{(i)T}$ and w is the identify vector, then:

$$AW = \sum w \tag{2}$$

For singular value decomposition of the covariance matrix, we have:

$$W_{m \times n} = U_{m=n} \sum V_{n \times n}^{T} \tag{3}$$

Where U and V are unitary matrices and orthogonal to each other. The eigenvectors corresponding to the top λ_1 eigenvalues are the features we need. After subtracting the mean value, the sample matrix is denoted ad *DataAdjust*, and the matrix composed of eigenvectors is *EigenVector*. The data after projecting is denoted as *FinalData*:

$$FinalData((M + N) \times \lambda_1) = DataAdjust((M + N) \times (M + N)) \times EigenVector(m \times \lambda_1) \tag{4}$$

To get lower dimensions and ensure that the model can convergence during the training process, we set the target dimension as λ_2 and perform the second-dimension reduction operation. Practice shows that when the dimension is $(M + N)/100$ of the initial matrix S_i, the *FinalData* can reserve relatively complete data information.

User Interactive Behavioral Features Extraction Module. Compared with the real reviewers, the spammers usually behave abnormal behaviors. We divide the user behavioral features into three categories: user discrete features, user interactive behavioral features, and single review features. The specific features are shown in Table 1. The module selects the best feature combinations for model classification by considering user interactive data, information entropy, and text cosine similarity.

Table 1. User behavior feature information.

Category	Features
User discrete feature	Extreme Rating Ratio (ERR)
	Maximum Number of ratings/day (MN)
User interactive behavioral features	Upvote Number (UN)
	Fans Number (FaN)
	Followings Number (FoN)
	User Rating Deviation (URD)
	User Frequency (UF)
Single review features	Extreme Reviews (ER)
	Maximum Content Similarity (MCS)
	Rating Number (RN)

User Rating Deviation. Compared with the real reviewers, the spammers usually comment on target products with purpose. The ratings of the spammers are usually extreme, while the rating of the normal users is relatively close. Therefore, the features are constructed by calculating the average rating deviation between the specific reviewer's review and the others on the same product.

User Frequency. The commentary behavior of the spammers is generally organized and explosive behavior, which often occurs on the same target product in a short time. In this paper, the FP growth algorithm is used to mine frequent item-sets to mark whether each user belongs to frequent item-sets. Frequent item-sets refer to users who often review the same products in a short time. If they belong to frequent item-sets, the user frequency is 1, otherwise 0.

Maximum Content Similarity. The spammers generally have no real consumer experience, so the content of the reviews is relatively similar because the spammers usually copy or modify the prepared review templates to review the products. Therefore, the more similar the content is, the more likely the review is to be an online spam review. In this paper, the one-hot encoding is used to preprocess the reviews to get the two sequences V_1, V_2:

$$V_1 = \{V_{11}, V_{12}, \ldots, V_{1n}\}$$

$$V_2 = \{V_{21}, V_{22}, \ldots, V_{2n}\}$$

Then, we calculate the maximum content similarity between the reviews V_1 and other reviews V_2 by calculating the cosine similarity.

Text Feature Extraction Module Based on Nested LSTM and Capsule Network.
The text feature extraction module based on nested LSTM (NLSTM) and capsule network is shown in Fig. 3, which consists of three components: (1) Word embedding layer; (2) NLSTM encoding layer; (3) Capsule network layer.

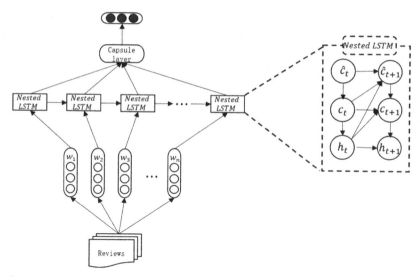

Fig. 3. The structure of the text feature extraction module based on NLSTM and capsule network.

Word Embedding Layer. The input of this module is the network reviews, denote each review as $S = \{w_1, w_2, \ldots, w_n\}$, $w_i \in \mathbb{R}^{|N|}$, $|N|$ is the size of the words. Suppose $E \in \mathbb{R}^{d \times |N|}$ represents the pre-training word vector lookup table generated by global vector (Glove), where d is the dimension of word vector. Each word w_i is mapped to its corresponding word vector by word embedding matrix E, then the word embedding of the input review is expressed as $L = \{l_1, l_2, \ldots, l_n\}$.

Nested Long-short Memory Network Coding Layer. NLSTM is used in the word encoding layer to obtain the hidden layer representations. The internal update process of NLSTM at each time t is described as follows:

$$\tilde{h}_{t-1} = f_t \odot c_{t-1} \tag{5}$$

$$\tilde{x} = i_t \odot \sigma(x_t W_{xc} + h_{t-1} W_{hc} + b_c) \tag{6}$$

$$\tilde{i}_t = \sigma\left(\tilde{x}_t \widetilde{W}_{xi} + \tilde{h}_{t-1} \widetilde{W}_{hi} + \tilde{b}_i\right) \tag{7}$$

$$\tilde{f}_t = \sigma\left(\tilde{x}_t \widetilde{W}_{xf} + \tilde{h}_{t-1} \widetilde{W}_{hf} + \tilde{b}_f\right) \tag{8}$$

$$\tilde{o}_t = \sigma\left(\tilde{x}_t \widetilde{W}_{xo} + \tilde{h}_{t-1} \widetilde{W}_{ho} + \tilde{b}_o\right) \tag{9}$$

$$\tilde{c}_t = \tilde{f}_t \odot \tilde{c}_{t-1} + \tilde{i}_t \odot \sigma\left(\tilde{x}_t \widetilde{W}_{xc} + \tilde{h}_{t-1} \widetilde{W}_{hc} + \tilde{b}_c\right) \tag{10}$$

While the external update process of NLSTM is described as follows:

$$c_t = \tilde{h}_t \tag{11}$$

Where σ denotes the logistic sigmoid function, $\odot$ denotes the dot multiplication operator; $\tilde{i}_t, \tilde{f}_t, \tilde{o}_t, \tilde{c}_t$ separately denotes activation vectors of the input gate, forgetting gate, output gate and memory unit at time t; $W_{xc}, W_{hc}, \widetilde{W}_{xi}, \widetilde{W}_{hi}, \widetilde{W}_{xf}, \widetilde{W}_{hf}, \widetilde{W}_{xo}, \widetilde{W}_{ho},$ $\widetilde{W}_{xc}, \widetilde{W}_{hc}, b_c, \tilde{b}_i, \tilde{b}_f, \tilde{b}_o, \tilde{b}_c$ are parameters to be trained.

Capsule Network Layer. In the capsule network layer, the feature vector h_i encoded by NLSTM is used as the input, and the weight matrix W_{ij} is used to generate the prediction vector $\hat{u}_{j|i}$ from the sub-capsule i to the parent capsule j, and a new activation function squash function is introduced to calculate the output result vector V_j.

$$V_j = \frac{\|s_j\|^2}{1 + \|s_j\|^2} \cdot \frac{s_j}{\|s_j\|^2} \tag{12}$$

$$s_j = \sum_i c_{ij}\hat{u}_{j|i} + b_{ij} \tag{13}$$

$$\hat{u}_{j|i} = W_{ij}h_i \tag{14}$$

$$b_{ij} \leftarrow b_{ij} + \hat{u}_{j|i} \cdot v_j \tag{15}$$

$$c_{ij} = \frac{exp(b_{ij})}{\sum_k exp(b_{ik})} \tag{16}$$

Where $\hat{u}_{j|i}$ represent the prediction vector, s_j is the weighted sum of prediction vectors, b_{ij} is the random value when the capsule network propagates to the parent capsule neuron, v_j is the output of the previous layer's capsule j, c_{ij} is the coupling coefficient.

Classifier Module Based on Integrated Learning. The classifier module based on ensemble learning consists of two layers. The first layer, consists of three base classifiers (i.e., Random Forest, KNN, GBDT) which learn and fit the extracted features, maps the prediction result set F into F'; the second layer inputs F' into the XGBoost classifier for prediction. The structure of the classifier module based on integrated learning is shown in Fig. 4.

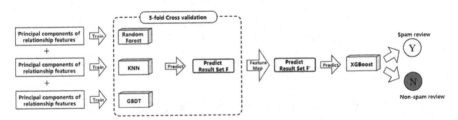

Fig. 4. Classifier module based on integrated learning.

In this module, the feature vectors of user behaviors and reviews are concatenated as the input to the first-level classifier:

$$F = [F_B : F_D : F_L] \tag{17}$$

$$h_t = \Gamma_t(F), t \in 1, 2, 3 \tag{18}$$

where F_B is the discrete features of user behaviors, F_D is the relationship features between users, and F_L is the review features of users. Γ_t is a classification algorithm based on ensemble learning.

The objective function of the first-level base classification model is described as follows:

$$\Gamma(\emptyset) = \sum_i l(\hat{y}_i, y_i) + \sum_j \Omega(f_k) \tag{19}$$

$$\Omega(f_k) = \gamma^T + \frac{1}{2}\lambda\|\omega\|^2 \tag{20}$$

Where l is the loss function of a single base model, which is used to evaluate the training error of the samples; $\Omega(f_k)$ represents the generalization ability of the model, and the smaller the value, the stronger the generalization ability.

Since the first layer of the base model needs to stack each base classifier, this paper uses the greedy principle to optimize the base classifier function f_t, so that its loss decreases with the increase of time. Therefore, the evaluation function of the current base classifier f_t performance is obtained as follows:

$$\Gamma^{(t)} = \sum_{t=1}^{n} l(\hat{y}_i, y + f_t(x_i)) + \Omega(f_t) \tag{21}$$

The prediction results of the three base classifiers are as follows:

$$z_{it} = h_t(x_i), t = 1, 2, 3 \tag{22}$$

The prediction results of the three base classifiers are concatenated as a new feature and is fed into the XGBoost classifier to predict the result:

$$F' = \{z_{i1}, z_{i2}, z_{i3}\} \tag{23}$$

The objective function of the final classification model is described as follows:

$$\Gamma = \sum_{j=1}^{T} \left[\left(\sum_{i\in I_j} g_i \right) w_j + \frac{1}{2} \left(\sum_{i\in I_j} h_i w_j^2 \right) \right] + \gamma^T + \frac{\lambda}{2} \sum_{j=1}^{T} w_j^2 \tag{24}$$

where g_i is the first-order Taylor expansion of mean square deviation, h_i is the second-order Taylor expansion, T is the total number of samples, $\frac{\lambda}{2} \sum_{j=1}^{T} w_j^2$ is the regular term introduced to prevent overfitting.

4 Experiment

4.1 Dataset

We conducted the experiments on the Hotel dataset and Restaurant dataset published by Mukherjee et al. [7], which contain reviews post on Yelp. We preprocessed the above datasets following the practice in [8] and filter out the reviews without user behaviors. Table 2 shows the details of the two datasets after preprocessing.

Table 2. Distribution of Experimental Datasets.

	Hotel	Restaurant
Number of non-spam reviews	4,876	50,149
Number of spam reviews	802	8,368
Review ratio of spammers (%)	14.1	14.3
Total reviews	5,678	58,517
Total reviewers	5,124	35,593

4.2 Experimental Evaluation Index and Experimental Setup

In this paper, the experimental results are mainly measured from Accuracy (Acc), Precision(P), Recall(R), and F1-Measure (F1). The specific calculation formula is described as follows:

$$Acc = \frac{n_{correct}}{n_{all}} \tag{25}$$

$$F1 = \frac{2 \times Precision \times Recall}{Precision + Recall} \tag{26}$$

$$P = \frac{n_{correct\_fake}}{n_{predict}} \tag{27}$$

$$R = \frac{n_{correct\_fake}}{n_{labeled}} \tag{28}$$

where n_{true} is the number of the correct predictions, n_{all} is the number of all reviews, n_{true_fake} is the number of the correct prediction for spam reviews, $n_{predict}$ is the number of the prediction for spam reviews, $n_{labeled}$ is the number of the reviews correctly labeled as spam.

The experimental parameter settings are shown in Table 3.

Table 3. Experimental parameter settings

Model	Parameter	Setting
Capsule network	Number of capsules	10
	Dimension of capsules	16
Integrated model	Number of cross-validation	5
XGBoost	Learning rate	0.0005
	Max depth	5
NLSTM	Depth	2
	Dropout	0.3
	Word embedding dimension	50

4.3 Comparison Model

In this paper, the benchmark experiments on the two datasets mentioned above are shown as follows:

- M_BF+BIGRAM [7]: This model proposes a detection method based on the suspicious behaviors of users and proves the effectiveness of the proposed method compared with the text-based one;
- CNN+BiGRU [2]: This model extracts text features of online reviews through deep learning, where CNN learns the sentence representations and BiGRU with attention mechanisms generates the document representation vectors. Taking document features representations into account, the model performs well on the AMT dataset;
- SPEAGLE [15]: This model proposes a method based on the semi-supervised graph model where texts, timestamps, reviews and other types of data are taken as the inputs to the model to detect suspicious users and comments;
- RESCAL [12]: This model uses the tensor decomposition technique to learn the relational representations between users and products, based on which spam reviews can be detected more accurately;
- STACKING [21]: This model uses the PCA dimension reduction algorithm to get a low-dimensional user-product relationship matrix, and uses a double-layer stacking classification model, which improves the experiment results on the natural distributed dataset.

4.4 Analysis of Experimental Results

To prove the effectiveness of the method proposed in this paper (denoted as Multi-Feature). Interactive-Feature is a method that only considers the features of user interaction. The experimental results of each model are shown in Table 4.

Table 4. Experimentalresults of different methods on the two datasets.

Model	Data distribution	Hotel				Restaurant			
		P	R	F1	Acc	P	R	F1	Acc
M_BF+Bigram	50:50	82.8	86.9	84.8	85.1	82.8	88.5	85.6	83.3
	ND	46.5	82.5	59.4	84.9	48.2	87.9	62.3	78.5
CNN+BiGRU	50:50	61.2	54.7	57.8	64.4	69.4	59.0	63.8	66.5
	ND	32.7	53.1	40.8	56.4	35.9	78.9	48.1	68.3
SPEAGLE	50:50	75.7	83.0	79.1	81.4	80.5	83.2	81.8	82.5
	ND	26.5	56.0	36.0	80.4	48.2	70.5	58.6	82.0
RESCAL	50:50	84.2	89.9	87.0	86.5	86.8	91.8	89.2	89.9
	ND	48.2	85.0	61.5	85.9	58.2	90.3	70.8	87.8
STACKING	50:50	87.3	90.7	89.9	88.8	88.7	93.2	90.9	90.7
	ND	52.0	90.0	65.9	86.6	64.6	92.4	76.0	88.3
Interactive-feature	50:50	88.8	92.7	90.7	90.4	90.4	94.0	92.2	91.5
	ND	54.5	91.3	68.2	88.1	67.1	94.3	78.4	90.5
Multi-feature	50:50	**89.8**	**93.1**	**91.5**	**91.2**	**91.0**	**94.5**	**92.7**	**92.3**
	ND	**55.4**	**92.8**	**69.4**	**89.2**	**67.9**	**94.8**	**78.9**	**91.0**

50:50 indicates that the dataset is balance distributed, ND indicates that the dataset is naturally distributed.

As shown in Table 4, Multi-Feature achieves better performance over baselines in terms of all metrics, whatever on the balanced or the natural distribution dataset, demonstrating the effectiveness of our proposed framework. The accuracy of Multi-Feature on the balanced Hotel dataset and Restaurant dataset is 91.2%and 92.3%, respectively, which are 2.4% and 1.6% higher than the STACKING model. The F1 value reaches 91.5% and 92.7%, with an increase of 1.6% and 1.8%, respectively. As for the natural distribution datasets, the accuracy increased by 2.6% and 2.7%, respectively, and the F1 value increased by 3.5% and 2.9%. The performance improvement benefits from the consideration of deep-seated user interaction behavioral features and better access to long space features and context semantic information hidden in the text. The proposed model can better access to fine-grained features of text and further improve the performance. In the method of combining reviews feature with user behaviors, RESCAL fusions bigram and Stacking is better than the SPEAGLE based on user behavior and CNN + BiGRU based on text content feature. The F1 value of STACKING model is 89.9% and 90.9% on the balanced Hotel and Restaurant datasets, and 65.9% and 76.0% on the natural distribution ones. The optimal results of benchmark experiments are obtained under balanced distribution and natural distribution, which fully shows that the method based on the fusion of text reviews and user behavior is better than the method based on considering user behavior or reviews alone. The above methods do not take into account the information hidden in user interaction, and do not fully consider the spatial structure information of review, word position relationship, and other features.

Among the models proposed in this paper, the Multi-Feature model achieves the best performance, while the Interactive-Feature method, which only considers the deep-seated features of user interaction, is still superior to the benchmark experiment. The accuracy of Interactive-Feature on the balanced Hotel and Restaurant increased by 1.6% and 0.8%, respectively, and the F1 value increased by 0.8% and 1.3%. As for the natural distribution datasets, the accuracy of Interactive-Feature increased by 1.5% and 2.2% on Hotel and Restaurant dataset, and the F1 value increased by 2.3% and 2.4%. The main reason is that Interactive-Feature fully excavates the deep-seated relationship features of the user-product from the perspective of reviews, user behavior, and user behavior interaction relationship, so as to improve the performance of the model to a certain extent. Based on the Interactive-Feature, the NLSTM is used to fully mine the long-term dependence of the text, so as to extract more fine-grained text features. Compared with the Interactive-Feature method, the four evaluation indexes of the NLSTM and the capsule network (Multi-Feature) are the best on the balance distribution and the natural distribution datasets.

4.5   Effects of User Interactive Behavioral Features

In this section, we summarize the effective feature representations that distinguish the spam reviews and real reviews from the perspective of user behaviors and relationships. For example, the 10 dimensions of a typical spam review A and a real review B are shown in Table 5.

Table 5. Comparison of user behavioral features between spam review and real review

Category	User discrete feature		User interactive behavioral features					Single review features		
	ERR	MN	UN	FaN	FoN	URD	UF	ER	MCS	RN
Spam reviews A	0.75	3.00	0.00	0.00	106.00	2.60	1.00	1.00	0.09	0.00
Real reviews B	0.30	1.00	0.79	33.00	0.00	1.80	0.00	0.00	0.02	5.00

Table 5 shows the significant differences between A and B in terms of user discrete features, interactive behaviors, and single review features. These features that saves the original behavior information can better distinguish between spam reviews and real ones, and effectively improve the detection performance. To explore the impact of different features on detection performance, we conducted experiments using these different features. The experimental results are shown in Table 6.

Table 6. Effects of different features on detection performance

Feature	Index	Hotel		Restaurant	
		50:50	ND	50:50	ND
No-consider user behavioral features	F1	87.2	58.8	90.3	73.1
	Acc	86.2	80.1	89.2	86.6
User discrete feature	F1	87.9	60.1	90.7	74.3
	Acc	87.6	83.0	90.0	87.3
Single review features	F1	88.0	63.8	90.6	75.0
	Acc	87.8	86.6	90.7	88.3
Features of user interactive behavior	F1	88.9	66.0	90.9	76.0
	Acc	89.3	87.2	90.9	89.1
No-consider features of user interactive behavior	F1	89.2	66.2	91.2	76.2
	Acc	89.0	87.0	91.0	89.5
Consider all user interactive behavioral features	F1	**90.7**	**68.2**	**92.2**	**78.4**
	Acc	**90.4**	**88.1**	**91.5**	**90.5**

From Table 6, it can be seen that the performance of adding user discrete features, single review features, and user interactive behavioral features respectively is better than that of not adding any user behavior feature, among which the user interactive behavioral features are the most significant for the improvement of review spam detection. We conclude that all kinds of user behavioral features have a certain improvement in the performance.

4.6　Effects of Extracting Text Features from Capsule Network

In this section, we design the different contrast models to verify the validity of the network in extracting text features. As is shown in Fig. 5, we can see that models in which using capsule networks, have better performances than those using convolution neural network (CNN). This proves the capsule network can help extract text features. The main reason is that in the actual application scenario, the selection of the CNN window size depends on experience, and the selection of window size affects the effects of extracting text features, which has a great impact on the performance of the model. The capsule network uses dynamic routing to train a new neural network, which effectively improves the shortcomings of CNN.

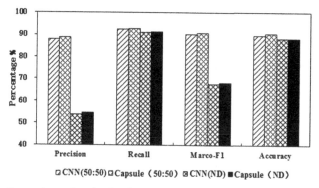

Fig. 5. Comparison of evaluation indicators of CNN and Capsule on Hotel dataset

4.7 Effects of Nesting Depth of NLSTM

One major setting that affects the performance of our model is the number of nesting depth in the NLSTM. We evaluate our framework with 1 to 4 depth, and the results are given in Fig. 6. It can be seen that performances increase firstly and then decrease with the increase of nesting depth, and our model achieves the best performance when the nesting depth is 2. With the increase of network nesting depth, the effectiveness of text feature extraction decreases, it is because as the model's complexity increases, the model becomes more difficult to train and less generalizable.

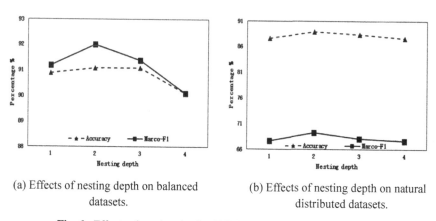

(a) Effects of nesting depth on balanced datasets.

(b) Effects of nesting depth on natural distributed datasets.

Fig. 6. Effects of nesting depth of NLSTM on detection performance

5   Conclusion

In this paper, a new method of review spam detection based on multi-dimensional features is proposed. The method firstly learns the word vector representations as inputs to the neural network consists of nested LSTM and capsule network to extract the text features, which solves the issue that the existing methods cannot get the long spatial features and context semantics of the text well. The extracted text features are then integrated with the user behavioral features and user-product relationship features to get the final feature representations and fed into a classification module based on integrating learning for classification. Experiments show that the accuracy, precision, recall, and macro average F1 have been significantly improved on the two different datasets.

References

1. Chen, Y.R., Chen, H.H: Opinion spammer detection in web forum. In: Proceedings of the 38th International ACM SIGIR Conference on Research and Development in Information Retrieval, pp. 759–762. ACM (2015)
2. Kim, S., Chang, H., Lee, S., et al.: Deep semantic frame-based deceptive opinion spam analysis. In: Proceedings of the 24th ACM International on Conference on Information and Knowledge Management, pp. 1131–1140. ACM (2015)
3. Li, H., Fei, G., Wang, S., et al.: Bimodal distribution and co-bursting in review spam detection. In: The 26th International Conference on International World Wide Web Conferences Steering Committee, pp. 1063–1072 (2017)
4. Chen, C., Zhao, H., Yang, Y.: Deceptive Opinion Spam Detection Using Deep Level Linguistic Features. In: Li, J., Ji, H., Zhao, D., Feng, Y. (eds.) NLPCC-2015. LNCS (LNAI), vol. 9362, pp. 465–474. Springer, Cham (2015). https://doi.org/10.1007/978-3-319-25207-0_43
5. Mccallum, A., Nigam, K.: A comparison of event models for naive Bayes text classification. In: AAAI-1998 Workshop on learning for text categorization, pp. 41–48 (1998)
6. Diehl, C.P., Cauwenberghs, G.: SVM incremental learning, adaptation and optimization. In: Proceedings of the International Joint Conference on Neural Networks, pp. 2685–2690. IEEE (2003)
7. Mukherjee, A., Venkataraman, V., Liu, B., et al.: What yelp fake review filter might be doing. In: Proceedings of the International AAAI Conference on Web and Social Media, pp. 409–418 (2013)
8. Wang, X., Liu, K., He, S., et al.: Learning to represent review with tensor decomposition for spam detection. In: Association for Computational Linguistics, Texas, pp. 866–875 (2016)
9. Green, P.J.: Reversible jump Markov chain Monte Carlo computation and Bayesian model determination. Biometrika **82**(4), 711–732 (1995)
10. Sawaya, Y., Kubota, A., Yamada, A.: Understanding the time-series behavioral features of evolutionally advanced email spammers. In: Proceedings of the 5th ACM Workshop on Security and Artificial Intelligence, pp. 71–80 (2012)
11. Wang, X., Liu, K., Zhao, J.: Handling cold-start problem in review spam detection by jointly embedding texts and behaviors. In: Association for Computational Linguistics, Vancouver, pp. 366–376 (2017)
12. Rayana, S., Akoglu, L.: Collective opinion spam detection: bridging review networks and metadata. In: Proceedings of the 21th ACM SIGKDD International Conference on Knowledge Discovery and Data Mining, pp. 985–994 (2015)
13. Kim, S., Chang, H., Lee, S., et al.: Deep semantic frame-based deceptive opinion spam analysis. In: Proceedings of the 24th ACM International on Conference on Information and Knowledge Management, pp. 1131–1140 (2015)
14. Feng, S., Banerjee, R., Choi, Y.: Syntactic stylometry for deception detection. In: Association for Computational Linguistics, pp. 171–175 (2012)
15. Ren, Y., Zhang, Y.: Deceptive opinion spam detection using neural network. In: The COLING 2016 Organizing Committee, pp. 140–150 (2016)

16. Chen, T., Xu, R., He, Y., et al.: Improving sentiment analysis via sentence type classification using BiLSTM-CRF and CNN. Expert Syst. Appl. **72**, 221–230 (2017)
17. Santosh, K.C., Maity, S.K., Mukherjee, A.: ENWalk: learning network features for spam detection in Twitter. In: Lee, D., Lin, Y.-R., Osgood, N., Thomson, R. (eds.) SBP-BRiMS 2017. LNCS, vol. 10354, pp. 90–101. Springer, Cham (2017). https://doi.org/10.1007/978-3-319-60240-0_11
18. Hai, Z., Zhao, P., Cheng, P., et al.: Deceptive review spam detection via exploiting task relatedness and unlabeled data. In: Proceedings of the 2016 Conference on Empirical Methods in Natural Language Processing, pp. 1817–1826 (2016)
19. Shehnepoor, S., Salehi, M., Farahbakhsh, R., et al.: NetSpam: a network-based spam detection framework for reviews in online social media. IEEE Trans. Inf. Forensics Secur. **12**(7), 1585–1595 (2017)
20. Fakhraei, S., Foulds, J., Shashanka, M., et al.: Collective spammer detection in evolving multi-relational social networks. In: Proceedings of the 21th ACM SIGKDD International Conference on Knowledge Discovery and Data Mining, pp. 1769–1778 (2015)
21. Liao, X., Xu, Y., Wei, J., et al.: Review spam detection based on the two-level stacking classification model. J. Shandong Univ. (Nat. Sci.) **54**(7), 57–67 (2019)

Application Track

Rehabilitation XAI to Predict Outcome with Optimal Therapies

Takashi Isobe[1,2,3]($\boxtimes$) and Yoshihiro Okada[2]

[1] Hitachi High-Tech America, Inc., Pleasanton, CA 95488, USA
takashi.isobe.sw@hitachi-hightech.com
[2] Hitachi High-Tech Solutions Corporation, Chuo-ku, Tokyo 104-6031, Japan
[3] Hitachi High-Tech Corporation, Minato-ku, Tokyo 105-8717, Japan

Abstract. Value-based payment is becoming general in healthcare. In rehabilitation medicine, medical services are becoming to be paid depending on the outcome obtained from hospitalization period and dependency score called as FIM (Functional Independent Measurement). The optimal therapies to maximize the outcome differs by each patient's age, sex, disease, handicap, FIM and therapies. Non-experienced hospitals have a difficulty in improving the outcome. Therefore, there are needs to maximize the outcome by optimizing therapies. We developed a rehabilitation XAI system to predict outcome with optimal therapies. Our system piles up medical records into vectors and predicts the outcome with optimal therapies using machine learning based on vector distance that can explain the basis of prediction in the same way as doctors suggesting optimal therapies to patients based on similar past cases. The interface not only displays optimal therapies but also predicts outcome by each patient. We used data from multiple hospitals and evaluated the adaptability of our system. In case of using the data from one hospital, the pattern achieving high outcome, which was most important because it was used to suggest optimal therapies, occupied the proportion of 31.1% in the actual record while the precision and recall were 64.5% and 73.4%. In case of using the data from another hospital, they were 64.4% and 66.1% against the actual proportion of 35.7%. In case of using the data from both hospitals, they were 63.6% and 71.0% against the actual proportion of 33.3%. Our system achieved similar performance and adaptability between two hospitals. Correlation coefficient between actual and predicted outcome were 0.681 using 203 patients' record. We compared the accuracy to predict outcome between our XAI and humans. Average outcomes of top 70% patients predicted at hospitalization by our XAI and humans were 43.0 and 42.4. Our XAI could predict outcome at higher accuracy than humans.

Keywords: Artificial intelligence · Rehabilitation AI · Medical AI · AI · XAI

1 Background and Purpose

Value-based program [9] and payment [10] are becoming general in healthcare insurance company or governmental institution [11]. In rehabilitation medicine, the medical

© Springer Nature Switzerland AG 2020
R. Xu et al. (Eds.): AIMS 2020, LNCS 12401, pp. 127–139, 2020.
https://doi.org/10.1007/978-3-030-59605-7_10

services are becoming to be paid depending on the outcome determined by the combination of hospitalization period and dependency score called as functional independent measurement (FIM) gain [11] utilized to measure the level of dependence that patient has in performing a certain task. As more patients can complete the rehabilitation at higher FIM gain within shorter period, hospitals can get higher outcome and more payment. The outcome has an impact on the revenue of rehabilitation hospitals.

Rehabilitation therapies are composed of physical, occupational and speaking therapies (PT, OT and ST). Their optimal combination to maximize the outcome varies depending on many parameters such as each patients' age, sex, disease, handicap, time-series FIM score and therapies. Non-experienced hospitals, therapists or doctors don't know the optimal combination well and have a difficulty in improving the outcome. Therefore, there are needs to maximize the outcome by predicting optimal combination of rehabilitation therapies.

We have developed and improved a rehabilitation explainable AI (XAI) system to predict the outcome obtained from hospitalization period and FIM gain with optimal combination of rehabilitation therapies [8, 17]. Our proposed system piled up actual time-series medical records into vectors and predicted the pattern of outcome with optimal therapies by each patient using machine learning based on vector distances that could explain the basis of prediction in the same way as doctors suggesting optimal therapies to patients based on similar past cases. The interface not only displays the optimal combination of therapies to maximize the outcome but also predicted the outcome calculated from FIM gain and hospitalization period by each patient.

In this research, we added new data from another hospital and evaluated the adaptability of our AI system to multiple hospitals. We also evaluated and compared the accuracy to predict the outcome between our XAI and humans using the actual record from a customer hospital.

2 Related Works

Medical diagnostic using correlation [1] is the most popular technique. If the distribution of data is small and correlation coefficient is large, correlation-based diagnostic generally has high accuracy. In rehabilitation medicine, the distribution of outcome against each parameter is large and the correlation coefficient often becomes small between outcome and many parameters by large noise because humans have emotion and don't react quantitatively like machines.

Medical diagnostic using Bayesian network [2] is also well known. If each conditional branch node has the table of conditional probability defined by optimal condition, diagnostic using Bayesian network has high accuracy. Rehabilitation's outcome differs widely by the difference of a few percentage in the allocation of therapies between PT, OT and ST. It is often difficult to find the optimal condition in rehabilitation medicine.

In rehabilitation medicine, the techniques to predict FIM score [3, 4] or FIM gain [5–7] using correlation-based technique were reported in past papers. As the accuracy to predict FIM gain, the correlation coefficient of 0.653 was reported [5]. However, we don't find any report about how to accurately predict outcome obtained from dividing FIM gain by hospitalization period. The prediction of rehabilitation outcome is challenging because it needs to accurately predict both FIM gain and hospitalization period that greatly fluctuate depending on patient's motivation, families' emotion, home's preparation and hospital's policy even if the condition is same.

3 Proposed Rehabilitation XAI System

3.1 System Configuration

Figure 1 shows the configuration of our proposed rehabilitation XAI system to predict outcome with optimal therapies. Our XAI system works as a cloud service of SaaS (Software as a Service) [17] with other services such as NaaS (Network as a Service) [16]. Users send electric medical record to XAI application of cloud. After then, they receive the result of predicted outcomes with optimal therapies.

Our XAI system includes two programs. One is learning data generator. Another is judgement program.

Learning data generator creates the learning data piled up as vectors using the archives of past electric medical record composed of patients' personality, disease, handicap, time-series FIM scores and therapies. It also classifies vectors into multiple patterns depending on FIM gain per week.

Judgement program recognizes the pattern of outcome by each patient based on machine learning using the learning data. It not only predicts the outcome with optimal therapies, FIM gain, FIM score and hospitalization period but also shows the statistical information about similar cases and patients as the basis of prediction. It uses the algorithm of K-NN (Nearest Neighbor) based on vector distance that can explain the basis of prediction in the same way as doctors suggesting probable therapies to patients based on similar past cases.

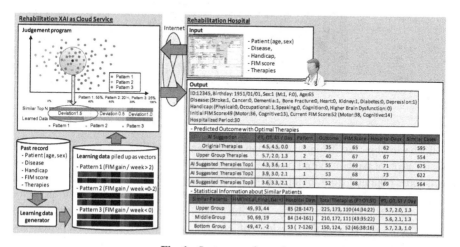

Fig. 1. System configuration

3.2 Medical Record Data Used for Learning

Through the collaboration with two actual rehabilitation hospitals A [12] and B [13], we analyzed the actual electric medical record including eighteen thousand patients between 2006 and 2018. Our system classified diseases into eight categories (stroke, heart, kidney, diabetes, cancer, dementia, bone fracture, depression) and handicaps into five categories (physical, speaking, occupation, cognition, higher brain dysfunction).

The statistical analysis of the actual record shows the trend where highly recovered patient group receives larger number of PT/OT and smaller number of ST as initial FIM score or age becomes larger. On the contrary, too large number of PT/OT or too small number of ST causes the worse outcome. The type of disease also influences the outcome. Stroke type of disease shows the trend where highly recovered patients receive larger number of ST. On the other hand, heart or cancer type of disease shows the trend where highly recovered patients receive larger number of PT/OT.

3.3 Learning Data Generation

Learning data generator creates the learning data piled up as vectors composed of sex, age, disease, handicap, FIM score (motor, cognition and speed) and therapies (the number of PT, OT and ST) by each combination of patient ID and hospitalized day. FIM score and therapies are smoothed by each day between two days when FIM scores are measured. One row becomes one vector. (See Fig. 2)

Patient ID	Hospitalized Day	FIM Measurement Day	Sex	Age	Disease				Handicap				FIM			Therapies / Day			Pattern
					Stroke	Heart	Kidney	...	Physical	Occupational	Speaking	...	Physical	Cognition	Speed	PT	OT	ST	
12345	12/20/2016	12/22/2016	1	65	1	0	1	...	0	1	0	...	36	13	.	4	4	1	1
12345	12/20/2016		1	65	1	0	1	...	0	1	0	...	37	13.5	.	4	4	1	1
12345	12/20/2016	12/24/2016	1	65	1	0	1	...	0	1	0	...	38	14	1.5	3	5	1	2
12345	12/20/2016		1	65	1	0	1	...	0	1	0	...	38.25	14	1.5	3	5	1	2
12345	12/20/2016		1	65	1	0	1	...	0	1	0	...	38.50	14	1.5	3	5	1	2
12345	12/20/2016		1	65	1	0	1	...	0	1	0	...	38.75	14	1.5	3	5	1	2
12345	12/20/2016	12/28/2016	1	65	1	0	1	...	0	1	0	...	39	14	0.25	4	5	0	3
12345	12/20/2016		1	65	1	0	1	...	0	1	0	...	39	13.5	0.25	4	5	0	3
12345	12/20/2016	12/30/2016	1	65	1	0	1	...	0	1	0	...	39	13	-0.5	-	-	-	-

Fig. 2. Sample of learning data

Each vector is classified into three patterns depending on FIM gain per one week. The classification of patterns based on FIM gain per one week enables the direct prediction of outcome obtained from dividing FIM gain by hospitalization periods. The threshold for the classification were determined by the trend line between hospitalization period and average FIM gain shown in Fig. 3. In the first ten weeks, average FIM gain per week was 2. Therefore, we used the threshold of 2 for classifying vectors into first pattern and others.

FIM gain of more than two per one week is defined as pattern 1. FIM gain of two or less and more than zero per one week is defined as pattern 2. FIM gain of zero or less per one week is defined as pattern 3. Pattern 1, which is most important because it is

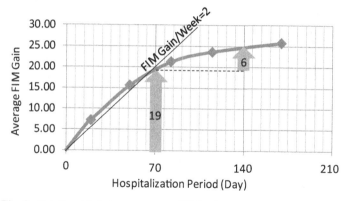

Fig. 3. Relationship between average FIM gain and hospitalization period

used to suggest optimal therapies, occupies 31.1%, 35.7% and 33.3% in hospital A, B and both ones (See Table 1).

Table 1. Proportion of each pattern in electric medical record

Data	Pattern 1	Pattern 2	Pattern 3
Hospital A	186,280 (31.1%)	248,945 (41.5%)	164,106 (27.4%)
Hospital B	192,511 (35.7%)	216,104 (40.0%)	131,018 (24.3%)
Both hospitals	378,791 (33.3%)	465,049 (40.8%)	295,124 (25.9%)

3.4 Explainable Pattern Recognition Using K-NN with Tuned Weight

Judgement program recognizes the pattern of outcome by each patient using the algorithm of K-NN based on Euclidean vector distance tuning weight in specific range of some features. The program extracts top 700–1500 of most similar vectors from all learned vectors using Euclidean distance of vectors composed of sex, age, disease, handicap, FIM score and therapies between original patient's vector and all learned vectors. The program calculates the proportion of pattern 1–3 in the extracted top 700–1500 of most similar vectors and recognizes the pattern significantly deviating from the average proportion of entire learned data as prospected pattern. After then, it calculates the predicted values of outcome, FIM gain, FIM score and hospitalization period using extracted similar cases of the recognized pattern (See Fig. 4).

The K-NN algorithm based on Euclidean vector distance can explain the basis of prediction in the same way as doctors suggesting probable therapies to patients based on similar past cases or literatures. It is adaptable to the field of medicine that requires responsibility to explain the basis of prediction to patients and doctors.

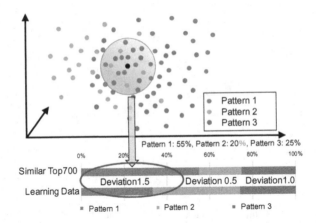

Fig. 4. Explainable algorithm to recognize probable pattern of outcome

3.5   Suggestion of Optimal Therapies

Figure 5 shows our method to suggest optimal therapies. Judgement program extracts top N (= 00, 300 or 700) of most similar vectors from learned vectors of pattern 1 using Euclidean distance of vectors eliminating therapies between original patient's vector and all learned vectors. After then, the program creates N vectors by overwriting original patient's vector eliminating therapies into the extracted top N similar vectors. The patterns of newly created N vectors are recognized N times using the K-NN algorithm. The vectors recognized as pattern 1 are sorted in descending order of the number of similar cases, and after then, the therapies included in top 3 vectors are output as optimal therapies. If there is no vector recognized as pattern 1, the vectors recognized as pattern 2 or 3 are used. The vectors recognized as pattern 3 are sorted in ascending order of the number of similar cases.

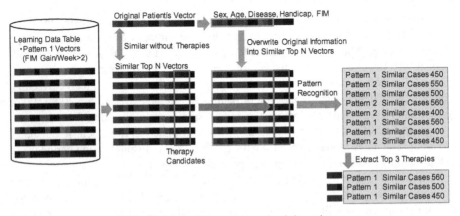

Fig. 5. Method to suggest optimal therapies

4 Evaluation

We divided the vectors of past electric medical record into two groups for leaning of 99.9% and evaluation of 0.1%. In addition, the vectors related to the evaluated vector were eliminated from learning data by each evaluation. We evaluated the execution time, precision, recall and accuracy to recognize the pattern or predict the outcome.

4.1 Comparison of Execution Time Between CPU and GPU

We evaluated the improvement of execution time using GPU [14]. The result is shown in Fig. 6 and Table 2.

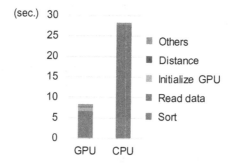

Fig. 6. Comparison of execution time between CPU and GPU

Table 2. Comparison of execution time between CPU and GPU

Similar vectors extracted for suggestion	CPU	GPU
Top 100	15 s	5 s
Top 300	29 s	8 s
Top 700	68 s	17 s

Execution time between input and output improved from 28 to 8 s by three times using GPU (See Fig. 6). When our XAI uses CPU [15], brute-force distance calculation occupied large area of execution time. GPU drastically reduced the time of brute-force distance calculation and sort time remained occupying large area of execution time.

The execution time increased in proportion to the top N number of similar vectors extracted for recognition and prediction. The top 300 or less satisfied the response of 10 s required by our customers.

4.2 Precision and Recall of Each Pattern

We evaluated the precision and recall by each pattern using the electric medical record from hospital A [12]. The result is shown in Table 3 and Table 4.

The precision and recall of pattern 1 were larger than those of pattern 2 or 3 (See Table 3). Pattern 1 often includes patients having single major disease like stroke and is easy to recognize the pattern of outcome. On the other hand, pattern 2 or 3 often includes patients having multiple major diseases and is more difficult to predict the outcome. Especially, the outcome of patients having depression with other major disease drastically changes depending on dairy symptom. Therefore, the precision and recall of pattern 2 or 3 were thought to decrease.

Pattern 1 achieving high FIM gain per week, which was most important because it was used to predict optimal therapies, occupied the proportion of 31.1% in the actual record while the precision was 64.5% and the recall was 73.4% (See Table 3). Our XAI system could correctly extract 73.4% of the most important pattern 1 used as candidates for optimal therapies. The users can improve the proportion of pattern1 achieving high outcome by preferentially hospitalizing patients predicted as pattern 1 with optimal therapies and enhance their outcome. Achieving higher accuracy close to 100% is challenging because patients have emotion and react non-quantitatively unlike machines.

Average FIM gain per week of pattern 1, 2 and 3 were about 5, 1 and 0. The difference between pattern 2 and 3 was very small. Therefore, it was important to separate pattern 1 from other patterns. The precision and recall merging pattern 2 and 3 were shown in Table 4. In this case, the accuracy improved from 59.3% to 79.1%. The accuracy changed depending on the number of recognized patterns.

Table 3. Precision and recall of each pattern

		Predicted			Recall
		Pattern 1	Pattern 2	Pattern 3	
	Pattern 1	**138**	38	12	73.4%
Actual	Pattern 2	53	**127**	69	51.0%
	Pattern 3	23	50	**92**	55.8%
Precision		64.5%	59.1%	53.2%	59.3% (Accuracy)

Table 4. Precision and recall of each pattern

		Predicted		Recall
		Pattern 1	Pattern 2, 3	
Actual	Pattern 1	**138**	50	73.4%
	Pattern 2, 3	76	**338**	81.6%
Precision		64.5%	87.1%	79.1% (Accuracy)

4.3 Dependency of Precision and Recall on Hospitals

We evaluated the dependency of precision and recall on hospitals using data from hospital A [12], B [13] or both ones. The result is shown in Table 5.

Table 5. Dependency of precision and recall on hospitals

Pattern 1	Hospital A	Hospital B	Both hospitals
Actual proportion	31.1%	35.7%	33.3%
Precision	64.5%	64.4%	63.6%
Recall	73.4%	66.1%	71.0%

In case of using data from hospital B, the precision and recall of the most important pattern 1 were 64.4% and 66.1% against the actual proportion of 35.7%. In case of using data from both hospitals, the precision and recall of the most important pattern 1 were 63.6% and 71.0% against the actual proportion of 33.3%. Our AI could extract the most important pattern 1 at the percentage of 64.4–73.4% in all combinations of hospitals. There were not large difference between single and mixed data. Our system achieved similar performance and adaptability between two hospitals.

4.4 Dependency of Precision and Recall on Amount of Data

We evaluated the dependency of precision and recall on amount of data by deleting past two year of 2006 and 2007 from hospital A and B record. The result is shown in Table 6.

Table 6. Dependency of precision and recall on amount of data

Pattern 1	2006–2017	2008–2017
Actual proportion	33.3%	32.6%
Precision	63.6%	60.5%
Recall	71.0%	65.8%

The precision and recall of the most important pattern 1 decreased as the learning data decreased. Gathering large amount of data is important to achieve high precision and recall.

4.5 Prediction of Outcome

Outcome to determine payment for medical services is calculated by multiplying the standard hospitalization period by the value obtained from dividing FIM gain by actual hospitalization period. Moreover, hospitals can eliminate up to 30% patients from the population to calculate the outcome only when they are hospitalized [11]. Therefore, it is important to predict the outcome at high accuracy at the time of hospitalization.

We evaluated the correlation coefficients between predicted and actual values of outcome using actual 203 patients' who were newly hospitalized at hospital A between May and July in 2018. The result is shown in Fig. 7. Correlation coefficient between actual and predicted outcome was 0.681, which was similar to the precision or recall of 64.5–73.4% (See Fig. 7).

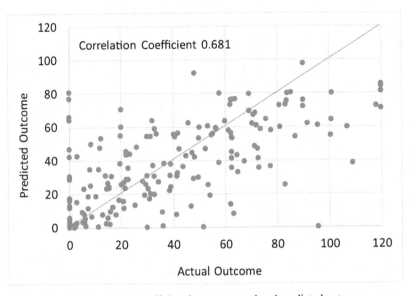

Fig. 7. Correlation coefficient between actual and predicted outcome

The prediction of outcome is more difficult than that of FIM gain because the prediction of the outcome, which is calculated using both FIM gain and hospitalization period, needs to predict not only FIM gain but also hospitalization period at high accuracy. Especially, even if the condition is same, hospitalization period greatly fluctuates depending on patients' motivation, families' consensus, hospitals' policy or homes' preparation for acceptance. We enabled the direct prediction of outcome by the classification of patterns based on FIM gain per one week. Our prediction of outcome could achieve higher accuracy at correlation coefficient of 0.681 than conventional prediction of FIM gain at correlation coefficient of 0.653 [5].

We also compared the accuracy to predict the outcome between our XAI and humans. Average outcomes of top 70% patients predicted at hospitalization by our XAI and humans were 43.0 and 42.4 (See Table 7). Our XAI could predict the outcome at the higher accuracy than humans.

Table 7. Comparison of accuracy between our XAI and humans

Patients Group	Average outcome
Top 70% predicted by humans	42.4
Top 70% predicted by our XAI	43.0
Actual top 70%	43.3
All	30.4

5 Conclusion

We have developed and improved a rehabilitation XAI system to predict the outcome obtained from dividing FIM gain by hospitalization period with optimal combination of rehabilitation therapies.

Our XAI system works as a cloud service. Users send electric medical record to XAI application of cloud. The electric medical record includes patient's personality with disease, handicap, therapies and FIM score. After then, they receive the result of predicted outcome with optimal therapies. The interface not only displays the optimal combination of therapies to maximize the outcome but also predicts the outcome obtained from dividing FIM gain by hospitalization period by each patient.

Our XAI system creates learning data by piling up past medical records into vectors. Each vector is classified into three patterns depending on FIM gain per one week. The classification of patterns based on FIM gain per one week enables the direct prediction of outcome determined by dividing FIM gain by hospitalization periods. Our XAI predicts the pattern of outcome with optimal therapies by each patient using K-NN machine learning algorithm based on vector distances that can explain the basis of prediction in the same way as doctors suggesting optimal therapies to patients based on similar past cases.

We used data from multiple hospitals and evaluated the adaptability of our system. In case of using the data from one hospital, the pattern achieving high FIM gain per week, which was most important because it was used to suggest optimal combination of therapies, occupied the proportion of 31.1% in the actual medical record while the precision was 64.5% and the recall was 73.4%. The users can improve the proportion of pattern 1 achieving high outcome by preferentially hospitalizing patients suggested with therapies predicted as pattern 1 and enhance their outcome.

In case of using the data from another hospital, the precision and recall were 64.4% and 66.1% against the actual proportion of 34.5%. In case of using the data from both hospitals, they were 63.6% and 71.0% against the actual proportion of 32.7%. Our system achieved similar performance and adaptability between two hospitals.

We also evaluated the correlation coefficients between predicted and actual values of outcome using actual 203 patients' record newly obtained from our customer hospital. Correlation coefficient between actual and predicted outcome was 0.681. The prediction of outcome is more difficult than that of FIM gain because the prediction of the outcome needs to predict not only FIM gain but also hospitalization period at high accuracy. We enabled the direct prediction of outcome by the classification of patterns based on

FIM gain per one week. Our prediction of outcome could achieve higher accuracy at correlation coefficient of 0.681 than conventional prediction of FIM gain at correlation coefficient of 0.653 [5].

We also compared the accuracy to predict the outcome between our XAI and humans. Average outcomes of top 70% patients predicted at hospitalization by our XAI and humans were 43.0 and 42.4. Our XAI could predict the outcome at the higher accuracy than humans.

We are currently improving our rehabilitation XAI system to have higher accuracy and adaptability using the record obtained from more hospitals as the future task.

References

1. Mukaka, M.M.: A guide to appropriate use of correlation coefficient in medical research. Malawi Med. J. **24**(3), 69–71 (2012). Medical Association of Malawi
2. Nikovski, D.: Constructing Bayesian networks for medical diagnosis from incomplete and partially correct statistics. IEEE Trans. Knowl. Data Eng. **12**(4), 509–516 (2000)
3. Sonoda, S., Saitoh, E., Nagai, S., Okuyama, Y., Suzuki, T., Suzuki, M.: Stroke outcome prediction using reciprocal number of initial activities of daily living status. J. Stroke **14**(1), 8–11 (2005)
4. Chumney, D., Nollinger, K., Shesko, K., Skop, K., Spencer, M., Newton, R.A.: Ability of functional independence measure to accurately predict functional outcome of stroke-specific population: systematic review. J. Rehabil. Res. Dev. **47**(1), 17–29 (2010)
5. Tokunaga, M., et al.: The stratification of motor FIM and cognitive FIM and the creation of four prediction formulas to enable higher prediction accuracy of multiple linear regression analysis with motor FIM gain as the objective variable—an analysis of the Japan Rehabilitation Database. Jpn. J. Compr. Rehabil. Sci. **8**, 21–29 (2017). Kaifukuki Rehabilitation Ward Association
6. Tokunaga, M., Mori, Y., Ogata, Y., Tanaka, Y., Uchino, K., Maeda, Y., et al.: Predicting FIM gain in stroke patients by adding median FIM gain stratified by FIM score at hospital admission to the explanatory variables in multiple regression analysis. Jpn. J. Compr. Rehabil. Sci. **7**, 13–18 (2016). Kaifukuki Rehabilitation Ward Association
7. Tokunaga, M., Sannomiya, K., Nakashima, Y., Nojiri, S., Tokisato, K., Katsura, K., et al.: Formula for predicting FIM gain and discharge FIM: methods using median values of FIM gain stratified by admission FIM, age, cognitive function, and transfer interval. Jpn. J. Compr. Rehabil. Sci. **6**, 6–13 (2015)
8. Isobe, T., Okada, Y.: Medical AI system to assist rehabilitation therapy. In: Perner, P. (ed.) ICDM 2018. LNCS (LNAI), vol. 10933, pp. 266–271. Springer, Cham (2018). https://doi.org/10.1007/978-3-319-95786-9_20
9. Value-based programs of CMS (Centers for medicare & medicaid services). https://www.cms.gov/Medicare/Quality-Initiatives-Patient-Assessment-Instruments/Value-Based-Programs/Value-Based-Programs.html. Accessed 05 Dec 2019
10. Value-based payment of medicaid. https://www.medicaid.gov/state-resource-center/innovation-accelerator-program/iap-functional-areas/value-based-payment/index.html. Accessed 05 Dec 2019
11. Ministry of health, labor and welfare. http://www.mhlw.go.jp/file/05-Shingikai-12404000-Hokenkyoku-Iryouka/0000169318.pdf. Accessed 05 Dec 2019
12. Hatsudai rehabilitation hospital. http://www.hatsudai-reha.or.jp/. Accessed 05 Dec 2019
13. Funabashi municipal rehabilitation hospital. http://www.funabashi-reha.com/. Accessed 05 Dec 2019

14. Nvidia GPU Tesla P 100. http://www.nvidia.com/object/tesla-p100.html. Accessed 05 Dec 2019
15. Intel CPU E5-1620 v3. https://ark.intel.com/products/82763/Intel-Xeon-Processor-E5-1620-v3-10M-Cache-3_50-GHz. Accessed 05 Dec 2019
16. Isobe, T., Tanida, N., Oishi, Y., Yoshida, K.: TCP acceleration technology for cloud computing: algorithm, performance evaluation in real network. In: 2014 International Conference on Advanced Technologies for Communications (ATC 2014), pp. 714–719. IEEE (2014)
17. Hitachi high-tech solutions corporation rehabilitation AI service https://www.hitachi-hightech.com/hsl/special/cloud/awina/english/about/. Accessed 10 Jan 2020

A Mobile Application Using Deep Learning to Automatically Classify Adult-Only Images

Fanyin Zhuang, Lei Ren, Qianying Dong, and Richard O. Sinnott$^{(\boxtimes)}$

School of Computing and Information Systems, University of Melbourne, Melbourne, Australia
rsinnott@unimelb.edu.au

Abstract. The Internet has become an essential part of everyday life. It links people with enormous amounts of information covering almost any topic imaginable. However harmful or inappropriate information such as pornography can also be easily found on the web which should not always be available, especially to minors. Internet filters are typically used to block such inappropriate content. These are largely based on the metadata related to the websites or by directly blocking the URLs related to those websites. However seemingly innocuous websites can contain undesirable images that should not be accessible to children. In this paper, we describe how images and videos can automatically be identified (classified) without any human supervision based on their subject matter. To achieve this, we apply deep learning methods to detect and classify adult-only image content from both images and live videos. We use the TensorFlow library and two pre-trained models: *MobileNet_v1* and *Inception_v3*, with an official (academic) pornography dataset including associated labelling. The performance of each model was investigated. The final solution was delivered as an iOS application to detect and classify photos and live videos based on their adult-only content. The app achieved an accuracy of over 92%.

Keywords: Deep learning · Convolutional Neural Networks · Pornography · iOS app · InceptionNet · MobileNet · TensorFlow

1 Introduction

Images and video are an essential part of the web. In 2014, statistics showed that people uploaded an average of 1.8 billion digital images every single day with over 657 billion photos uploaded per year [1]. This number is continually rising due to faster and easier Internet access to all corners of the globe, and the increasing use of portable computers and other communication devices such as laptops, smartphones and tablets. However, images can include harmful materials including pornographic and (in some countries/situations) illegal content [2]. Therefore, effective image filtering is needed to protect certain users, e.g. children, from such materials. Companies such as NetNanny operate by maintaining lists of URLs and blocking them from children using settings defined by adults [3]. However, the Internet is expanding rapidly, and such lists will always lose the battle with regards to sites that pop up that have not been flagged so that

© Springer Nature Switzerland AG 2020
R. Xu et al. (Eds.): AIMS 2020, LNCS 12401, pp. 140–155, 2020.
https://doi.org/10.1007/978-3-030-59605-7_11

they should be blocked. This problem also exists with mainstream social media sites such as Facebook, Twitter and Instagram. Detection based on actual image or video analysis and classification has the advantage of processing every image before it is uploaded or downloaded from the Internet. This would provide a much more effective and comprehensive filtering approach. This is the goal of this work: to create an iOS mobile app to detect and classify pornographic images from image content and live video streams. Facial recognition functionality is also added to support age detection. Combining these two detections, the app is capable of classifying pornographic images potentially involving underage child. The second aim of this paper is exploring different image classification methods and selecting solutions that achieve both accuracy and computational efficiency, i.e. to use the computational power of portable devices in real time.

The rest of the paper is structured as follows. Section 2 provides an overview of the data set used for this work. Specifically, we introduce the NPDI database and the classified images that it contains and how these images were augmented to support the deep learning training model. Section 3 focuses on the deep learning models that were applied. Section 4 presents the results in applying the models. Section 5 describes the iOS solution and finally Sect. 6 draws conclusions on the work and identifies areas of potential future work.

2 Dataset

The NPDI pornographic dataset provides one of the largest publicly available pornographic datasets used for research purposes [4]. It was collected by the NPDI group, the Federal University of Minas Gerais (UFMG) in Brazil. This dataset consists of approximately 80 h of 400 adult and 400 non-adult videos. 16,727 image frames were extracted from those videos [5]. 6,240 pornographic images were used in this work comprised together with 10,487 non-pornographic images.

The NPDI dataset is separated into three classes: *easy non-adult class, hard non-adult class* and *adult class*. The adult class includes a variety of adult-oriented video categories covering a wide ethnic diversity including Asian, black, white, and multi-ethnic pornographic images. The non-porn images contain challenging scenarios for disambiguation such as wrestling, swimming and people on beaches, i.e. the images include a significant amount of human skin being exposed, but in themselves they are not explicitly pornographic. Cartoon and anime style images are also included in all of the classes. The total amount of video and related images is shown in Table 1.

Table 1. Summary of the NPDI pornography dataset

Class	Videos	Hours	Key frames per video
Porn	400	57	15.6
Easy Non-porn	200	11.5	33.8
Difficult Non-porn	200	8.5	17.5
Overall	800	77	20.6

Data cleansing is an essential procedure to detect and correct corrupt or inaccurate data within a given dataset, especially one to be used for deep learning [6]. In this project, the images in the porn class were purified. Although the images in the porn class were all fetched from NPDI-based pornographic videos, there were many non-pornographic images existing in that class. The following six groups of pornographic images were manually moved from the porn class to the non-porn class to improve the purity of the data set and hence the accuracy of the model:

- Actors or actresses that were dressed;
- Portraits;
- Actors with only their upper body naked;
- Actors or actresses kissing whilst dressed;
- Girls in bikini girls, and
- Movie titles and/or blank image frames.

By applying data cleaning, the pornographic images were reduced from 6,240 images to 4,789 images, while the non-porn images increased from 10,480 images to 11,938 images.

One way to improve the performance of deep learning models is to increase the size of the training set. Apart from gathering more new data from different sources and manual labelling of the images and video frames, other methods can allow developers to increase the amount of data through data augmentation [7]. Data augmentation is an essential part of a Convolutional Neural Network (CNN) and can be used to capture the translational invariance of images. Some popular augmentations include support for grayscales, image flipping, random cropping, colour jitter, translation and image rotation. In this project, horizontal flipping, vertical flipping, image rotation, greyscales and random noises were used to increase the size of the original dataset, without jeopardizing the data quality.

2.1 Image Flipping

Flipping images is one of the most popular methods for image augmentation due to its simplicity. Images or videos can be taken from different angles and image flipping is used to simulate angle changes. Both horizontal and vertical flipping can be used to increase the number of images to improve the training model. The orientation does not adversely impact on the model performance.

2.2 Image Rotation

All videos in the NDPI dataset are taken in landscape mode. By rotating the images by 90°, the model can be used to recognize images or videos taken in portrait mode. This can be used to double the size of the data set.

2.3 Image Greyscale

Most of the training images are in colour. By converting them into greyscale images, a more robust model is created that can tackle greyscale or black and white images. To support this, an averaging method is used that averages the values of RGB channels to a black/white scale.

2.4 Image with Noise

Noise is another image augmentation technique. It widely used in adversarial training where batches of random noise are thrown into an image so that the model will fail to classify the image correctly as a result. Adding noise can be used to achieve a more robust model that can cope with imperfect data.

3 Model Selection and Training

Deep learning, also known as deep structured learning or hierarchical learning, is a sub-field of machine learning based on learning data representations [8]. For traditional machine learning methods, one of the key steps during model training is to identify and extract features. This is typically achieved by human experts [9]. With large variations of data formats and with the limitation of processing data in its raw form, this can be an extremely time-consuming task.

Conventional machine learning approaches are gradually being replaced by deep learning methods which have many advantages in handling such problems [10]. They are highly suited to learning representations of data whether the data is encoded in images, videos or other forms, e.g. text. The flexible architecture of deep learning networks can utilize untouched raw data directly. Deep learning can be used for discovering complex hidden structures in high-dimensional data that would otherwise unlikely be found by humans. The downside is that deep learning networks depend on large amounts of high-quality data, i.e. there should be lots of data with lots of features capturing the information of interest.

Traditional deep learning architectures had limitations in processing imaging data due to the computational complexity when dealing with an enormous number of parameters in the fully connected layer. This resulted in high computational workloads and overfitting problems. CNNs are one of the most popular deep learning architectures for image recognition and suited to tackle many of these issues [11].

There are many different CNNs that have been put forward. AlexNet was first shown in the 2012 ImageNet Large-Scale Visual Recognition Challenge and won the competition using a CNN with a test error rate as low as 15.4% while the second-best entry only achieved an error of 26.2% [12]. This network was made up of five convolutional layers, followed by max-pooling layers, and the last 3 layers were fully connected layers. The input layer took an image with size of $256 \times 256 \times 3$. An important feature of the AlexNet was the use of ReLU (Rectified Linear Unit) Nonlinearity layer.

MobileNet was put forward as a lightweight deep neural network model suitable for portable devices and embedded vision applications [13]. Compared to normal convolutions with the same depth of networks, MobileNet greatly decreases the number of parameters required with only a small reduction in accuracy by using depth-wise separable convolutions [13].

The Inception network provided an important milestone in developing CNN classifiers [14]. Before the Inception network, the most popular CNN stacks had many layers that were used to get better performance. InceptionNet on the other hand, was engineered and constructed to push the performance in terms of speed and accuracy by reducing the relative complexity [15].

There are many deep learning frameworks available today. The most popular ones include TensorFlow, Keras, Caffe, PyTorch, Chainer, MxNet and Theano [27]. TensorFlow is arguably one of the most widely supported deep learning frameworks with a highly flexible system architecture [16]. It supports computational deployment across various platforms, from desktop computers to portable devices. In addition, TensorFlow comes with tools such as *TensorBoard* which provides an effective way to visualize the network model and performance. *TensorFlowLite* is a lightweight version of Tensorflow library, that is able to run machine learning models on portable or embedded devices. It supports the majority of operations available in standard TensorFlow library. As such, many TensorFlow models can be converted directly and executed on a portable device. TensorFlowLite uses various methods to optimize the operation of a given model to achieve low latency that is especially important on portable devices [17]. TensorFlow also provides support for several programming language such as Python, C++ and R. For these reasons, TensorFlow was selected for this work.

Mobilenet_v1_1.0_224 and *Inception_v3* were chosen as the models for this work. Both of them are supported directly by TensorFlowLite. MobileNet is specially designed for mobile applications with a small memory footprint (around 15 Mb for *Mobilenet_v1_1.0_224*) and low latency (around 150 ms for *Mobilenet_v1_1.0_224*). The *Inception_v3* model was selected due to its high accuracy. The model is medium-sized (approximately 80 Mb) whilst the latency of the model is still acceptable compared to other high accuracy models such as *Inception_ResNet* or *Inception_v4*. A comparison of the TensorFlowLite models is shown in Fig. 1.

Model Name	Model_Size	Top-1 Accuracy	Top-5 Accuracy	TF Lite Performance^^	Tensorflow Performance
DenseNet	43.6 Mb	64.2%	85.6%	894 ms	1262 ms
SqueezeNet	5.0 Mb	49.0%	72.9%	224 ms	255 ms
NASNet mobile	21.4 Mb	73.9%	91.5%	261 ms	389 ms
NASNet large	355.3 Mb	82.6%	96.1%	6697 ms	7940 ms
ResNet_V2_101	178.3 Mb	76.8%	93.6%	1880 ms	1970 ms
Inception_V3	95.3 Mb	77.9%	93.8%	1433 ms	1522 ms
Inception_V4	170.7 Mb	80.1%	95.1%	2986 ms	3139 ms
Inception_ResNet_V2	121.0 Mb	77.5%	94.0%	2731 ms	2926 ms
Mobilenet_V1_1.0_224	16.9 Mb	71.0%	89.9%	160.1 ms	224.3 ms

Fig. 1. Model comparison of hosted TensorFlow Lite models

Transfer learning is a machine learning method where a model trained for one task is used as the starting point for a model on another related task [18]. In the field of deep learning, one common practice of transfer learning is to use a pre-trained model as the starting point for computer vision and natural language processing tasks. As noted, in this work, the pre-trained *Inception_V3* and *Mobilenet_V1_1.0_224* models were used. The training parameters associated with these two models are listed in Table 2.

Table 2. Training parameters setup

Parameters	Values
Training steps	20,000
Learning rate	0.01
Training data percentage	80%
Validation data percentage	10%
Testing data percentage	10%
Training batch size	100
Validation batch size	100

Two key aspects of any given machine learning model are accuracy and loss.

4 Results

The training accuracy and cross-entropy loss figures of training data and validation data for *Mobilenet_v1_1.0_224* model and *Inception_v3* model are shown in Fig. 2 and Fig. 3 respectively.

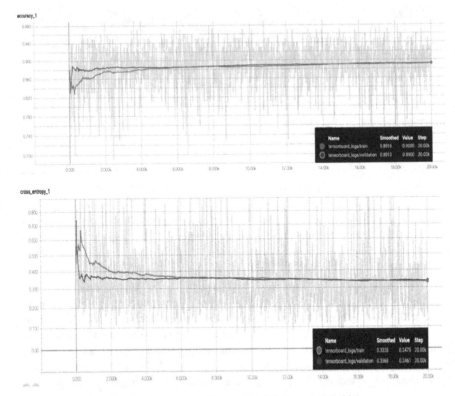

Fig. 2. Accuracy and Loss of *MobileNet_v1_1.0_224*

For the *MobileNet_v1_1.0_224* model, the accuracy for both the training data and the validation data continually rises until the training iteration reaches step 6,000. Then the accuracy values remain stable until the end of the training process. At iteration 20,000, the accuracy of the training data reaches 89.16% while the accuracy of the validation data reaches 89.13%. The cross-entropy loss figure at the bottom shows a similar trend. The two-line segments meet when the iteration reaches 6000. The final cross-entropy losses of the training and validation data are 0.3328 and 0.3368 respectively. The accuracy for both data sets are very close to one another. Therefore, no overfitting appears at the end of the training session. The testing accuracy was 88% with 10,381 testing images. The total training time for *MobileNet_v1_1.0_224* was approximately 1 h.

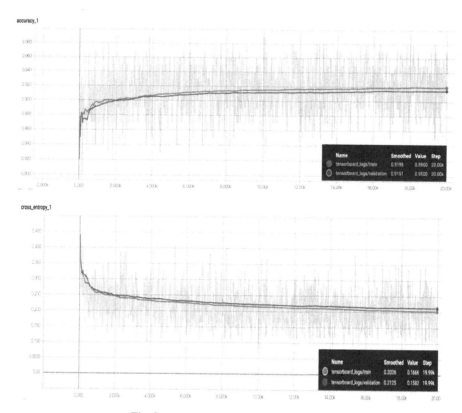

Fig. 3. Accuracy and Loss of *Inception_v3*

The upper part of Fig. 3 shows that the accuracy of the training and validation data keeps rising until the training iteration reaches approximately 18,000 cycles. The accuracy values stay almost the same until the end of the training process. At iteration 20,000, the accuracy of the training data reaches 91.98% while the accuracy of the validation data reaches 91.51%. The cross-entropy loss figure at the bottom shows the same trend. The final cross-entropy loss related to training and validation data are 0.2026 and 0.2125 respectively. It is obvious that no sign of overfitting appears at the end of the training session. The final testing accuracy was 92% with 10,381 testing images. The total training time for *Inception_v3* was about 6 h.

Although the training time of *Inception_v3* was almost 6 times more than that of *MobileNet_v1_1.0_224*, the overall performance of Inception was better with a higher overall accuracy and a lower loss.

Based on this, in the following sections, we show how the *Inception_v3* model was used for real world performance testing and integrated into an iOS mobile app. Since *Mobilenet_v1_1.0_224* was already specialized to work on mobile devices, there were no more tests required to ensure it could work on mobile devices.

Although the model was tested with images selected from the NDPI dataset, more comprehensive testing was necessary to measure the real-world performance. A Python program was written to automatically crawl images from Google Image Search. The number of pornographic images used was 389 after data cleansing. In addition, 757 non-pornographic images were downloaded from the Internet across the following categories shown in Table 3.

Table 3. The structure of testing data

Image group	Number of images
Boxing	90
Infant	96
Landscape	76
Swimmer	80
Architecture	80
Sumo wrestling	82
Portrait	90
Wrestling	83
Beach girl	80
Total	757

Table 4 shows the testing results.

Table 4. The testing results

		Predicted class	
		Porn	No-porn
Actual class	Porn	321	68
	Non-porn	125	632

The *recall, precision* and *F1 score* were calculated to explain the performance of the *Inception_v3* model. The *recall* value of 82.52% showed that the majority of pornographic images were indeed correctly labelled as pornographic images. The *precision* value indicated that 71.97% of images labelled as porn were actually porn. This number is slight lower because of a larger portion of non-porn images were detected as porn. This is due to the large misclassification rates of infant, sumo wrestling and girls on beach images (discussed later). The F1 score was used to measure the overall accuracy of the model with the asymmetric testing dataset. The F1 score was 76.88% which shows a balance between precision and recall.

Figure 4 and Fig. 5 show the accuracy and average confidence for pornographic and non-pornographic image classification.

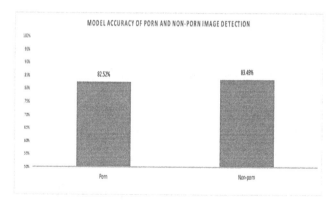

Fig. 4. Accuracy for pornographic and non-pornographic image detection

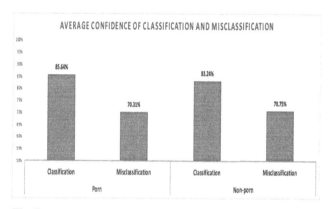

Fig. 5. Average confidence for classification and misclassification

The accuracy for pornographic and non-pornographic image detection was 82.52% and 83.49% respectively. The accuracies are reasonably high. The average confidence of correct classification of porn images was 85.64% while the average confidence of misclassification was 70.31%. The non-pornographic image detection showed similar results with the average confidence of correct classification at 83.24% and misclassification at 70.75%. As seen, the average confidence of misclassification was lower than that of correct classification. There are two possible reasons for this. Firstly, the model fails to detect the correct features of an image and hence misclassifies it. A second possible reason is that the image is somehow in between a pornographic and non-pornographic category. So, the model misclassifies the image with a confidence close to 50%.

Figure 6 shows the comparison between the accuracy for different non-porn image groups and Fig. 7 the average confidence of classification for misclassification of non-porn image groups.

The accuracy and prediction confidence were also considered among the different non-porn image groups. Figure 7 shows the accuracy of difference non-pornographic image groups. As can be seen, boxing, landscapes, swimmers, architecture and wrestling

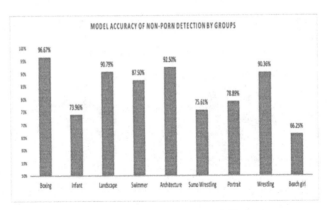

Fig. 6. Accuracy of different non-pornographic image groups

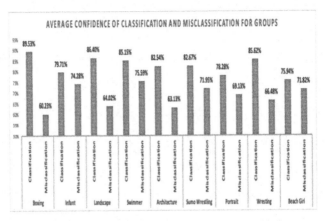

Fig. 7. The average confidence of different non-pornographic image groups

groups all have accuracies above 87%. For portrait images, sumo wrestling and infant images the accuracy decreases to 78.89%, 75.61% and 73.96% respectively. The reasons for this low accuracy are:

1. Large area of human body and skin are exposed in the non-porn images.
2. The skin tone and body shape of sumo wrestlers make them slightly more difficult to distinguish from pornographic images.
3. Nudity is common in newborn and infant photography.

The beach girl image group showed the worst result. Not only was the accuracy the lowest at only 66.25%, but also the average confidence for correct classification and misclassification were close to one another. This result may still be acceptable, since whilst many beach photos may not be considered as pornography, they may nevertheless can contain adult content and hence be classified as soft-core pornography.

5   iOS Application Development

In this section, we introduce the iOS application that realizes these models.

5.1   Architecture Design

This application was written in Objective-C and Objective-C++. The application was able to classify images and live video into two categories: pornographic and non-pornographic. The app supports three primary functionalities:

1. Pornographic image recognition and facial detection. Users can either select a photo from a photo library or take a photo through the camera. The image will be shown in the top screen, while the image classification and percentage of confidence are shown at the bottom of the screen. If there are human faces in the image, the application will identify them, and bounding boxes placed around the faces.
2. Live pornography video recognition. Live video will be shown in the screen. Confidence scores of both pornographic and non-pornographic image classification will be shown in the screen if the number is higher than 10%.
3. The application allows users to switch between *Mobilenet_v1* and the *Inception_v3* model. This is used for a performance comparison between the different models. More models could also be added to the application in the future.

The user interface to the iOS app is shown in Fig. 8.

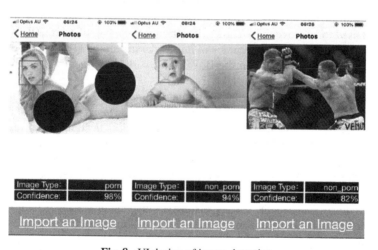

Fig. 8. UI design of image detection

6   Related Work

For years, researchers have been looking into better ways to detect and classify adult-only images. There are numerous methods that have been applied to address the problem. These can be categorized into three major approaches:

- Human body feature detection;
- Traditional machine learning, and
- Deep learning.

Historically, human body detection approaches have mainly focused on detecting human body information in an image. The primary goal is typically to determine whether a naked human body (skin/flesh) is in an image or not. Based on human body geometry models and skin colour detection techniques, pornographic classification of an image is based on combining all skin areas detected in an image and then comparing it with human body geometry models [20]. The downside of this approach is that it cannot cover all possible relative positions of human body parts. Furthermore, it requires significant computational power, which is often not practical for many applications, e.g. in a mobile device.

Most existing pornography detection research belongs to the category of traditional machine learning and rely on image analysis with some form of machine intelligence. An image analysis pipeline usually includes a feature extractor followed by an image classifier [21]. The feature extractor obtains the key information from the input images and feeds them into the pre-trained image classifiers. The most important feature of pornographic imagery is the human skin colour [22]. Support Vector Machines (SVM) are widely used as image classifiers, where an image is considered pornographic if it contains too many skin coloured pixels, i.e. the SVM is used as an indicator of nudity.

However, skin colour recognition is not reliable in many scenarios such as a face closeups or people on a beach with a large number of skin pixels appearing in a given image. Therefore, new computer vision models and pornography detection algorithms have been used to improve the accuracy. For instance, the bag-of-words (BoW) model was introduced to improve the accuracy of image classification [23] and the BossaNova representation designed based on the BoW framework subsequently used to classify pornographic videos [24].

Different from traditional methods of handcrafting image features and classifiers, another approach that has drawn a great attention in recent years is deep learning. Deep learning methods combine both feature extraction and classification into a single module which involves less or even no human supervision in terms of selection of features and classification. Some studies claim 98% of accuracy on pornographic image detection using Convolutional Neural Networks [25]. Other studies combine pornography detection and age detection for child pornography recognition [26]. However, these approaches do not focus on the specific challenges inherent in making these deep learning models run in a real time manner on devices of limited computational capacity, i.e. mobile devices.

In other application domains, many researchers have focused on different image classification problems. These often include image detection and associated classification. Examples of some of the related applications include mobile apps for flowers/plants [28], dogs [29], cats [30], trees and canopy volume estimation [31], trucks and trailers [32], estimating the yield of fruit crops [33], counting moving people through a cascaded multi-task neural network [33] through to poisonous and non-poisonous spider detection.

7 Conclusions and Future Work

This work has explored how deep learning approaches can be applied to identify and classify pornographic images. The work used two leading deep learning models (*Mobilenet_v1_1.0_224* and *Inception-v3*). These were re-trained for adult-only image recognition. The model performance was measured through training procedures and real-world testing. The *Inception-v3* model achieved an accuracy score of 92% during training and reached an F1-score of 76.88% during real-time testing using data of a sufficiently realistic and complex nature.

Deep learning models are able to learn via stochastic training algorithms, however as discussed, they are sensitive to the training data that is used. The same network model may deliver radically different results depending on the quality of the data sets. Different deep learning methods have their own pros and cons when dealing with different types of data. A neural network that has a high variance in outcomes can make it hard to finalize a good model. To tackle this, ensemble methods such as model averaging using multiple models that contribute equally to a combined prediction could be explored [19]. Using ensemble methods, the variance of neural networks can subsequently be reduced, and the overall prediction performance improved.

Different from ensemble methods which train multiple models to perform the same task, multiple deep learning applications such as image classification, object detection, facial recognition can all be combined to provide a more comprehensive solution for a given task. For example, human body part detection and facial recognition could be added to the application to provide more confidence in the adult content detection.

Other work could include the embedding of deep learning solutions into Internet browsers, e.g. as plug-ins that could be rolled out across schools for example. This would require greater consideration of the performance aspects to ensure that non-adult content Internet browsing was not adversely impacted.

References

1. Meeker, M.: Internet Trends Report 2018. Kleiner Perkins, 30 May 2018. https://www.kleine rperkins.com/internet-trends
2. Zheng, H., Daoudi, M.: Blocking adult images based on statistical skin detection. ELCVIA Electron. Lett. Comput. Vis. Image Anal. 4(2), 1 (2004)
3. Blocking Images on Google: Netnanny.com (2019). https://www.netnanny.com/kb/255/
4. Avila, S., Thome, N., Cord, M., Valle, E., Araújo, A.d.A.: Pooling in image representation: the visual codeword point of view. Comput. Vis. Image Underst. 117(5), 453–465 (2013)
5. Ou, X., Ling, H., Yu, H., Li, P., Zou, F., Liu, S.: Adult image and video recognition by a deep multicontext network and fine-to-coarse strategy. ACM Trans. Intell. Syst. Technol. 8(5), 1–25 (2017)
6. Wu, S.: A review on coarse warranty data and analysis. Reliab. Eng. Syst. Saf. 114, 1–11 (2013)
7. Mikolajczyk, A., Grochowski, M.: Data augmentation for improving deep learning in image classification problem. In: 2018 International Interdisciplinary Ph.D. Workshop (IIPhDW) (2018)
8. Schmidhuber, J.: Deep learning in neural networks: an overview. Neural Netw. 61, 85–117 (2015)

9. Why Deep Learning over Traditional Machine Learning? Towards Data Science (2019). https://towardsdatascience.com/why-deep-learning-is-needed-over-traditional-machine-learning-1b6a99177063

10. Cayir, A., Yenidogan, I., Dag, H.: Feature extraction based on deep learning for some traditional machine learning methods. In: 2018 3rd International Conference on Computer Science and Engineering (UBMK) (2018)

11. Li, Z., Zhu, X., Wang, L., Guo, P.: Image classification using convolutional neural networks and kernel extreme learning machines. In: 2018 25th IEEE International Conference on Image Processing (ICIP) (2018)

12. Krizhevsky, A., Sutskever, I., Hinton, G.E.: ImageNet classification with deep convolutional neural networks. Commun. ACM **60**(6), 84–90 (2017)

13. Howard, A., et al.: MobileNets: efficient convolutional neural networks for mobile vision applications, arXiv.org (2019). https://arxiv.org/abs/1704.04861

14. Szegedy, C, et al.: Going deeper with convolutions. In: 2015 IEEE Conference on Computer Vision and Pattern Recognition (CVPR) (2015)

15. A Simple Guide to the Versions of the Inception Network. Towards Data Science (2019). https://towardsdatascience.com/a-simple-guide-to-the-versions-of-the-inception-network-7fc52b863202

16. Demirovic, D., Skejic, E., Serifovic-Trbalic, A.: Performance of some image processing algorithms in tensorflow. In: 2018 25th International Conference on Systems, Signals and Image Processing (IWSSIP) (2018)

17. TensorFlow Lite: Knowledge Transfer, 01 November 2018. http://androidkt.com/tenserflow-lite/

18. Pan, S.J., Yang, Q.: A survey on transfer learning. IEEE Trans. Knowl. Data Eng. **22**(10), 1345–1359 (2010)

19. Kamp, M., et al.: Efficient decentralized deep learning by dynamic model averaging. In: Berlingerio, M., Bonchi, F., Gärtner, T., Hurley, N., Ifrim, G. (eds.) ECML PKDD 2018. LNCS (LNAI), vol. 11051, pp. 393–409. Springer, Cham (2019). https://doi.org/10.1007/978-3-030-10925-7_24

20. Hu, W., Wu, O., Chen, Z., Fu, Z., Maybank, S.: Recognition of pornographic web pages by classifying texts and images. IEEE Trans. Pattern Anal. Mach. Intell. **29**(6), 1019–1034 (2007)

21. Moustafa, M.: Applying deep learning to classify pornographic images and videos, arXiv.org (2019). https://arxiv.org/abs/1511.08899

22. Nuraisha, S., Pratama, F.I., Budianita, A., Soeleman, M.A.: Implementation of K-NN based on histogram at image recognition for pornography detection. In: 2017 International Seminar on Application for Technology of Information and Communication (iSemantic) (2017)

23. Lou, X., Huang, D., Fan, L., Xu, A.: An image classification algorithm based on bag of visual words and multi-kernel learning. J. Multimed. **9**(2) (2014). https://doi.org/10.4304/jmm.9.2.269-277

24. Souza, R.A.D., Almeida, R.P.D., Moldovan, A.-N., Patrocinio, Z.K.G.D., Guimaraes, S.J.F.: Gameplay genre video classification by using mid-level video representation. In: 2016 29th SIBGRAPI Conference on Graphics, Patterns and Images (SIBGRAPI) (2016)

25. Nian, F., Li, T., Wang, Y., Xu, M., Wu, J.: Pornographic image detection utilizing deep convolutional neural networks. Neurocomputing **210**, 283–293 (2016)

26. Jung, J., Makhijani, R., Morlot, A.: Combining CNNs for detecting pornography in the absence of labeled training data. http://cs231n.stanford.edu/reports/2017/pdfs/700.pdf

27. Erickson, B.J., Korfiatis, P., Akkus, Z., Kline, T., Philbrick, K.: Toolkits and libraries for deep learning. J. Digit. Imaging **30**(4), 400–405 (2017). https://doi.org/10.1007/s10278-017-9965-6

28. Gao, M., Lin, L., Sinnott, R.O.: A mobile application for plant recognition using deep learning. In: IEEE e-Science Conference 2017, Auckland, New Zealand, October 2017
29. Wu, F., Chen, W., Sinnott, R.O.: A mobile application for dog breed recognition and detection based on deep learning. In: IEEE/ACM International Conference on Big Data Computing, Applications and Technologies (BDCAT), Zurich, Switzerland, December 2018
30. Yang, L., Zhang, X., Sinnott, R.O.: A mobile application for cat detection and breed recognition based on deep learning. In: 1st IEEE International Workshop on Artificial Intelligence for Mobile, Hangzhou, China, February 2019
31. Wang, K., Huo, R., Jia, Y., Sinnott, R.O.: A mobile application for tree classification and canopy calculation using machine learning. In: 1st IEEE International Workshop on Artificial Intelligence for Mobile, Hangzhou, China, February 2019
32. Chen, L., Jia, Y., Sun, P., Sinnott, R.O.: Identification and classification of trucks and trailers on the road network through deep learning. In: 6th IEEE/ACM International Conference on Big Data Computing, Applications and Technologies, Auckland, New Zealand, December 2019
33. Yu, H., Song, S., Ma, S., Sinnott, R.O.: Predicting yield: identifying, classifying and counting fruit through deep learning. In: 6th IEEE/ACM International Conference on Big Data Computing, Applications and Technologies, Auckland, New Zealand, December 2019
34. Zhao, P., Lyu, X., Wei, S., Sinnott, R.O.: Crowd-counting through a cascaded, multi-task convolutional neural network. In: 6th IEEE/ACM International Conference on Big Data Computing, Applications and Technologies, Auckland, New Zealand, December 2019
35. Yang, D., Ding, X., Ye, Z., Sinnott, R.O.: Poisonous spider recognition through deep learning. In: Australia Computer Science Week, Melbourne, Australia, February 2020

Short Paper Track

OSAF_e: One-Stage Anchor Free Object Detection Method Considering Effective Area

Yong Zhang[1], Lizong Zhang[1,3(✉)], Zhihong Rao[1,2], Guiduo Duan[1,3], and Chunyu Wang[4]

[1] School of Computer Science and Engineering, University of Electronic Science and Technology of China, Chengdu 611731, China
`l.zhang@uestc.edu.cn`
[2] China Electronic Technology Cyber Security Co., Ltd., Chengdu 610000, China
[3] Trusted Cloud Computing and Big Data Key Laboratory of Sichuan Province, Chengdu 611731, China
[4] School of Information and Software Engineering, University of Electronic Science and Technology of China, Chengdu 610054, China

Abstract. The task of object detection is to identify the bounding box of the object and its corresponding category in images. In this paper, we propose a new one-stage anchor free object detection algorithm OSAF_e, with the consideration of effective mapping area. A feature extraction network is used to obtain high level feature, and the true bounding box of the object in the original image is mapped to the grid of feature map, in order to perform category prediction and bounding box regression. The proposed algorithm is evaluated with the Pascal Voc dataset, and the experiments indicate that it has a better result.

Keywords: Object detection · OSAF_e · Effective area · Feature map grid

1 Introduction

Object detection is a classic problem in the field of computer vision. It aims to provide the location and category information of objects in given images. The deep learning theory draws the attention of many researches, and the emerged anchor-free approach is a hot-spot in this area.

Recently, most of the researchers focus on anchor free method [1, 2, 10]. One special method, CornerNet [1], performs bounding box regression by detecting a pair of corners of a bounding box and grouping them to form the final result, but the network only predicts a set of position offsets when the corners of multiple objects fall in the same gird. FCOS [2] and FoveaBox [10] rely on features in each grid to perform classification and bounding box regression, where the detection category of each grid is determined by the mapping of true bounding boxes.

However, mapping the bounding box of the object in the original image to the feature map grid brings two problems. First, how to compute the mapping area in the feature map, Second, how to determine the detection category of the occlusion area.

R. Xu et al. (Eds.): AIMS 2020, LNCS 12401, pp. 159–167, 2020.
https://doi.org/10.1007/978-3-030-59605-7_12

Based on the idea that the results of bounding boxes predicated by locations far away from the center of an object is of low-quality [2], we only map the 1/4 center regions of the true bounding box to the feature map as effective mapping area. When multiply bounding boxes are mapped to the same grid, the detection category of this gird is determined by the distance to the right bounding boxes.

The contributions of this paper are as follows:

First, we propose a method to compute the mapping area in the feature map that specially draw attention to the features near to centers of an object.

Second, we propose a method to determine the grid detection category when multiple object bounding box are mapped to the same feature map grid.

Third, we conduct a series of experiments in the Pascal Voc dataset. And the results demonstrate the effectiveness of our method.

2   Related Work

At present, deep learning based object detection methods mainly including one-stage methods and two-stage methods. One-stage methods simplifies the object detection process into a unified end-to-end regression problem, YOLO series [5–7] and SSD [8] are representatives. Two-stage methods divide detection into two stages, firstly, a RPN [15] network is used to select candidate regions, then classify the candidate regions and positioned to output finally results, such R-CNN series [3, 4, 15].

According to the differences of whether to use anchor boxes in bounding boxes regression period, we divide object detection into anchor-based methods and anchor free methods. In anchor-based methods, the network learns a function from anchor box to the true bounding box [3, 4, 7]. However, anchor-based detectors need to preset many hyperparameters, such as anchor's shape, size, number, IoU threshold, and so on. These parameters need to be carefully designed and are very dependent on the distribution of bounding boxes in the dataset. At the same time, it also brings imbalance [12, 13] between positive and negative samples.

Anchor free methods directly predicate the bounding boxes, simplifies the detection process [1, 2, 5, 15]. However, it cannot effectively solve the problem of occlusion. Traditionally, FPN [17] is used to detect objects in separate layers in order to solve the occlusion problem, however, the occlusion still appears in single layers.

Motivated by above contents, we proposed a new one-stage anchor free object detection method with the consideration of effective mapping area. We first map the bounding boxes of an image into feature map to divide detection category of each gird. Then based on the right distance judging metrics to divide the overlapping gird detection category in order to solve the problem of occlusion.

3   Methodology

3.1   Overall Network Architecture

In this paper, we introduce OSAF_e to develop a general model by incorporating the one-stage object detection process with the consideration of effective area. An overview of our OSAF_e can be found in Fig. 1. More specially, we first calculate effective mapping area in feature maps to generate high-level semantic area of a bounding by mapping true bounding boxes of an image to feature map grids. Then judging the predication task of each feature map grid to overcome the problem of occlusion by determining the distance to right bounding boxes. Finally, the channel features in each grid is used to perform class prediction and bounding box regression.

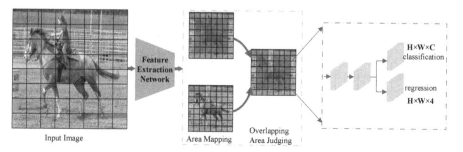

Fig. 1. Overall network architecture

3.2 Area Mapping

Our OSAF_e method first mapping true bounding boxes in an image to feature maps to generate high-level semantic areas. Define the input image size as X and the total down sampling step of feature extraction network as S, then the size of the feature map is X/S, defining the bounding box of an object in the image as $B_i = \{l_i, r_i, t_i, b_i, c_i\}$, the area mapped by the bounding box B_i on the feature map is $B_{fi} = \{l_{fi}, r_{fi}, t_{fi}, b_{fi}, c_i\}$, The mapping functions are shown below,

$$l_{fi} = \begin{cases} l_i/S, & if\ l_i/S - l_i/S \leq 0.5 \\ l_i/S + 1, & else \end{cases} \tag{1}$$

$$r_{fi} = \begin{cases} r_i/S, & if\ r_i/S - r_i/S \leq 0.5 \\ r_i/S - 1, & else \end{cases} \tag{2}$$

$$t_{fi} = \begin{cases} t_i/S, & if\ t_i/S - t_i/S \leq 0.5 \\ t_i/S + 1, & else \end{cases} \tag{3}$$

$$b_{fi} = \begin{cases} b_i/S, & if\ b_i/S - b_i/S \leq 0.5 \\ b_i/S - 1, & else \end{cases} \tag{4}$$

Based on the idea that the results of bounding boxes predicated by locations far away from center of an object is of low-quality [2]. we draw on FoveaBox [10] and propose the idea of effective mapping area. Specifically, we fix the center point of bounding box in original image, and set the effective width and height of the object bounding box to half of the original width and height, then use the mapping operation shown in function 1, 2, 3 and 4 to generate effective feature map area of object $B_{efi} = \{l_{efi}, r_{efi}, t_{efi}, b_{efi}, c_i\}$.

During training, when the feature map grid (x, y) falls within feature map area B_{efi}, the grid is considered as a positive sample and sets the detect category label of this grid is c_i, otherwise it is a negative sample and its detection category label is 0.

3.3 Overlapping Area Judging

Our OSAF_e method also brings overlapping area judging problem, which doesn't exist in anchor-based detectors. When multiple bounding boxes in an image overlaps, the overlapping grid belongs to multiple categories in Fig. 2.

In this way, it is necessary to determine the detection category in overlapping grid. We simply calculate the distance from the center point of grid to the right of multiple overlapping bounding boxes, and select the smallest distance corresponding category as detection category label of this grid.

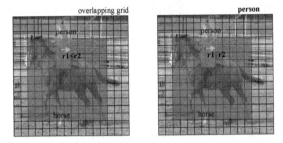

Fig. 2. Right distance judging

3.4 Bounding Box Regression

We based on the channel features in grid (x, y) to perform bounding box regression [2]. Its output is a 4D vector $\{l_p, t_p, r_p, b_p\}$ of the distance from the current grid center to the four sides of normalized bounding box. Let the center point of current grid is (x^i, y^i), the 4D vector of the regression of bounding box can be formulated as,

$$l_p = x^i - l_i, \ r_p = r_i - x^i \tag{5}$$

$$t_p = y^i - t_i, \ b_p = b_i - y^i \tag{6}$$

It is different from anchor-based detectors, which only consider the anchor boxes with a highly enough IoU with ground-truth boxes as positive samples.

3.5 Loss Function

We define the training loss as follows:

$$L_{total} = L_{cls} + L_{box} \tag{7}$$

$$L_{cls} = \sum\nolimits_{i=0}^{s^2} \sum\nolimits_{j=0}^{c} \left(1 - I_i^{ige}\right)\left(p_{cij} - t_{cij}\right)^2 \tag{8}$$

$$L_{box} = \sum\nolimits_{i=0}^{s^2} I_i^{obj}\left[\left(l_{pi} - l_{ti}\right)^2 + \left(r_{pi} - r_{ti}\right)^2 + \left(t_{pi} - t_{ti}\right)^2 + \left(b_{pi} - b_{ti}\right)^2\right] \tag{9}$$

Following SSD [8], the legislation activation function is used for classification process, where loss includes classification loss and bounding box regression loss, s^2 represents the total number of feature map grids.

I_i^{ige} indicates that the grid (x, y) falls within B_{fi} but outside B_{efi}, and the IoU of the predicted bounding box and the true bounding box in this gird is greater than 0.5.

I_i^{obj} shows that the bounding box regression loss is calculated only when the grid is divided into positive samples. The grid is divided into positive samples based on the following two cases,

Case 1: The grid (x, y) falls within the effective feature map area B_{efi},
Case 2: The grid (x, y) falls in the I_i^{ige} area.

4 Experiment

Experiment Data. We perform the experiments on the Pascal Voc data set. The samples from 2008 to 2012 are mixed for joint training. The samples of the training set and validation set are scrambled and mixed, and the number of training samples and validation samples are regenerated in a 4:1 ratio. The final training samples are 9633, and the validation samples are 1905. All experimental result data and analysis are performed on the 2012 test set.

Network Architecture. We treat the state-of-the-art YOLOv3 [7] as our baseline and implement OSAF_e stacked on it in TensorFlow. Darknet-53 pretrained on ImageNet [14] is used as our backbone network for feature extraction. We fixe input image size as 416×416 during training and testing. The OSAF_e network just replaces YOLOv3's three anchor-based layer with anchor free layer.

Parameter Settings. A wide range of data augmentation techniques are used to prevent overfitting when training. We apply momentum optimization algorithm to optimize the model. Using piecewise metrics to adjust learning rate, the first 25 epochs are 1e−4, the middle 40 epochs are 3e−5 and the last 35 epochs are 1e−4.

4.1 Comparison with Different Size of Feature Maps

We report the result comparisons on OSAF_e with different size of feature maps in Table 1. We adopt the metrics Average Precision (AP) across IoU thresholds from 0.5 to 0.7 with an interval of 0.1 to evaluate the performance. C1, C2, and C3 respectively indicate that the task of object detection is performed on feature maps with size of 13 × 13, 26 × 26, and 52 × 52.

As can be seen, our OSAF_e achieves an AP^{50} of 61.5% compared to 60.8% when considering effective area in C2 layer for training and evaluation. Significant performance gap can also be observed for AP^{60} and AP^{70}. This verifies the effectiveness that the grid channel features far away from the center of an object in feature map is of low-quality.

We can also see that our OSAF_e achieves highest APs scores in C2 layer, the reasons can be that C1 layer lost most features of small objects when feature extraction, and the large objects have larger mapping areas one feature map in C3 layer, simple NMS method cannot effective remove the wrong bounding box predication results.

Table 1. Comparison of Average Precision (AP) on different size of feature maps.

Feature layer	Effective area	AP^{50}	AP^{60}	AP^{70}
C1 [13 × 13]	✓	59.3	50.5	30.2
	×	59.0	49.2	28.8
C2 [26 × 26]	✓	**61.5**	**52.1**	**38.5**
	×	60.8	50.3	32.6
C3 [52 × 52]	✓	60.2	48.3	30.5
	×	55.3	43.7	25.4

Figure 3 shows some qualitative results using C2 layer as detection layer which also considers the effective mapping area. The results show that our OSAF_e can effectively solve the problem of occlusion and can detect objects in some complex scenes.

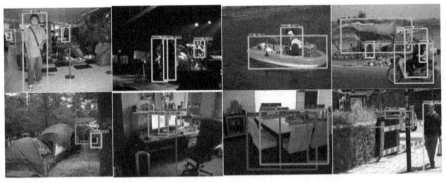

Fig. 3. Qualitative examples showing our OSAF_e detection result.

4.2 Comparison with Different IoU Thresholds for NMS

To better understanding the simple NMS method cannot effective remove wrong bounding boxes prediction results, we compare different IoU thresholds for NMS period in

Table 2. Note that larger object can predicate more bounding boxes regression results for our OSAF_e performs bounding boxes predication in every feature map grid. We choose C3 layer to conduct experiment for it can generate at most 2704 bounding boxes predication results, but 676 in C2 layer, 169 in C1 layer.

As can be seen, our OSAF_e achieves poor AP^{50} performance score when using traditional 0.5 IoU thresholds for NMS. This indicates that the bounding boxes regression results for larger object are more disordered, we need set lower IoU threshold to dislodge as many as wrong bounding boxes predication results. Furthermore, we set a series of IoU threshold scores for comparison, the results show that 0.4 threshold get the best performance.

Table 2. Comparison with different IoU thresholds for NMS

Feature layer	IoU threshold	AP^{50}
C3	0.2	59.3
	0.3	60.5
	0.35	60.9
	0.4	**61.1**
	0.45	60.7
	0.5	**60.4**

4.3 Comparison with State-of-the-Art

We report the results comparisons on VOC 2012 test dataset in Table 3. We compare with two-stage detectors, R-CNN [15], Fast R-CNN [3], Faster R-CNN [4], and one-stage detector YOLOV1 [5]. Our OSAF_e detector uses 0.5 threshold for NMS, C2 layer for detection and also considers effective area.

Table 3. Part of the leaderboard in OVC 2012 test set.

VOC 2012 test	mAP	aero	bike	bird	boat	bottle	bus	car	cat	chair	cow	table	dog	horse	mbike	person	plant	sheep	sofa	train	tv
Fast R-CNN	68.4	82.3	78.4	70.8	52.3	38.7	77.8	71.6	89.3	44.2	73.0	55.0	87.5	80.5	80.8	72.0	35.1	68.3	65.7	80.4	68.4
Faster R-CNN	70.4	84.9	79.8	74.3	53.9	49.8	77.5	75.9	88.5	45.6	77.1	55.3	86.9	81.7	80.9	79.6	40.1	72.6	60.9	81.2	61.5
YOLOv1	57.9	77.0	67.2	57.7	38.3	22.7	68.3	55.9	81.4	36.2	60.8	48.5	77.2	72.3	71.3	63.5	28.9	52.2	54.8	73.9	50.8
R-CNN	49.6	68.1	63.8	46.1	29.4	27.9	56.6	57.0	65.9	26.5	48.7	39.5	66.2	57.3	65.4	53.2	26.2	54.5	38.1	50.6	51.6
OSAF_e	61.5	76.2	**73.0**	60.1	40.1	**36.1**	71.2	55.5	83.0	**41.9**	57.4	51.1	79.5	70.1	68.5	65.8	**35.2**	51.2	57.6	**78.6**	67.2

As can be seen, the mAP criterion scores of OSAF_e is 5.5% higher than YOLOV1 [5]. Among them, the AP of bike, bottle, chair, plant, and train categories are all improved more than 10% than YOLOv1 [5]. Moreover, OSAF_e far exceeds R-CNN [15]. But is weaker than two-stage based detectors, like Fast R-CNN [3] and Faster R-CNN [4]. The reason may be that suing simple NMS method for generating bounding boxes predication results cannot work well.

5   Conclusion

We have proposed a new one-stage anchor-free object detector OSAF_e, which solves the object detection in a per-pixel prediction fashion. As shown in experiments, OSAF_e outperforms YOLOv1 [5] and R-CNN [15] anchor-free method. It also avoids computation and hyper-parameters related to anchor boxes. This algorithm will be migrated to the feature pyramid networks [17] in subsequent work.

Acknowledgement. This work was supported in part by the National Key R&D Program of China (No. 2018YFC0807500), and by Ministry of Science and Technology of Sichuan Province Program (No. 2018GZDZX0048, 2018JY0067, 20ZDYF0343, 2018HH0075).

References

1. Law, H., Deng, J.: CornerNet: detecting objects as paired keypoints. In: Proceedings of European Conference on Computer Vision, pp. 734–750 (2018)
2. Tian, Z., Shen, C., Chen, H., He, T.: FCOS: fully convolutional one-stage object detection. arXiv preprint arXiv:1904.01355 (2019)
3. RossGirshick: Fast R-CNN. In: Proceedings of IEEE Conference on Computer Vision and Pattern Recognition, pp. 1440–1448 (2015)
4. Ren, S., He, K., Girshick, R., Sun, J.: Faster R-CNN: towards real-time object detection with region proposal networks. In: Proceedings of Advances in Neural Information Processing Systems, pp. 91–99 (2015)
5. Redmon, J., Divvala, S., Girshick, R., Farhadi, A.: You only look once: unified, real-time object detection. In: Proceedings of the IEEE Conference on Computer Vision and Pattern Recognition, pp. 779–788 (2016)
6. Redmon, J., Farhadi, A.: YOLO9000: better, faster, stronger. In: Proceedings of the IEEE Conference on Computer Vision and Pattern Recognition, pp. 7263–7271 (2017)
7. Redmon, J., Farhadi, A.: Yolov3: an incremental improvement. arXiv preprint arXiv:1804.02767 (2018)
8. Liu, W., et al.: SSD: single shot multibox detector. In: Proceedings of European Conference on Computer Vision, pp. 21–37 (2016)
9. Lin, T.-Y., Goyal, P., Girshick, R., He, K., Dollár, P.: Focal loss for dense object detection. In: Proceedings of the IEEE Conference on Computer Vision and Pattern Recognition, pp. 2980–2988 (2017)
10. Kong, T., Sun, F., Liu, H., Jiang, Y., Shi, J.: FoveaBox: beyond anchor-based object detector. CoRR abs/1904.03797(2019)
11. Lin, T.-Y., Dollár, P., Girshick, R.B., He, K., Hariharan, B., Belongie, S.J.: Feature pyramid networks for object detection. In: Proceedings of the IEEE Conference on Computer Vision and Pattern Recognition, vol. 1, p. 4 (2017)

12. Shrivastava, A., Gupta, A., Girshick, R.: Training region-based object detectors with online hard example mining. In: Proceedings of the IEEE Conference on Computer Vision and Pattern Recognition, pp. 761–769 (2016)
13. Kong, T., Sun, F., Yao, A., Liu, H., Lu, M., Chen, Y.: RON: reverse connection with objectness prior networks for object detection. In: Proceedings of the IEEE Conference on Computer Vision and Pattern Recognition, vol. 1, p. 2 (2017)
14. Russakovsky, O., et al.: Imagenet large scale visual recognition challenge. Int. J. Comput. Vis. 115(3), 211–252 (2015)
15. Girshick, R., Donahue, J., Darrell, T., Malik, J.: Rich feature hierarchies for accurate object detection and semantic segmentation. In: Proceedings of the IEEE Conference on Computer Vision and Pattern Recognition, pp. 580–587 (2014)
16. Felzenszwalb, P.F., Girshick, R.B., McAllester, D., Ramanan, D.: Object detection with discriminatively trained part based models. IEEE Trans. Pattern Anal. Mach. Intell. 32(9), 1627–1645 (2010)
17. Lin, T.-Y., Dollár, P., Girshick, R., He, K., Hariharan, B., Belongie, S.: Feature pyramid networks for object detection. In: Proceedings of the IEEE Conference on Computer Vision and Pattern Recognition, pp. 2117–2125 (2017)

Attention-Based Interaction Trajectory Prediction

Zhe Liu[1], Lizong Zhang[1,3(✉)], Zhihong Rao[1,2], and Guisong Liu[1,4]

[1] School of Computer Science and Engineering, University of Electronic Science and Technology of China, Chengdu 611731, China
l.zhang@uestc.edu.cn
[2] China Electronic Technology Cyber Security Co., Ltd., Chengdu 610000, China
[3] Trusted Cloud Computing and Big Data Key Laboratory of Sichuan Province, Chengdu 611731, China
[4] School of Computer Science, Zhongshan Institute, University of Electronic Science and Technology of China, Zhongshan 528402, China

Abstract. Trajectory prediction is a hot topic in the field of computer vision and has a wide range of applications. Trajectory prediction refers to predicting the future trajectory of a target based on its past trajectory. This paper proposes a method based on graph neural network and attention mechanism, in order to update trajectory characteristics by implement global pedestrian interaction. And, a direct relationship between history and future is introduced with the attention module for reducing error propagation. The method was evaluated on several real-world crowd datasets, the results demonstrate the effectiveness of our method.

Keywords: Trajectory prediction · Graph attention network · Attention mechanism

1 Introduction

Trajectory prediction is a hot topic in the field of computer vision. Predicting the Trajectories of pedestrians is essential for Self-driving cars and robots. However, the problem of pedestrian trajectory prediction is extremely complicated, due to interdependent of pedestrians. And timing predictions often lead to error accumulation.

Traditional mathematical statistical methods [1, 2] rely on artificially designed features to model pedestrian movements and interactions. With the development of neural networks in recent years, the methods based on Neural Network have surpassed the traditional methods and achieved better results. Trajectory prediction methods based on deep learning mostly use LSTM [3] model to encode and decode each pedestrian trajectory sequence in the scene using LSTM network to obtain the trajectory characteristics of each pedestrian.

When dealing with the interactions between pedestrians, the above methods mostly deal with each pedestrian individually, which increase the amount of calculation and time cost. On the other hand, the error propagation problem is not solved properly. The

© Springer Nature Switzerland AG 2020
R. Xu et al. (Eds.): AIMS 2020, LNCS 12401, pp. 168–175, 2020.
https://doi.org/10.1007/978-3-030-59605-7_13

errors of the previous time step will be amplified and affect the result of the subsequent time step.

Inspired by the attention mechanism in natural language processing [4], a novel method for trajectory prediction is proposed. We assign different weight coefficients to historical features based on the attention mechanism and fuse historical features.

Contributions of this paper are summarized as follows:

- Proposed a pedestrian interaction processing method based on graph neural network, which realizes feature fusion between pedestrians, and reduces the time consumption.
- Proposed an attention-based historical feature fusion method that adaptively selects the historical trajectory characteristics to improve the accuracy of prediction.
- Evaluated on several publicly available real-world crowd datasets. And the results demonstrate the effectiveness of our method.

The remainder of this paper is organized as follows. Section 2 reviews main work related to trajectory prediction. Section 3 describes the proposed model. Section 4 evaluates the effectiveness of the framework while conclusions and suggestions for future work are summarized in Sect. 5.

2 Related Work

At present, trajectory prediction methods [1, 2] include traditional mathematical statistics methods and methods based on deep learning. Traditional mathematical statistical methods rely on artificially designed features to model pedestrian movements and interactions. The bottlenecks of traditional mathematical statistics methods are that they cannot consider long-term dependence on information and adapt to complex mobile scenarios.

In recent years, methods based on deep learning have proven to be superior to traditional mathematical statistical methods. Among them, the methods based on LSTM and the methods based on GAN [5] are the most representative. Because the nature of pedestrian trajectories is a set of natural motion sequences with time series characteristics, some methods [6–8] mainly build models based on recurrent neural networks. Alahi et al. [6] have introduced the social pooling layer to bring the hidden states of neighboring pedestrians together to form interaction features, and achieved the purpose of modeling pedestrian interaction. The social pooling layer meshes the target scene and pools the hidden layer features of other pedestrians in the neighborhood of each pedestrian grid according to the grid range. At the same time, the results generated by the GAN-based method [9, 10] perform well in authenticity and diversity. Gupta et al. [9] have proposed a trajectory sampler that handles the interactions between all the observed pedestrians by pooling the GAN input random vector with a vector combining the hidden representations of the other pedestrian trajectories.

Deep Learning on Graphs Generalizing neural networks to graph-structured data is an emerging topic. Recently, researchers apply attention mechanisms to graph-structured data [11] to model spatial correlations for graph classification. Regarding the attention mechanism [4], the literature proposes a network structure called "transformer" based on the attention mechanism to mine the relationship between input and output.

Inspired by the above, we model the pedestrians in the scene as graph nodes and implement pedestrian interaction through graph attention networks. We model the direct relationship between history and future time steps to mitigate the problem of error propagation.

3   Methodology

3.1   Problem Definition

Suppose pedestrians are represented by $P_1, P_2 \dots P_N$. The position of pedestrian P_i at time-step T is denoted as (X_{Ti}, Y_{Ti}). The problem is defined to predict the trajectories (X_{Ti}, Y_{Ti}), where $T = T_{obs+1}, T_{obs+2} \dots T_{pred}$.

3.2   Overall Flowchart

The overall network architecture is shown in Fig. 1. First, we use the LSTM network to extract the trajectory features, and merge the trajectory features into the graph attention network to obtain the global interaction features. Then, based on the attention mechanism, the trajectory features of multiple time steps are fused to obtain the final trajectory features. Finally, the trajectory features are input into the LSTM network to obtain the predicted position.

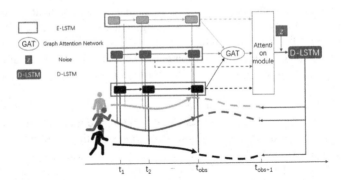

Fig. 1. Overall network architecture

3.3   Extract Trajectory Features

At first, we embed the location of each person to get a fixed length vector d_{Ti} and input it to the E-LSTM.

$$d_{Ti} = F\left(x_i^t, y_i^t\right) \tag{1}$$

$$S_i^t = E - LSTM\left(S_i^{t-1}, d_{Ti}; W_E\right) \tag{2}$$

where the function $F(\cdot)$ is an embedding function. S_i^t is the hidden state of the E-LSTM at time-step t. W_E is the weight of the E-LSTM.

3.4 Pedestrian Interaction

We consider the pedestrians as nodes on the graph, and use GAT [11] to implement our pedestrian interaction mechanism. $S_i^{t=T_{obs}}$ is input into the attention layer of the graph, and the attention coefficient between node pairs (i, j) is calculated:

$$\alpha_{i,j}^t = \frac{exp(LeakyRelu(\vec{a}^T [WS_i^t || WS_j^t]))}{\sum k \in N_i exp(LeakyRelu(\vec{a}^T [WS_i^t || WS_k^t])}$$

(3)

Where || is the concatenation operation, $\alpha_{i,j}^t$ is the attention coefficient of node j to i, N_i represents the neighbors of node i on the graph, W is the weight matrix, a is a single-layer feedforward neural network, parametrized by a weight vector $\vec{a}^T$. It is normalized by a softmax function with LeakyReLU.

After the standardized attention coefficient is obtained, the output of the attention network of node i graph is calculated by the following formula:

$$\hat{S}_i^t = \sigma\left(\sum j \in N_i \alpha_{i,j}^t WS_i^t\right)$$

(4)

Where σ is a nonlinear function, $\hat{S}_i^t$ is the state of pedestrian i after merging the characteristics of the surrounding pedestrian trajectory.

3.5 Trajectory Feature Fusion

To ease the error propagation, we added the attention module. The attention module models the direct relationship between each future time steps and historical time steps to generate the pedestrian final trajectory feature.

For pedestrian i, the correlation between the time step $t_P (t_P = T_{obs}, \ldots T_{obs+Q})$ and the historical time steps $t(t = T_1, \ldots T_{obs-1})$ is calculated.

$$\mu_{t_P,t} = \hat{S}_i^{t_P}, S_i^t$$

(5)

$$\gamma_{t_P,t} = \frac{exp(\mu_{t_P,t})}{\sum_{t_r=T_1}^{T_{obs-1}} exp(\mu_{t_P,t_r})}$$

(6)

Where $\langle \cdot, \cdot \rangle$ denotes the inner product operator, $\gamma_{t_P,t}$ is the attention score. The trajectory characteristics of pedestrian i are calculated by the following formula:

$$\hat{P}_i^t = \left(\sum_{t=T_1}^{T_{obs-1}} \gamma_{t_P,t} S_i^t\right) || \hat{S}_i^{t_P}$$

(7)

In many cases, the trajectory of a pedestrian is multi-modal. And different people may choose different modes of action. In order to enhance the diversity of the generated trajectory, the pedestrian trajectory characteristics are added to the noise vector and input to the LSTM network to decode and obtain the prediction result.

$$r_i^{T_{obs}} = \hat{P}_i^t || Z$$

(8)

$$r_i^{T_{obs}+1} = D - LSTM\left(r_i^{T_{obs}}, d_i^{T_{obs}}; W_D\right) \tag{9}$$

$$\left(x_i^{T_{obs}+1}, y_i^{T_{obs}+1}\right) = \delta_3\left(r_i^{T_{obs}+1}\right) \tag{10}$$

Where Z represents noise, $r_i^{T_{obs}}$ represents intermediate state vector, $\delta_3(\cdot)$ is a function, W_D is the D-LSTM weight. After the predicted position is obtained at time step T_{obs+1}, the subsequent time step location is predicted.

For each pedestrian, the model produces multiple predicted trajectories by randomly sampling z from N (0,1) (the standard normal distribution). And select the trajectory with the smallest distance from the real position as the model output to calculate the loss.

$$L = min_k \left|\left|P_i - \hat{P}_i^k\right|\right|_2 \tag{11}$$

Where P_i is the ground-truth trajectory of pedestrian i, $\hat{P}_i$ is the trajectory produced by our model, k is a hyperparameter.

4   Experiment

Training Samples. We evaluate our proposed model on two public pedestrian walking datasets, ETH [12] and UCY [13], which contain rich social interactions. The ETH dataset consists of two scenarios named ETH and HOTEL. UCY dataset includes two scenarios and in three components, named ZARA-01, ZARA-02 and UCY. These datasets contain thousands of real-world pedestrian trajectories and cover rich human-human interactions. We evaluate our model on these 5 datasets. We follow the leave-one-out evaluation methodology in [9].

Parameter Settings. We iteratively train the network with a batch size of 64 for 300 epochs using Adam optimizer with a learning rate of 0.01. The dimensions of the hidden state for LSTM is 32. For first graph attention layer, the shape of W is 16 × 16. For the second layer, the shape of W is 16 × 32. Batch Normalization is applied over the input of graph attention layer. The dimension of Z is set to 16.

Evaluation Index. There are two types of metrics for evaluating the performance of trajectory prediction, including the Average Displacement error (ADE) and Final Displacement error (FDE) in meters.

1. Average Displacement Error (ADE): Average L_2 distance between ground truth and our prediction over all predicted time steps.
2. Final Displacement Error (FDE): The distance between the predicted final destination and the true final destination at end of the prediction period T_{pred}.

Quantitative Evaluation. All experiments are based on ETH and UCY datasets. The results and analysis are as follows.

Table 1. Comparative experiment on attention module.

Metric	Dataset	OURS	OURS
Attention		×	✓
ADE	ETH	0.56	0.59
	HOTEL	0.27	0.25
	UNIV	0.31	0.31
	ZARA1	0.21	0.21
	ZARA2	0.20	0.20
AVG		0.31	0.31
FDE	ETH	1.10	1.15
	HOTEL	0.43	0.42
	UNIV	0.66	0.64
	ZARA1	0.42	0.42
	ZARA2	0.40	0.40
AVG		0.60	0.61

In Table 1, We evaluated the attention module of the experiment. × indicates that the attention module has been removed from the network. The results show that the effect is improved on some data sets, which shows that the attention module has a certain effect. But on the ETH dataset, the error becomes larger, which is related to the number of pedestrians' historical time step. Compared with other datasets, the average residence time of pedestrians in the ETH dataset is shorter.

In Table 2, we evaluate our model against all baseline models. The results show that our method outperforms all compared methods on all datasets. Compared with S-LSTM and SGAN, the ADE is reduced by 31% and 18% respectively. For FDE, the performance is increased by 32% and 21% respectively. These results show that our model has advantages compared to other methods.

Figure 2 shows some examples of predicted trajectories drawn from datasets. The predicted paths of our models appear able to better capture the direction of pedestrian movement. The generated trajectories do not have a linear trend, and the model also performs well in the case of multiple pedestrians.

Table 2. Comparison with several baseline models.

Metric	Dataset	S-LSTM	SGAN	OURS
ADE	ETH	0.73	0.60	0.59
	HOTEL	0.49	0.48	0.25
	UNIV	0.41	0.36	0.31
	ZARA1	0.27	0.21	0.21
	ZARA2	0.33	0.27	0.20
AVG		0.45	0.38	0.31
FDE	ETH	1.48	1.19	1.15
	HOTEL	1.01	0.95	0.42
	UNIV	0.84	0.75	0.64
	ZARA1	0.56	0.42	0.42
	ZARA2	0.70	0.54	0.40
AVG		0.91	0.77	0.61

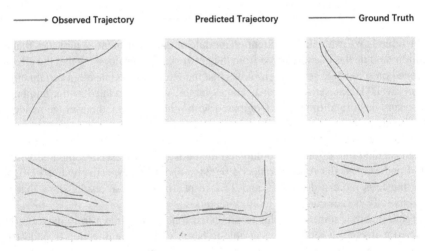

——————▶ Observed Trajectory   Predicted Trajectory   ———————— Ground Truth

Fig. 2. Trajectories generated by our model

5 Conclusion

In this paper, we propose a novel method for the prediction of pedestrian trajectories. We use the graph attention network to handle global pedestrian interaction. Furthermore, we use the attention module to select and fuse historical features. Experimental results show that the attention mechanism effectively reduces the error propagation and improves prediction results. Test results on two datasets prove that our method can effectively improve prediction accuracy. We have noticed that the attention module failed to get the expected result on the ETH dataset, the issue will be further analyzed to improve our method in the future work.

Acknowledgement. This work was supported in part by the National Key R&D Program of China (No. 2018YFC0807500), and by Ministry of Science and Technology of Sichuan Province Program (No. 2018GZDZX0048, 20ZDYF0343, 2018HH0075).

References

1. Elnagar, A.: Prediction of moving objects in dynamic environments using Kalman filters. In: Proceedings of the International Symposium on Computational Intelligence in Robotics and Automation (CIRA), pp. 414–419 (2001)
2. Barth, A., Franke, U.: Where will the oncoming vehicle be the next second? In: Proceedings of the IEEE Intelligent Vehicles Symposium (IV), pp. 1068–1073 (2008)
3. Hochreiter, S., Schmidhuber, J.: Long short-term memory. Neural Comput. **9**(8), 1735–1780 (1997)
4. Vaswani, A., et al.: Attention is all you need. In: Advances in Neural Information Processing Systems, pp. 6000–6010 (2017)
5. Goodfellow, I., et al.: Generative adversarial nets. In: Advances in Neural Information Processing Systems (NIPS), pp. 2672–2680 (2014)
6. Alahi, A., Goel, K., Ramanathan, V., Robicquet, A., Fei-Fei, L., Savarese, S.: Social LSTM: human trajectory prediction in crowded spaces. In Proceedings of the IEEE Conference on Computer Vision and Pattern Recognition, pp. 961–971 (2016)
7. Vemula, A., Muelling, K., Oh, J.: Social attention: modeling attention in human crowds. In 2018 IEEE International Conference on Robotics and Automation (ICRA), pp. 1–7. IEEE (2018)
8. Xu, Y., Piao, Z., Gao, S.: Encoding crowd interaction with deep neural network for pedestrian trajectory prediction. In: Proceedings of the IEEE Conference on Computer Vision and Pattern Recognition, pp. 5275– 5284 (2018)
9. Gupta, A., Johnson, J., Fei-Fei, L., Savarese, S., Alahi, A.: Social GAN: socially acceptable trajectories with generative adversarial networks. In: IEEE Conference on Computer Vision and Pattern Recognition (CVPR). Number CONF (2018)
10. Sadeghian, A., Kosaraju, V., Sadeghian, A., Hirose, N., Savarese, S.: SoPhie: an attentive GAN for predicting paths compliant to social and physical constraints. arXiv preprint arXiv: 1806.01482 (2018)
11. Veličković, P., Cucurull, G., Casanova, A., Romero, A., Lio, P., Bengio, Y.: Graph attention networks. arXiv preprint arXiv:1710.10903 (2017)
12. Pellegrini, S., Ess, A., Schindler, K., Van Gool, L.: You'll never walk alone: modeling social behavior for multi-target tracking. In: 2009 IEEE 12th International Conference on Computer Vision, pp. 261–268. IEEE (2009)
13. Lerner, A., Chrysanthou, Y., Lischinski, D.: Crowds by example. In: Computer Graphics Forum, vol. 26, pp. 655–664. Wiley Online Library (2007)

Author Index

Printed in the United States
By Bookmasters